IMAGES
of America

THE LAKES REGION OF NEW HAMPSHIRE VOLUME II

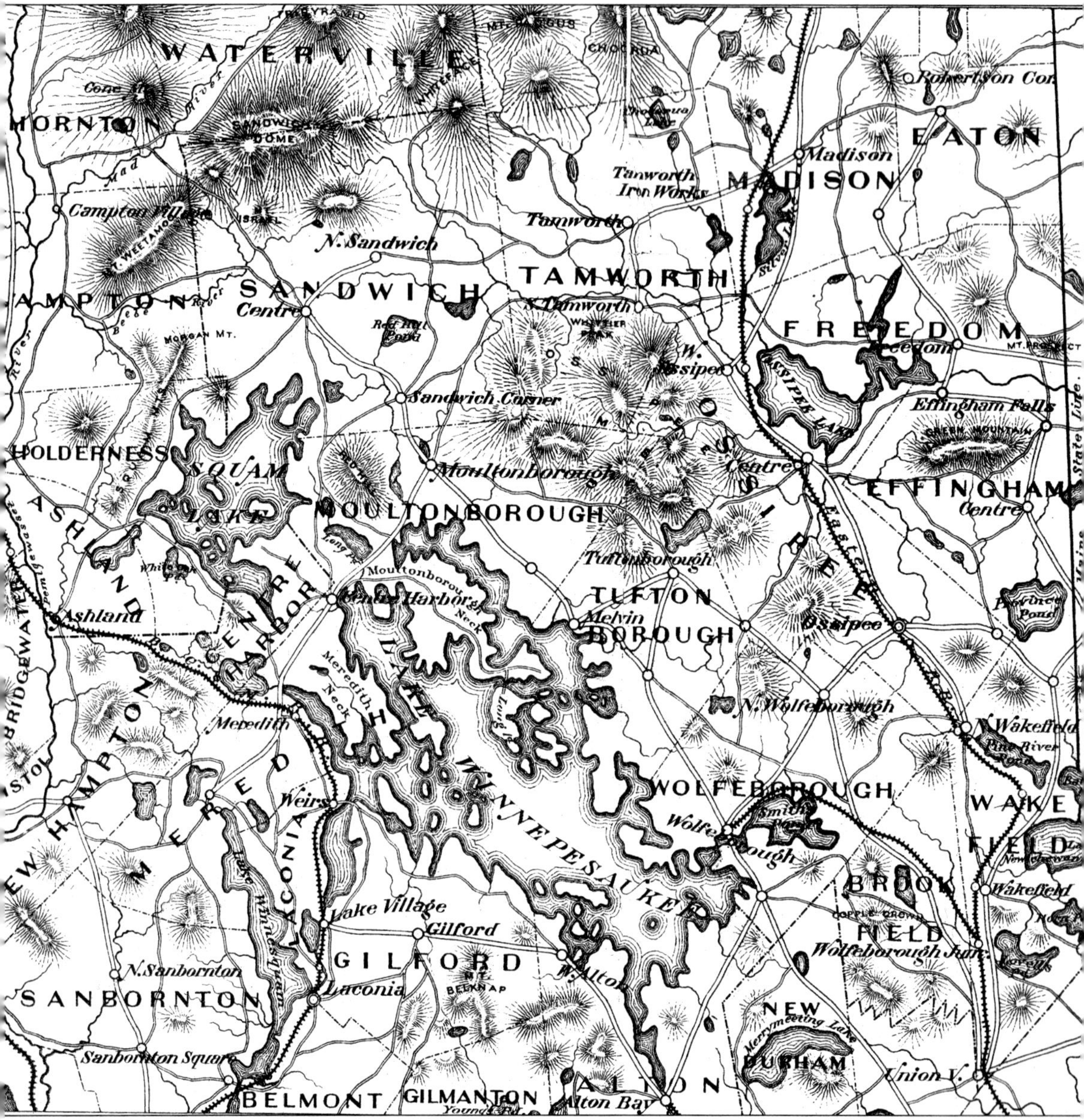

The Lake Country of New Hampshire, 1876, published in Osgood's *White Mountain Guide*.

IMAGES
of America

The Lakes Region of New Hampshire Volume II

Bruce D. Heald, Ph. D.

ARCADIA
PUBLISHING

ISBN 978-0-7385-6438-8

Published by Arcadia Publishing
Charleston, South Carolina

Printed in the United States of America

Library of Congress Catalog Card Number: 96-228073

For all general information contact Arcadia Publishing at:
Telephone 843-853-2070
Fax 843-853-0044
E-mail sales@arcadiapublishing.com
For customer service and orders:
Toll-Free 1-888-313-2665

Visit us on the Internet at www.arcadiapublishing.com

To my brother, Douglas Wayne Heald.

CONTENTS

The Lakes Region of New Hampshire.

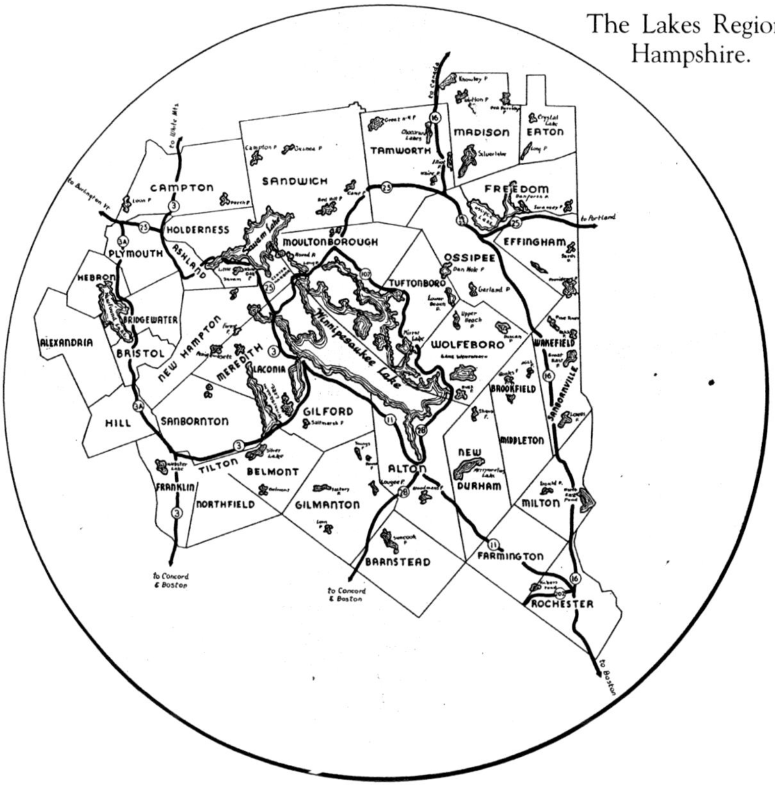

ACKNOWLEDGMENTS

Special thanks are extended to the following individuals and historical societies for their contributions to this volume:

The Appalachian Mountain Club, the Alton Historical Society, Gladys Bickford and the Center Harbor Historical Society, John D. Bardwell, the Bear Island Conservation Association, the Belmont Historical Society, Ronald P. Bergeron, Joanne and Dick Binette and Handy Landing, C.T. Bodwell, The Boston, Concord and Montreal Railroad, The Boston & Maine Railroad, William J. Buchanan, Joseph Bush Sr., Merrill Faye and Fay's Boat Yard, The Geneva Point Center, *The Granite State Monthly*, R. Brewster Harding, Holy Trinity School, Warren D. Huse, Irwin Marine, James Irwin, Jack Irwin, Barbara Kelley, The Lakes Region Association, Beth Lavertur, Robert Lawton and The Weirs Publishing Co., Richard Leavitt, the Meredith Historical Society, Don Minor, James Morash and The Winnipesaukee Flagship Corporation, Mark Morris and The New Hampshire Antique & Classic Boat Museum, the New Hampshire Fish and Game Department, *New Hampshire Profile*, New Hampshire Troubadour, The New Hampshire Planning and Development Commission, Harold Orne, E.D. Putnam, Mason Westfall, The Lake Winnipesaukee Historical Society, the Wolfeboro Historical Society, and all those unsung contributors who have helped make this historic publication possible.

Introduction

Few words or pictures can impart the majesty and beauty which the Lakes Region of New Hampshire offers. Our history, with its timeless advantages of climate and lavish nature, remains as ever to delight those who, by good fortune, have come here to enjoy them.

More than 1,300 ponds, lakes, river systems, and brooks adorn New Hampshire's 9,341 square acres, all of which have their allure, whether it be the gleaming expanse of Winnipesaukee or the reflection of Monkey Pond in Meredith. The thrill of listening and watching the cascading mountain falls in Sandwich Notch or the clear-watered brooks from the Ossipee Range bring a quiet splendor of serenity often hidden from the busy highway.

For many years the presence of Native Americans prevented the Europeans from settling the territory. To make their first settlement safer, the proprietors from Exeter voted to clear a road to the Lakes Region and build two blockhouses, one at the southeast corner of the grant called "White Hall" (a part of Gilmanton) and the second at the "Wares," near the northern end of the present White Oaks road in the section known as Aquedoctan.

By 1764, Colonial Governor John Wentworth completed a Province road from Portsmouth to Wolfeboro. The establishment of his summer home gives Wolfeboro the distinction of being the "Oldest Summer Resort in America." By 1768, the north and west side of the Winnipesaukee River were chartered by the governor and council as a part of Meredith. Early proprietors settled in that section and along a part of the Province Road, now known as the Parade Road.

Lake travel has played a major role in the development of this region, beginning with the primitive Native American canoes. Since the 1800s, horse boats, sailboats, rowboats, steamboats, racing boats, and the present motorboats have plied these waters.

By 1880, Winnipesaukee and the surrounding lakes, rivers, and ponds had begun to attract many admirers, who built simple summer dwellings on the mainland shores and islands. Throughout the region, old farmhouses were purchased, restored, and fitted as seasonal homes for summer residents. With the coming of the rail system during the 1840s, and later the automobile, the number of visitors and residents increased enormously. The thousands who visited annually at the turn of the century have become the millions of today.

The coming of the railroad greatly affected local industries, and more particularly, tourism. With the advent of mass transportation came the grand hotels and the lavish summer resorts. It was the Boston, Concord and Montreal Railroad which opened a road from Boston to Meredith Bridge (Laconia) on August 1, 1848; later, in the 1850s, it connected the road to the White Mountains, making the area more accessible for summer and winter visitors.

In the winter of 1930–31, the Boston & Maine Railroad put on its first snow train, which proved an immediate success. Within five years these trains carried nearly 60,000 passengers, the majority to New Hampshire centers. In other than the winter season, hike and bike trains offered a similar service to walkers and cyclists.

Fishing has always been a year-round sport, with salmon, brook and rainbow trout, pickerel, yellow and white perch, shad, smelt, and black bass all taken in their proper season. In fact, practically all fish native to New Hampshire waters are taken. Winter fishing is a special feature, with tiny houses clustered here and there on the ice for the comfort of the fisherman.

Over the past one hundred years, many boys' and girls' camps have sprung up on shores of the lakes and ponds. Summer theaters, public beaches, chalets, marinas, cabins, motels, hotels, condominiums, camping areas, boatyards, and ski resorts continue to embrace the landscape. Regattas, summer concerts, snowmobile trails, cross country skiing, and sled dog racing have continued to enrich the ever-increasing desire for outdoor entertainment.

The simplicity and vitality of the Lakes Region's landscape is a tonic for the vacationer; a relief from the wearisome harness of regularity. In this book I have assembled a rare collection of pictures illustrating the natural beauty of the scenic countryside encompassing the bold mountains, peaceful ponds, lavish rivers and streams, and grand lakes of the region. Situated among this natural habitant are the quiet villages and the memories past. Harnessed within one chapter I have accented the railroad systems, their stations, depots, and whistle stops, which intertwined from town to town. Memories past, moments to remember—a legacy not to be forgotten.

—Bruce D. Heald, Ph. D.

One

Scenic Countryside

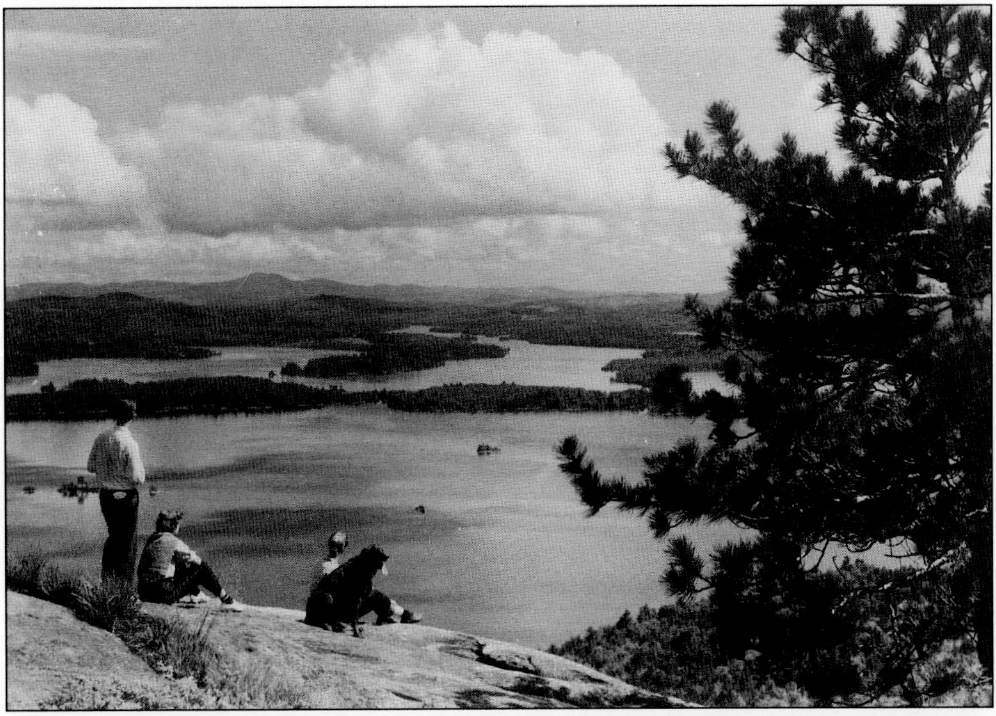

A view of Squam Lake from Rattlesnake Mountain, Rockywold, Deephaven Camps, Holderness, NH. One of the best views of the vastness of this lake, and its many islands and surrounding mountain ranges, is seen from this mountain. Rattlesnake (or Peaked Hill) is a double-headed spur of the Squam Range, which runs out nearly to the lake, with far-viewing ledges on its low and wooded crests.

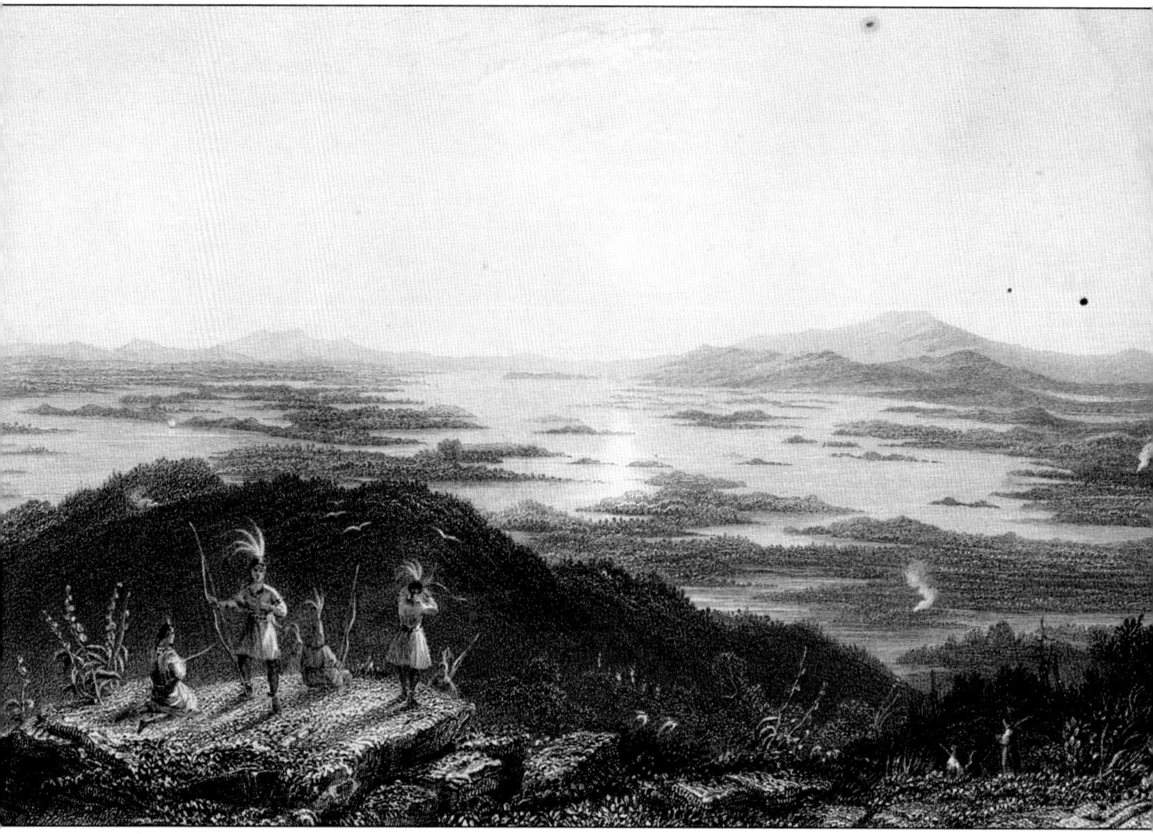

Lake Winnipesaukee from Red Hill. The northern boundary of this lake was the rendezvous area for Native American scouting parties, as it furnished them with a fishing ground when their game and plunder failed; and the adjacent mountains became their observatory or post of observation, where, by descrying the rising smoke in the forest, they could easily learn the position of every new settler for a vast region around the Lakes Region. The Native American etymology of the name is explained as Winni, meaning "beautiful"; nippe, meaning "water"; kees, meaning "high"; and auke, ahki, or ohki, meaning "place." Thus Winni-nippe-kees-auke, or Winnepekesauke, or Winnepesauke, means "The beautiful water (in the) high place." The popular definition of this name in New Hampshire is "The Smile of the Great Spirit," but it has no relation whatever to its etymology. (A Bartlett print.)

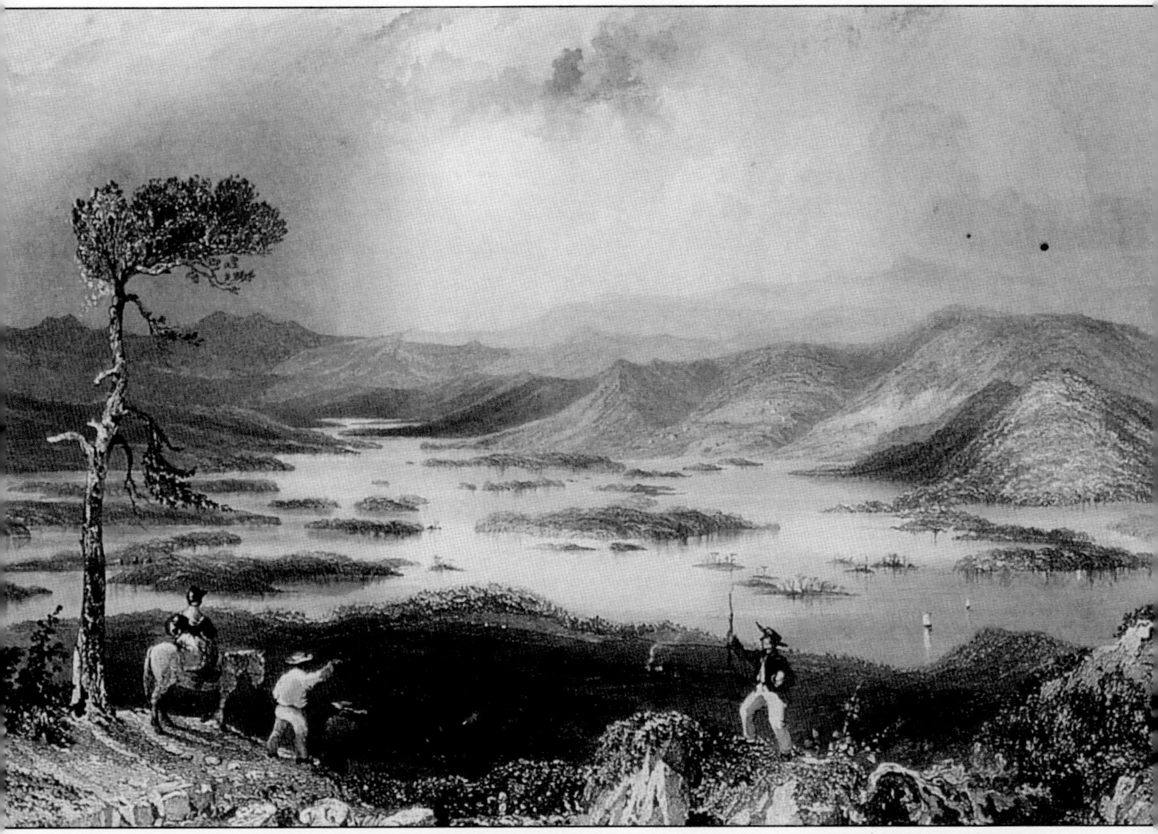

Squam Lake from Red Hill. The limpid purity of the water and the grandeur of the adjacent mountains all combine to make a rich and fascinating panorama. The lake, whose Native American name is said to have been either Wonn-as-squam-auke ("the beautiful surrounded-by-water place") or Kees-ee-hunk-nip-ee ("the goose-lake of the highlands"), is considered one of New Hampshire's most beautiful bodies of water. Officially known as Asquam ("water"), and popularly as Big Squam, the lake is surrounded by high green hills. Its waters flow, not into its neighboring lake, Winnipesaukee, but into the Pemigewasset River. Twenty-six islands dot its surface. (A Bartlett print.)

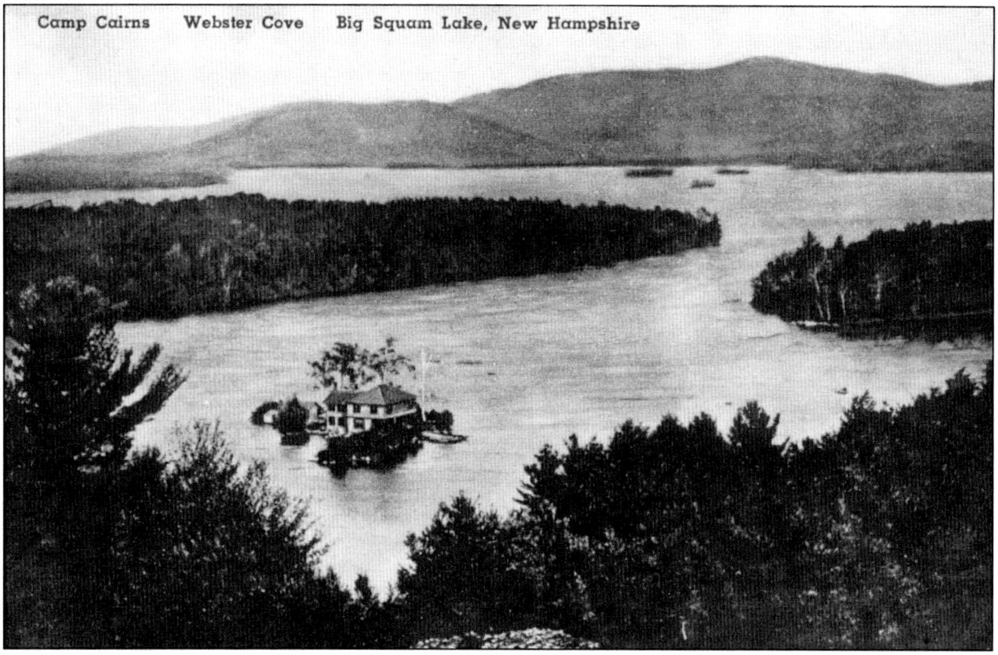

A view of Squam Lake, Camp Cairns, Webster Cove, Holderness, NH. This lake is a natural lake raised by a dam on Little Squam Lake. It has an altitude of 562 feet above sea level, an area of 6,765 acres, and lies in three counties and four townships.

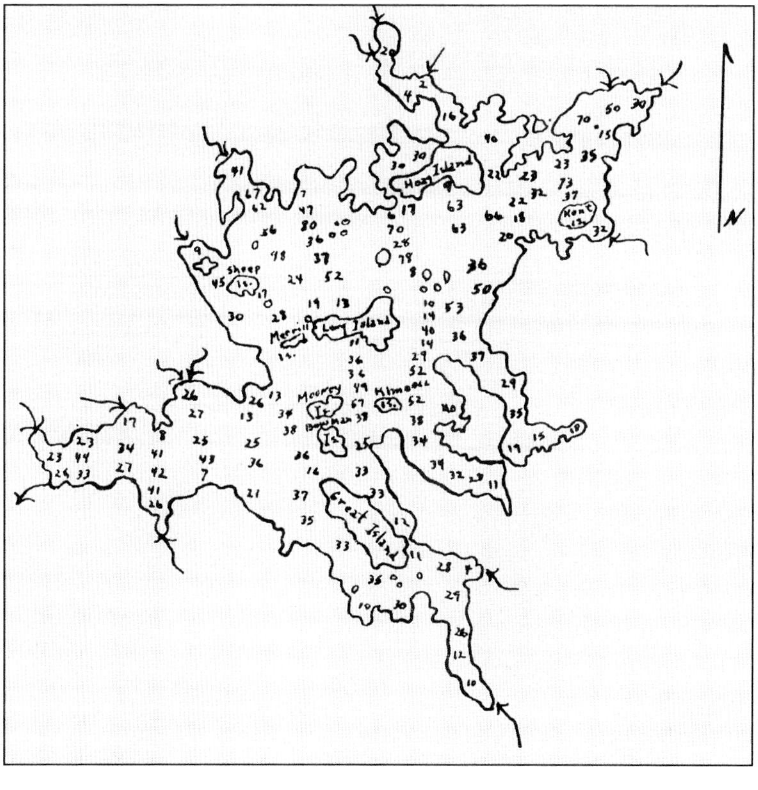

A map of Squam Lake indicating water depths. The lake has an area of 6,765 acres, a length over 6 miles, and a breadth of approximately 3 miles. Squam Lake is nearly divided into two sections, between which are several long islands parallel with each other. There are 16 islands in the lake, several of which were originally used for pasturing horses and sheep but now are habitable.

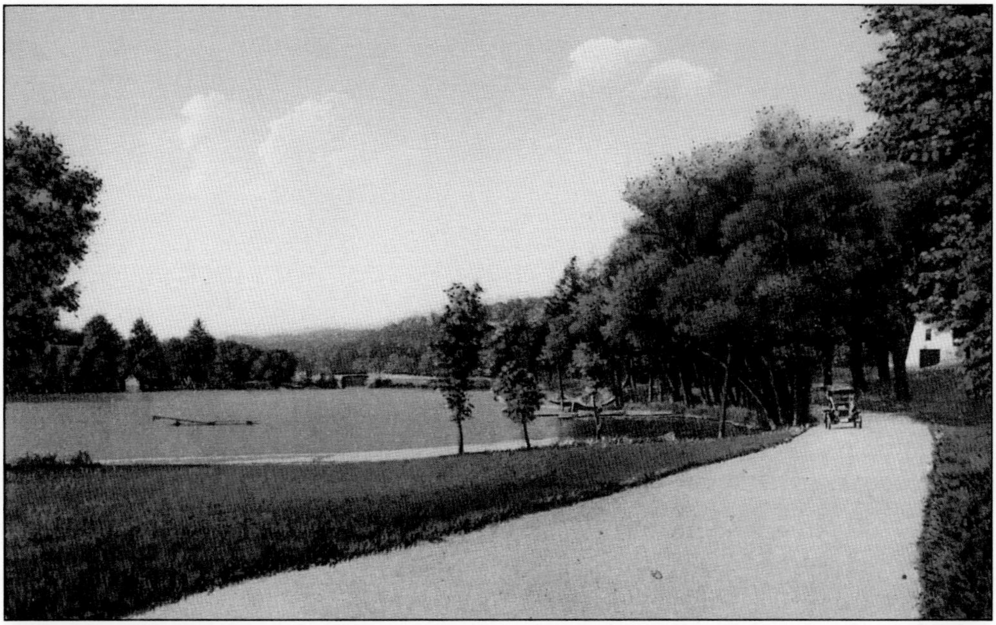

Little Squam Lake facing south to the dam in Ashland, NH, 1920s. This is the main outlet for Squam Lake. On the right is the state road connecting the villages of Holderness and Ashland, NH.

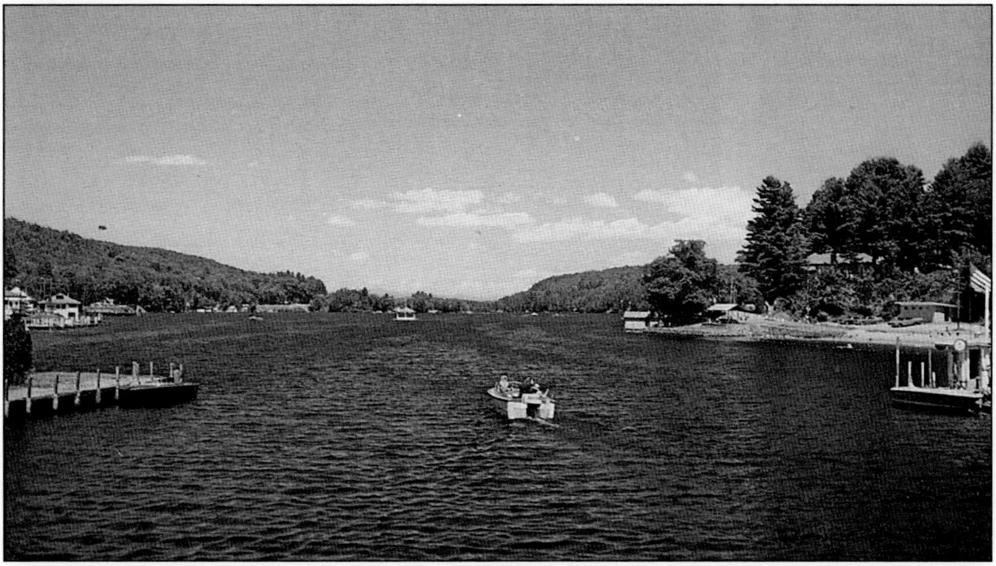

A view of Lake Winnipesaukee from Alton Bay looking north. This lake was glacially formed; it may be reasonable to assume that a massive ice-cap during pre-historic time covered all the territory, and that, during its breaking and melting, these ravines were created and a massive natural dam developed, forcing the water onto higher elevations. The lake is fed by both mountain streams and underwater springs. The largest streams which enter the lake are those of the Merry-Meeting and Smith's Rivers on the south, the other tributaries being short brooks or the outlets of adjacent ponds. The main outlet of the lake is by way of the Winnipesaukee River in Laconia, which unites with the Pemigewasset to form the Merrimack River, which eventually flows south and east into the Atlantic Ocean.

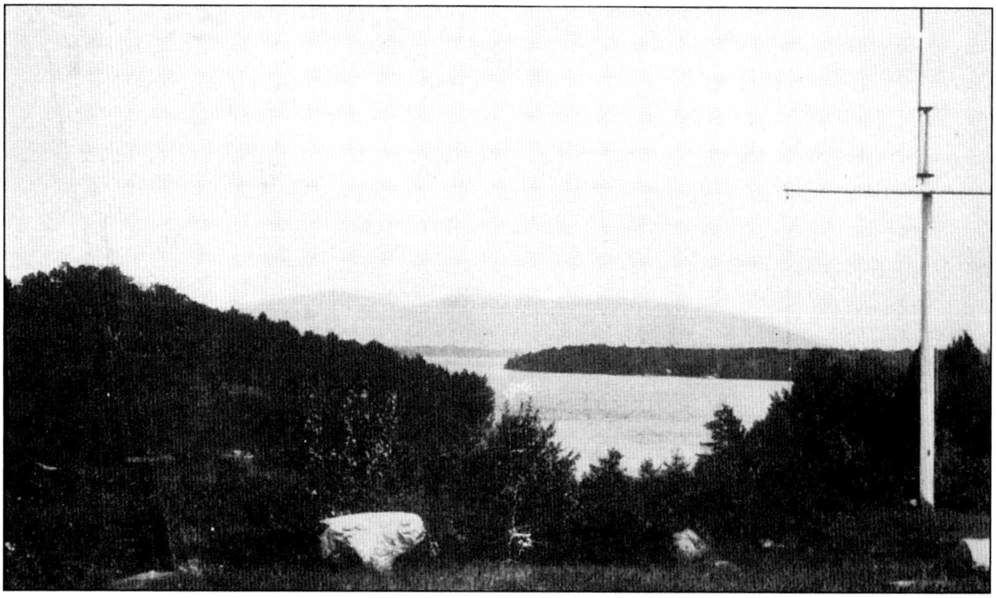

A view of Lake Winnipesaukee, Bear Island, and the Ossipee Mountain Range from Meredith Neck. Winnipesaukee, New Hampshire's largest lake with an area of 72 square miles (44,586 acres) and a mainland shoreline of 186 miles, is dotted with 274 habitable islands and surrounded by the foothills of the White Mountains. The lake is one of the most beautiful scenic areas in the world, with islands ranging in size from those of 1,000 acres to tiny dots of rock and turf which are scarcely large enough to hold a small summer camp.

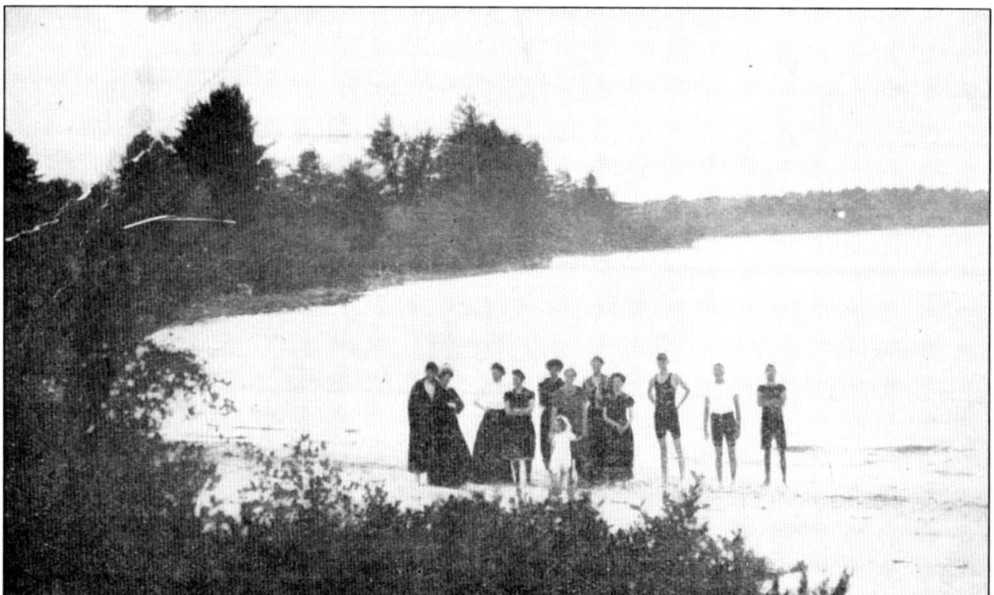

A bath scene on Long Pond (Lake Kanasatka), Moultonboro, NH. This charming lake is located one mile east of Center Harbor. The waters of this lake empty into Lake Winnipesaukee by a stream between the Second and Third Moultonboro Necks.

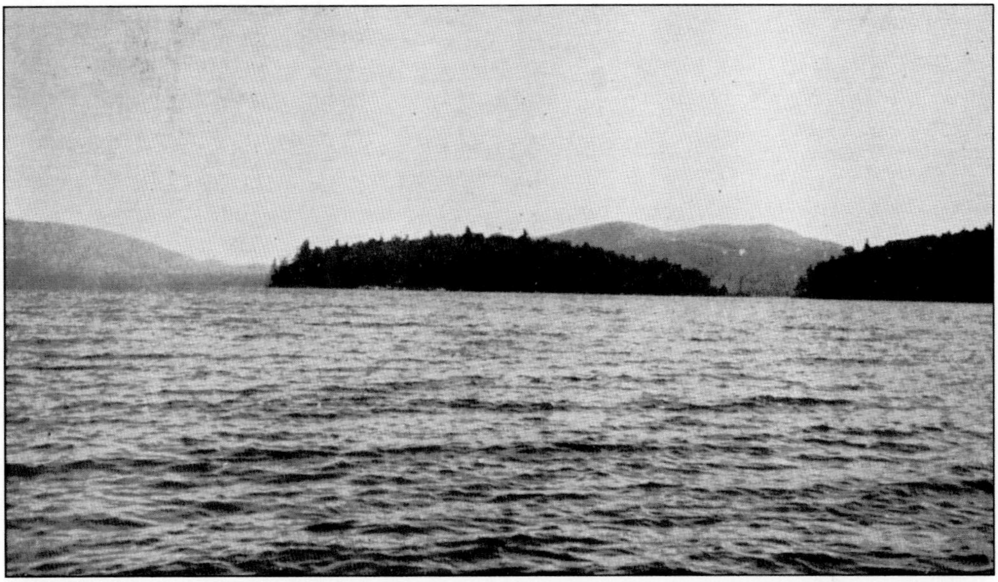

Belle Isle, Newfound Lake, Bristol, NH. This is the fourth largest of the New Hampshire's lakes; it is 6 miles long and 2.5 miles wide. There are four islands on the lake, the largest of which is Mayhew, located in the southern part.

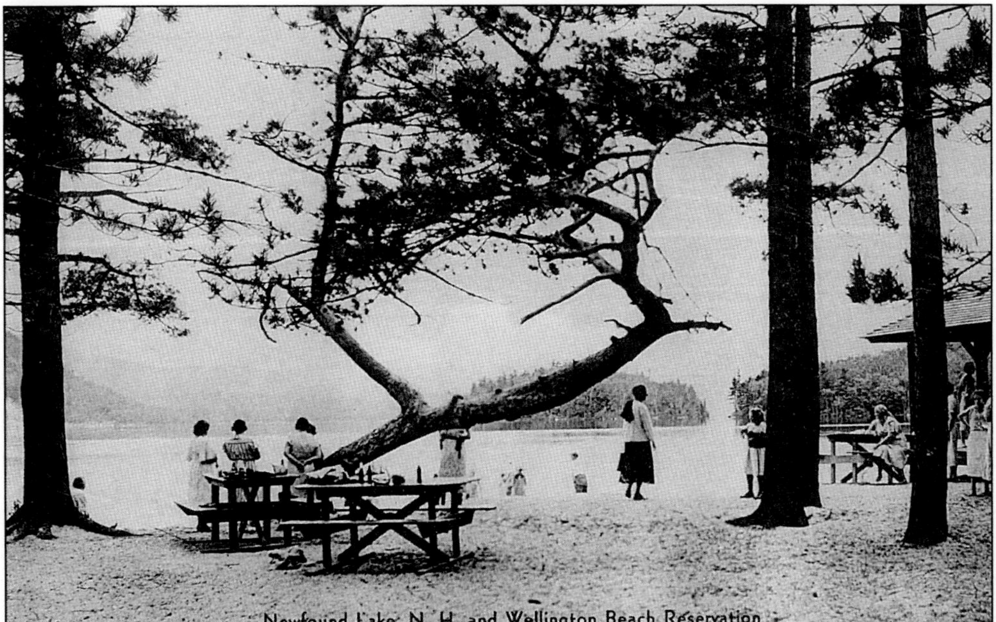

Newfound Lake and the Wellington Beach Reservation, Bristol, NH. The Native American name for this lake is Pasuaney, meaning "place where birch bark for canoes is found." The body of water is unusually beautiful, ringed with hills, and lies mostly in the town of Bristol, NH.

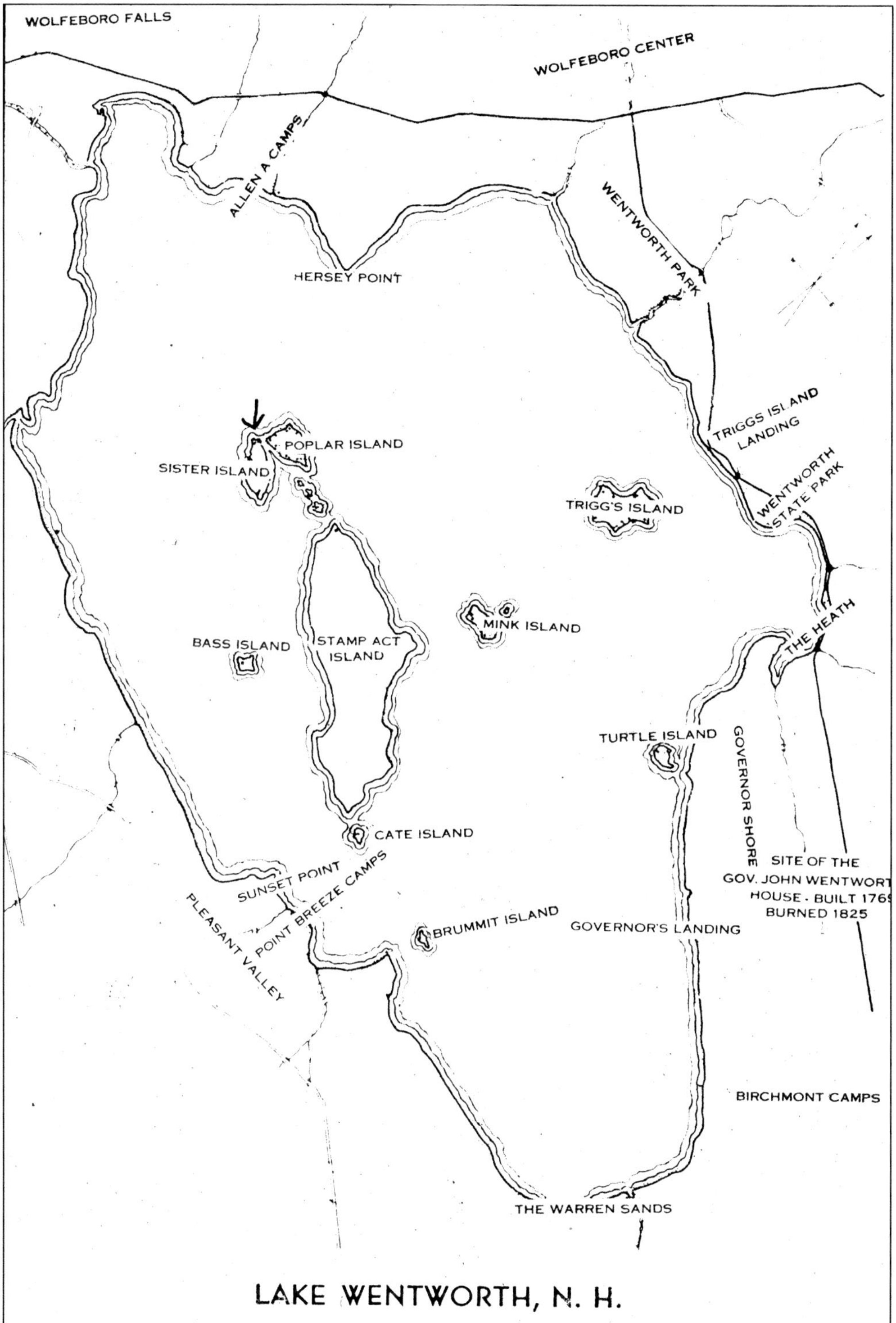

A map of Lake Wentworth. There are several islands on the lake, the largest of which is Stamp-Act Island, nearly 3/4 miles long.

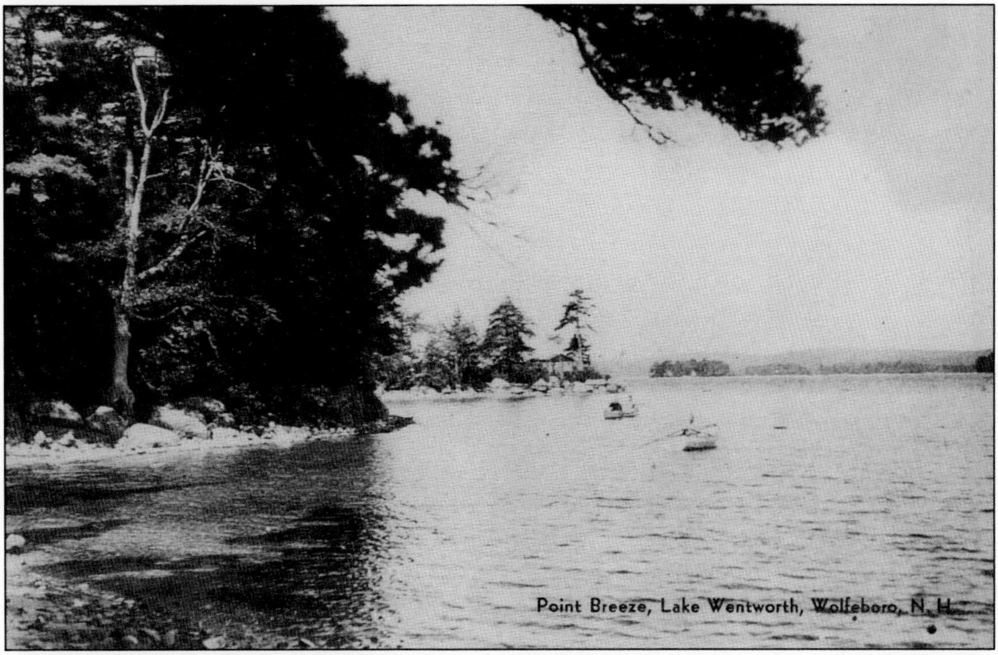

Point Breeze, Lake Wentworth (Smith's Pond), Wolfeboro, NH. This is an attractive sheet of water, 6 miles long, surrounded by low hills and numerous summer homes. In 1768 Gov. John Wentworth began building an imposing summer home 500 feet from the lake, but it was only partly completed and eventually burned during the early 19th century.

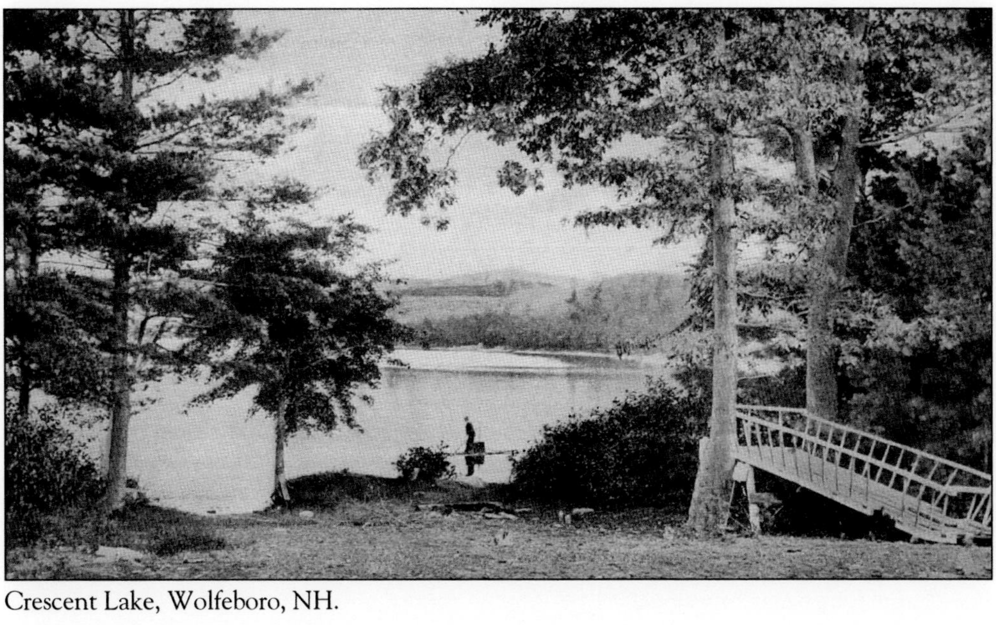

Crescent Lake, Wolfeboro, NH.

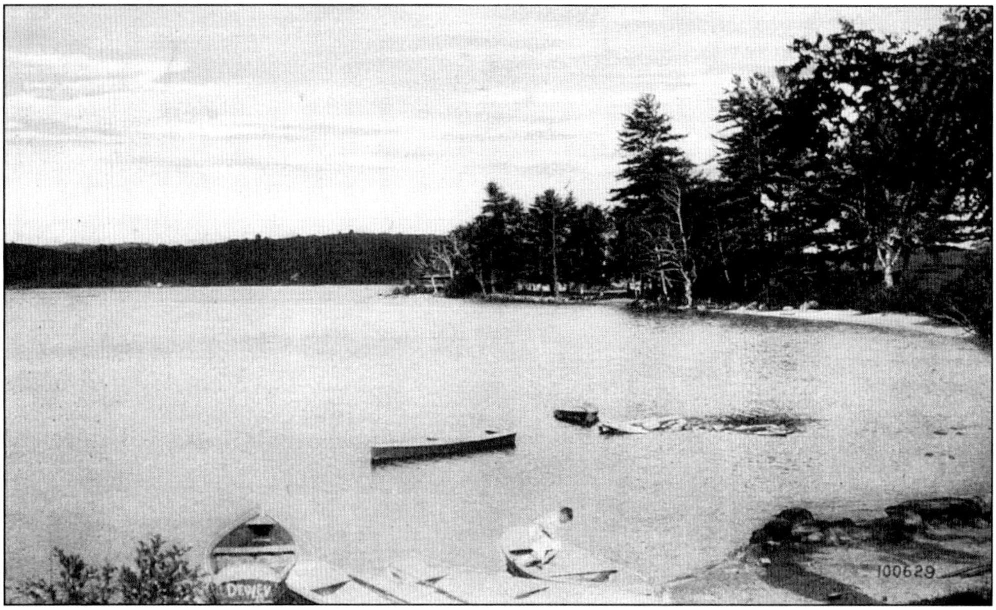

Aiken Point, Webster Lake, Franklin, NH. This is an attractive body of water with numerous cottages framing its shore. There is a bathing beach with all facilities near the highway. Webster Lake is a natural lake rising 401 feet above sea level with an area of 612 acres. This is a tributary to Chance Pond Brook (Sucker Brook), which eventually flows into the Pemigewasset River.

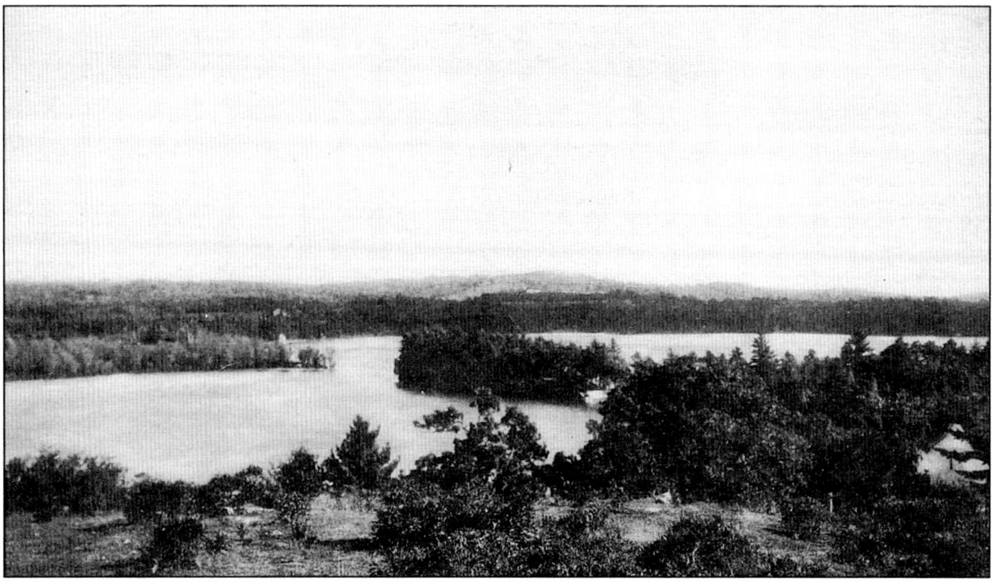

Lake Winnisquam and Mohawk Island. Winnisquam, a Native American name meaning "pleasant water," is a natural lake rising 481 feet above sea level with an area of 4,264 acres. On a clear day, from the bridge at the southern section of the lake, the white summits of the Presidential Range may be visible.

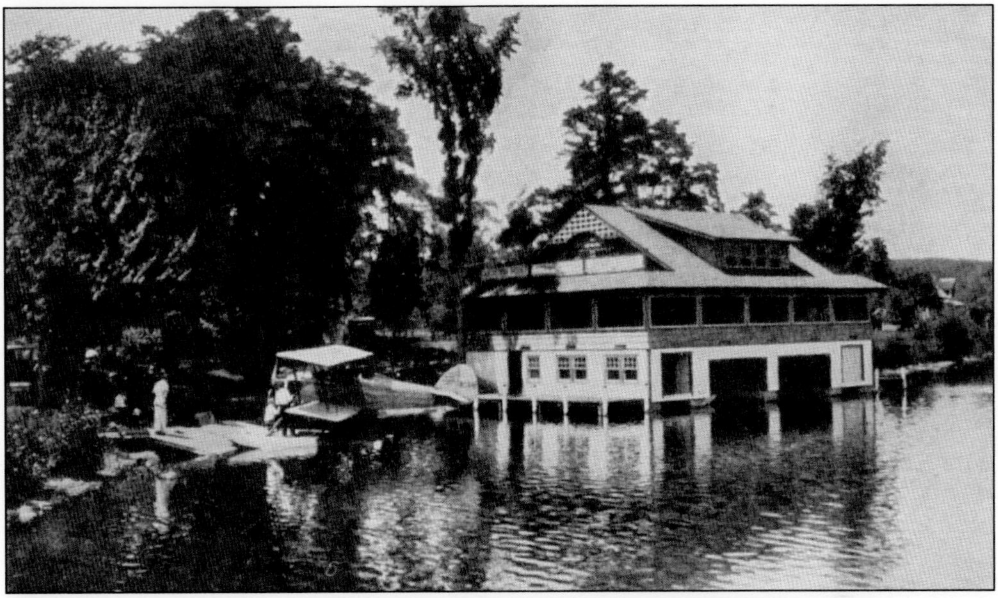

"The Sign of the Wings," an aviation point on Lake Winnisquam, NH. Lake Winnisquam, near Laconia, is located on the Daniel Webster Highway en route to Lake Winnipesaukee and the White Mountains. This attractive lodge, on the shore of the lake, afforded a perfect retreat for the early tourist to the Lakes Region, 1930s.

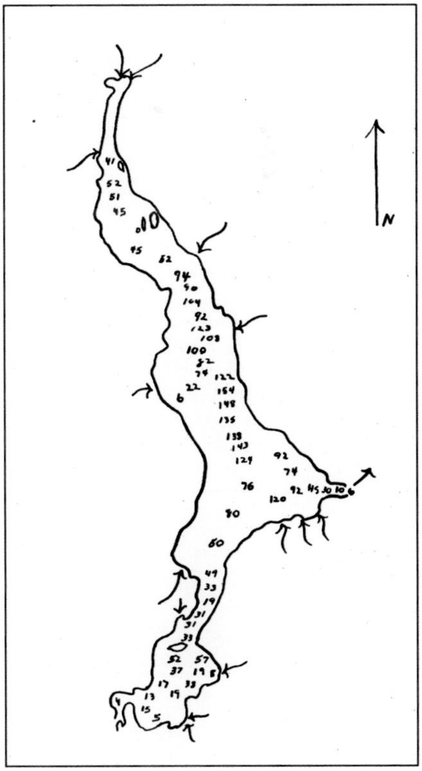

A map of Lake Winnisquam. The lake is about 9 miles long and varies in width from .5 to 2 miles, giving it an area of 4,264 acres. Its watershed is the Merrimack River, with a tributary to the Winnipesaukee River. It receives the waters of the Winnipesaukee River, and at the southern end sends them out to form the little Silver Lake, an expansion of its southern outlet which again takes the name, the Winnipesaukee River.

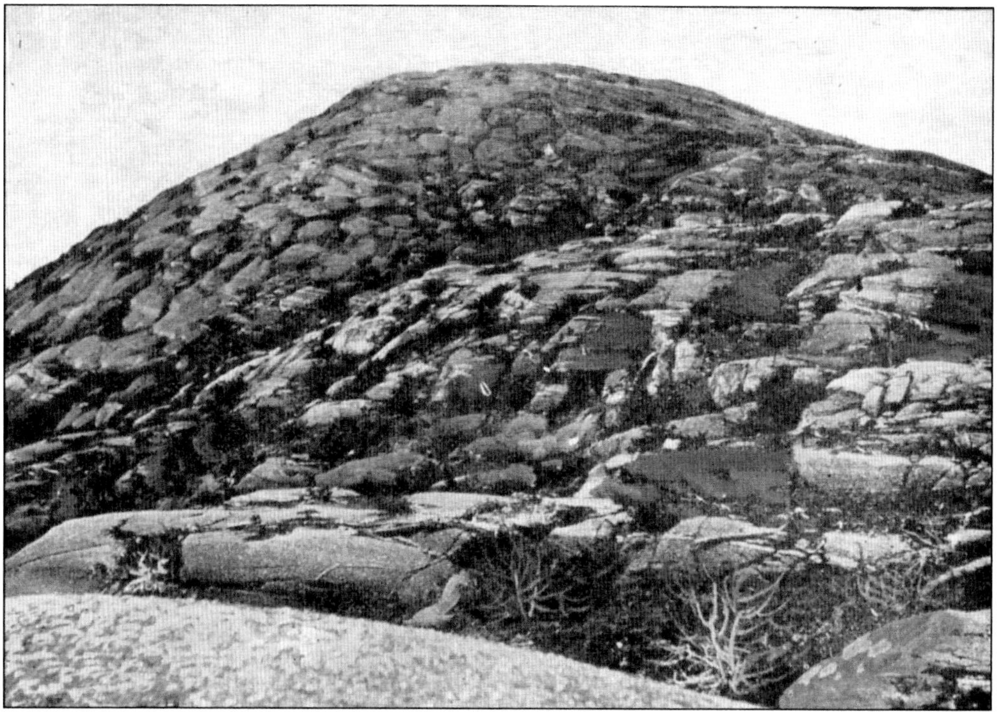

The summit of Mt. Cardigan, Alexandria, NH. This mountain is a huge, three-crested mass of granite with a base length of about 5 miles. The middle peak, Baldface, is the highest elevation in this part of the state. The mountain is steep-sided, dropping almost perpendicularly for about 1,200 feet into the forest below, while the spurs from the flanking peaks, running out to the east, enclose a vast ravine.

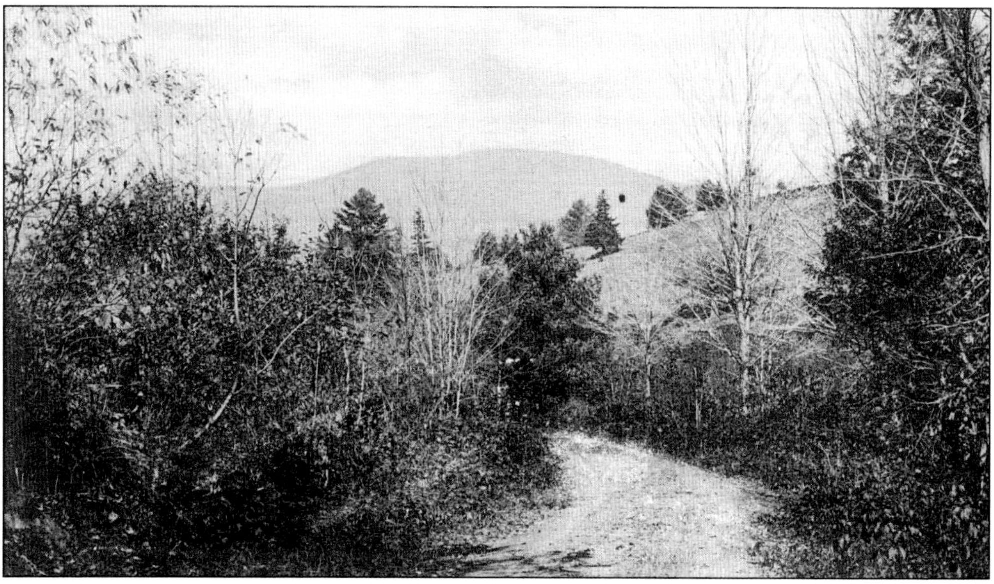

Ragged Mountain (alt. 2,200 feet), located in the town of Andover, NH. This mountain is heavily wooded and irregular in shape. From the south summit there is an excellent view of the Kearsarge, Sunnapee, and Cardigan Mountains.

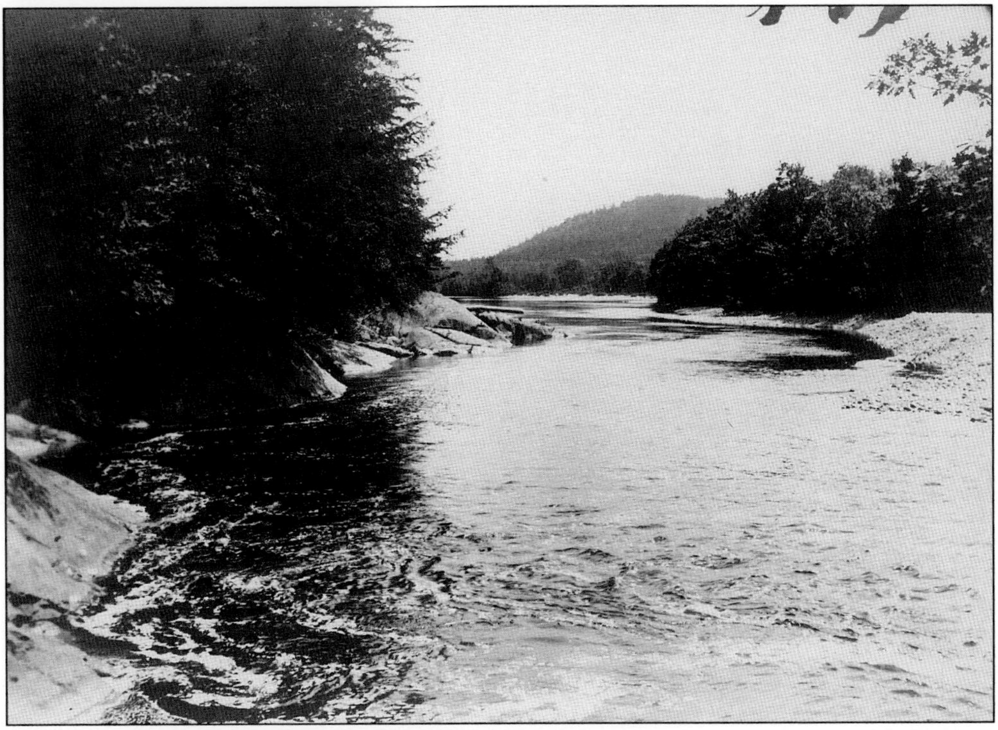

The Pemigewasset River in Plymouth, NH, 1907. Originating from the Franconias, this river flows south through the Pemigewasset Wilderness to Plymouth, New Hampton, Bristol, and eventually to Franklin, where it joins the Winnipesaukee River to form the Merrimack River.

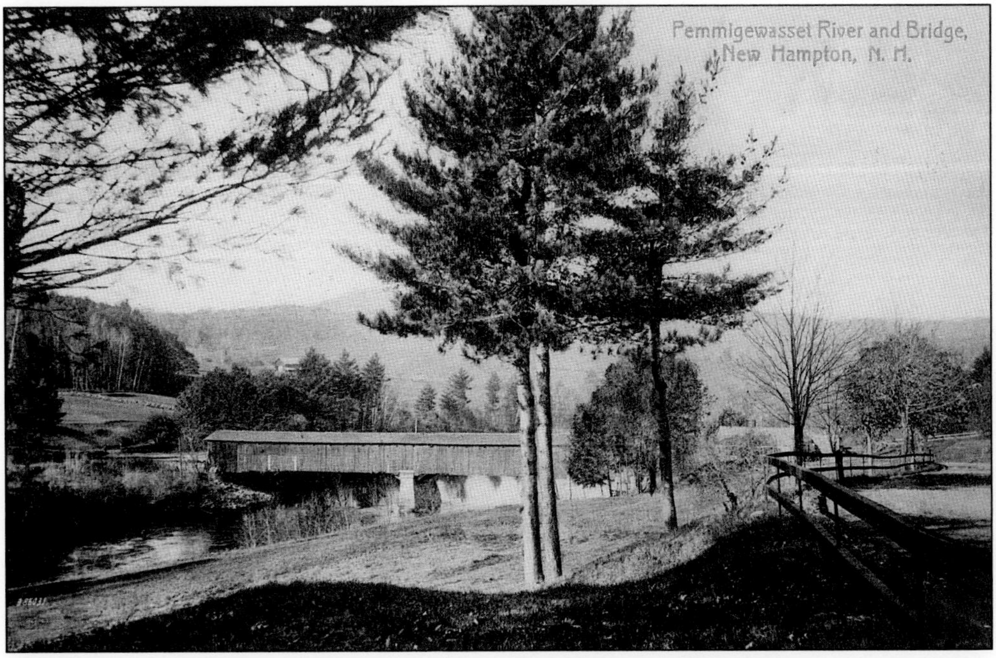

The Pemigewasset River and Covered Bridge in New Hampton, NH, 1912.

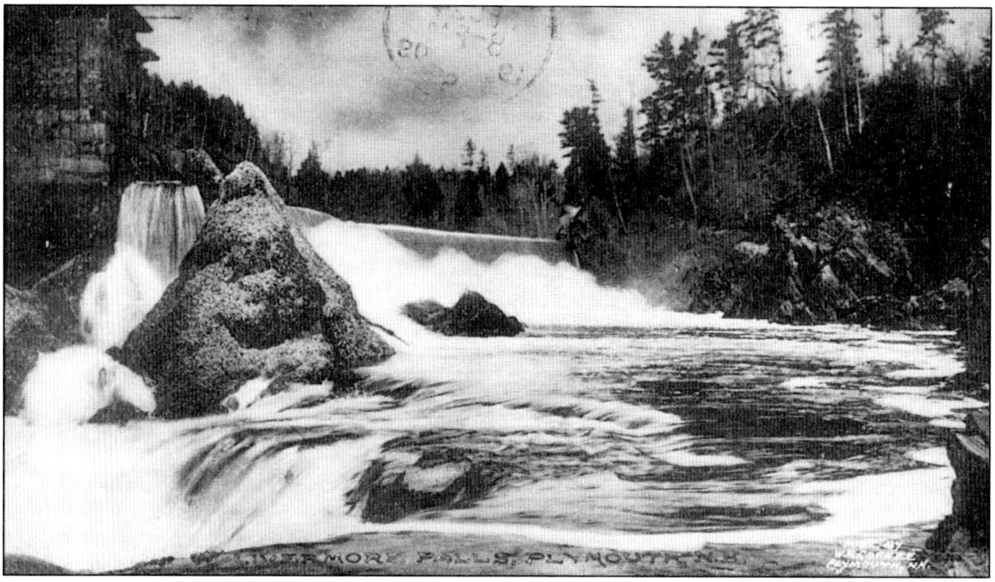

Livermore Falls, 1909. These falls are located about 2 miles above Plymouth, NH. There are many picturesque narrows of the Pemigewasset River among massive rocks. Sawheganet and Livermore Falls were considered by Native Americans and early settlers as the best fishing places. The broad and beautiful intervales of the tribe were located at the confluence of Baker's River and the Pemigewasset.

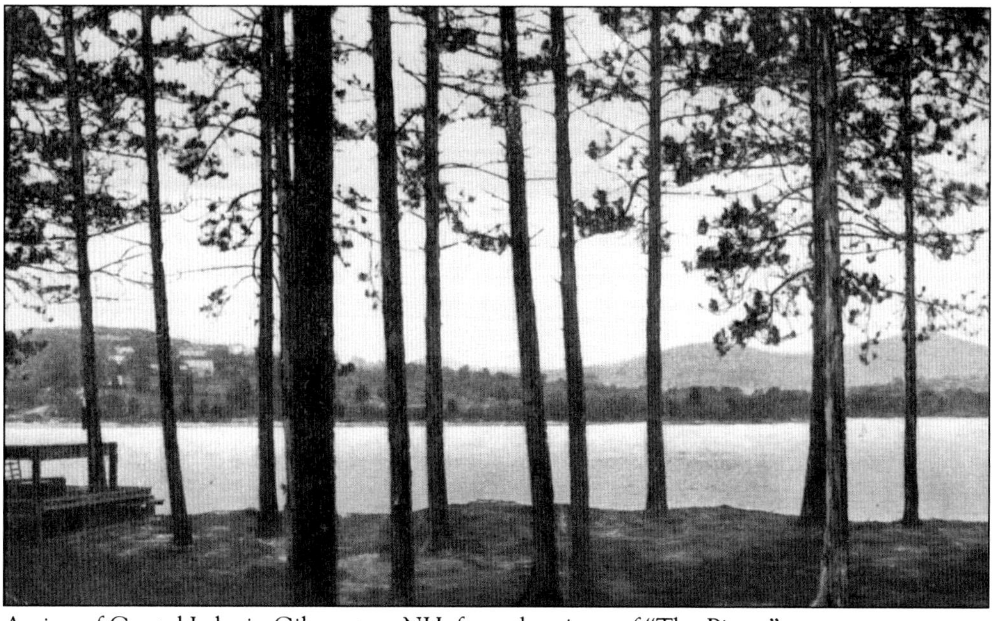

A view of Crystal Lake in Gilmanton, NH, from the piazza of "The Pines."

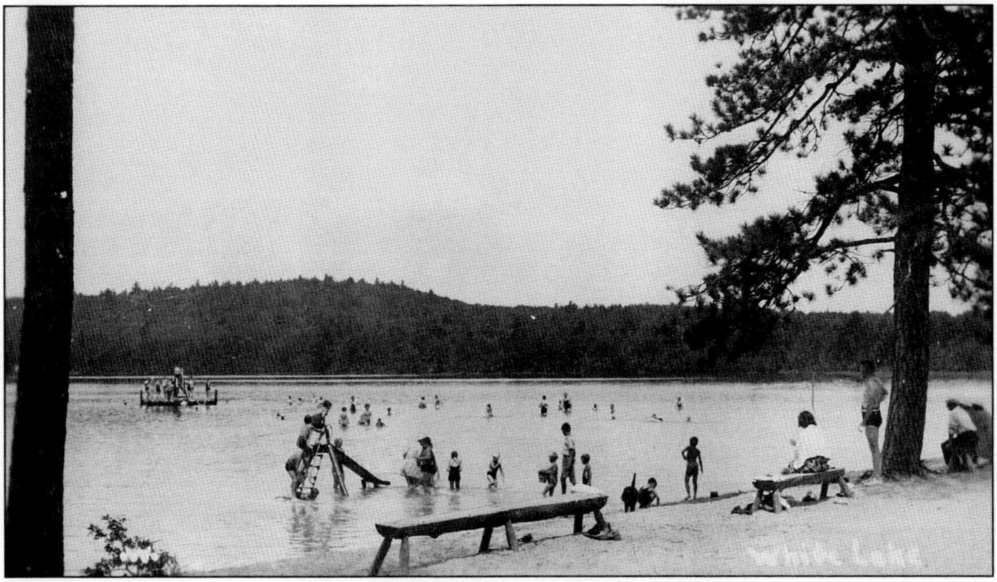

Silver Lake (White Lake) in Madison, NH. The shore of this small lake was a favorite camping ground for local Native Americans. Today, this is a popular lake for bathers.

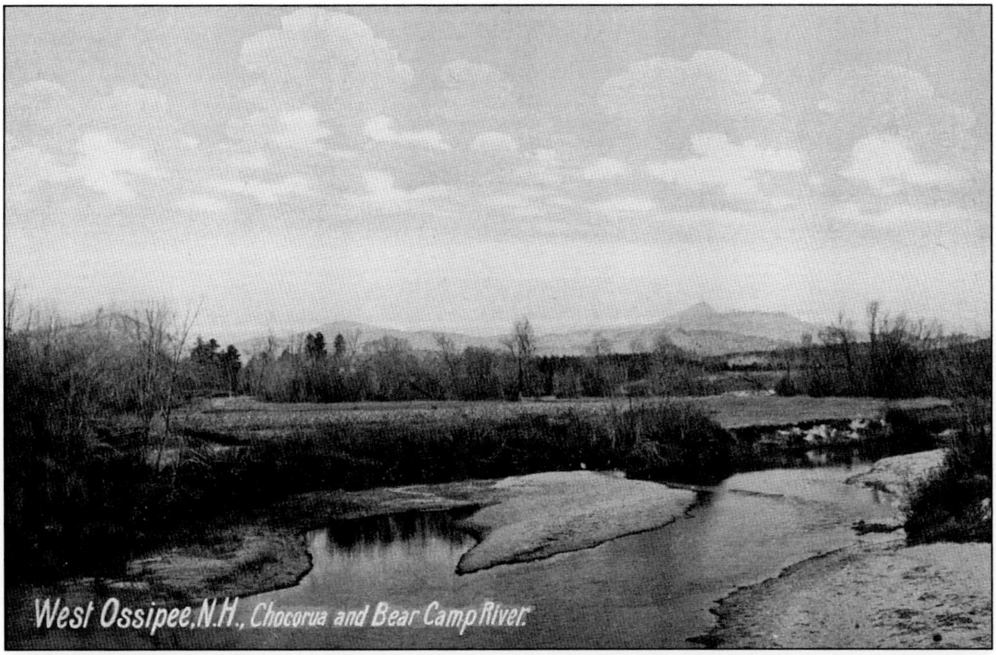

A view of Bear Camp River and Mount Chocorua as seen from West Ossipee, NH. Here the river flows close to the base of the Ossipee Mountains, bordered by pleasant meadows and graceful trees. The scenery encompasses the Ossipee range, the Green Mountains of Effingham, the picturesque peaks of the Sandwich Range, the alpine-crested Chocorua, the lower ledges of Mount Paugus, the dark round top of Passaconaway, the shining cliff's of Whiteface, and the forest-covered Sandwich Dome.

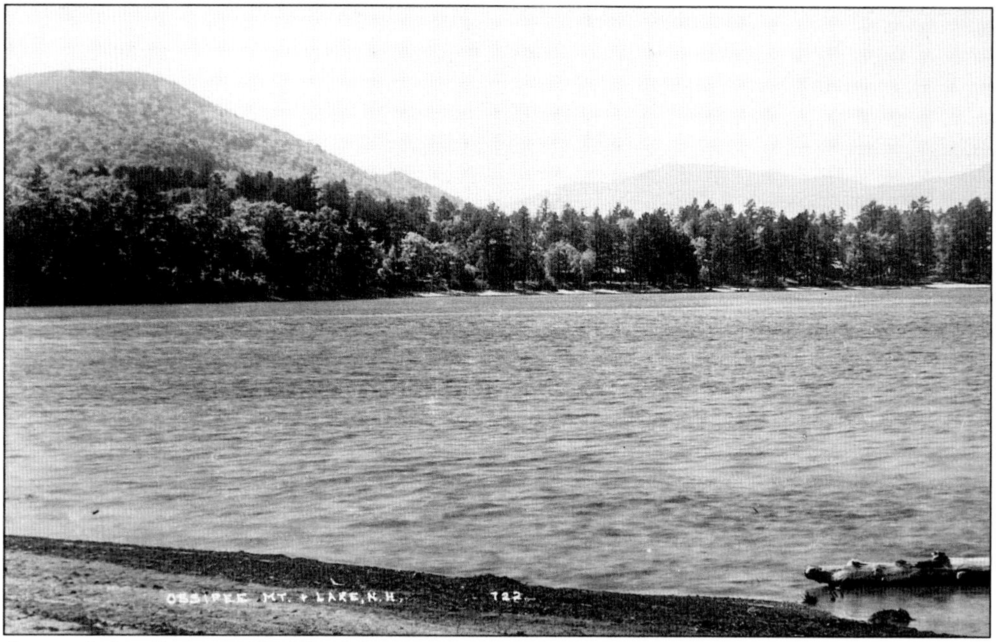

Ossipee Lake, Ossipee, NH. This lake is approximately 3.5 miles long and 2 miles wide, and, with its bays and inlets, contains nearly 7,000 acres. It is destitute of islands, and is partly surrounded by a beautiful border of silvery beaches. The waters of the Pine, Lovewell's, Bearcamp, and Six-Mile Rivers empty into the lake, which is itself emptied by the Ossipee River.

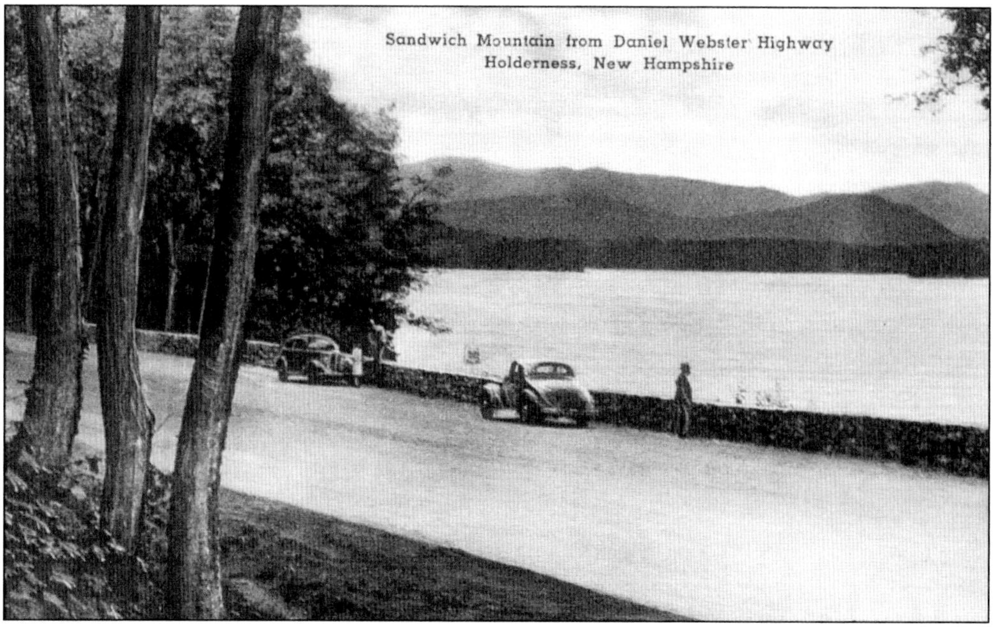

The Sandwich Mountain Range as seen from the Daniel Webster Highway in Holderness, NH, 1920s. This mountain range has several notable peaks, but Chocorua attracts the most attention.

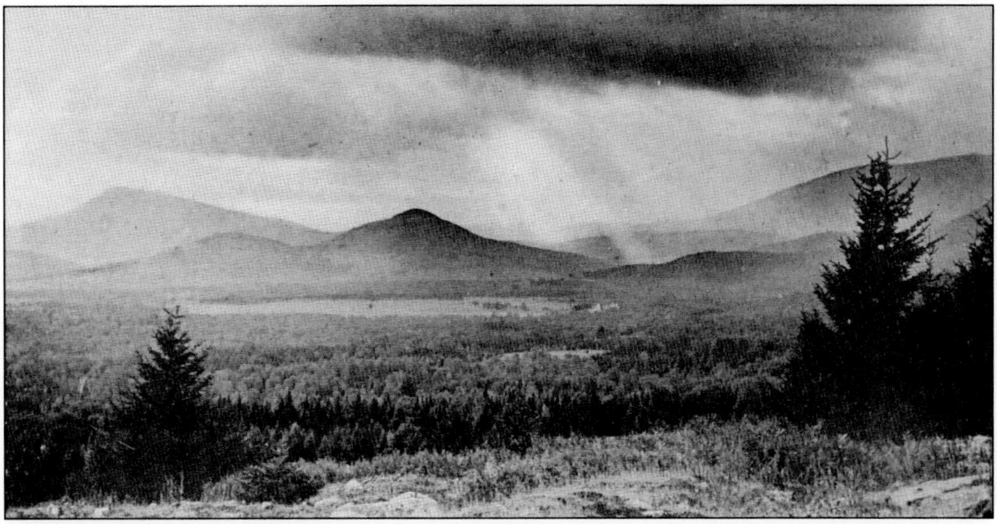

Sandwich Dome as seen from Mt. Katherine in Wonalancet, NH. This immense mountain lies in the western part of the towns of Sandwich and Waterville. It is separated from the Campton Range by the Sandwich Notch, and from Whiteface by the low plateau of Flat Mountain. This mountain is known to many in adjacent towns as Black Mountain, but since this name has been applied to so many summits in New Hampshire, Prof. Guyot bestowed upon this mountain the name of "Sandwich Dome," which has been accepted by the State Geological Survey.

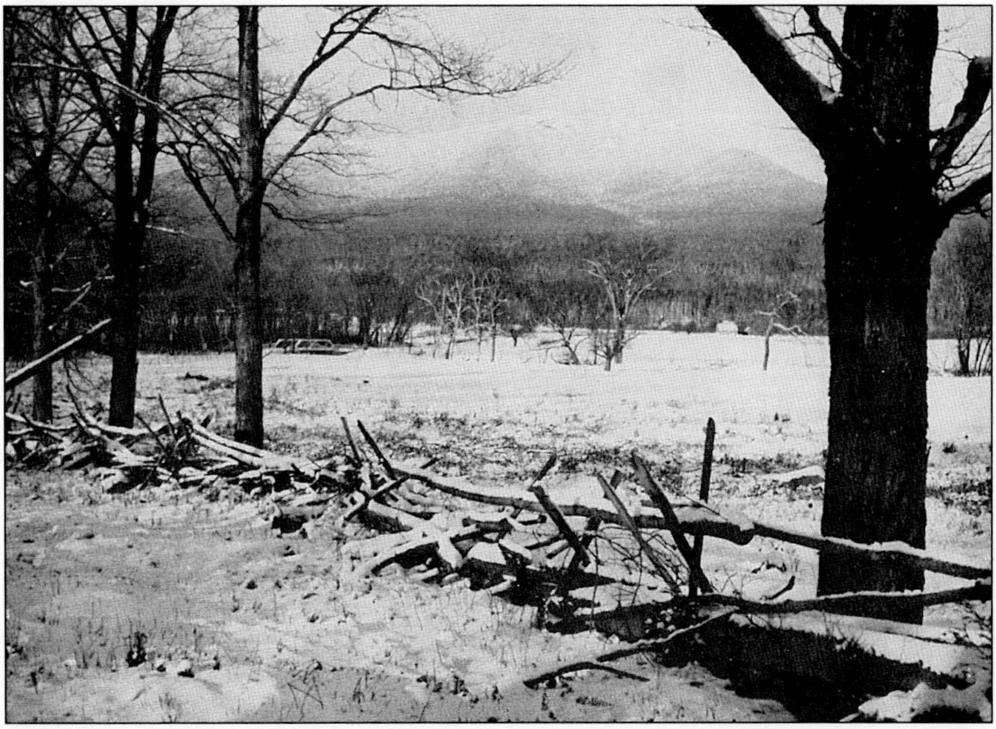

White Face Mountain Interval in the winter. "So lovingly the clouds caress his head, The Mountain-monarch; he, severe and hard, With white face set like flint horizon-ward; They weaving softest fleece of gold and red, And gossamer of airest silver thread, To wrap his form, wind-beaten, thunder-scarred." —From Lucy Larcom's *An Idyl of Work*.

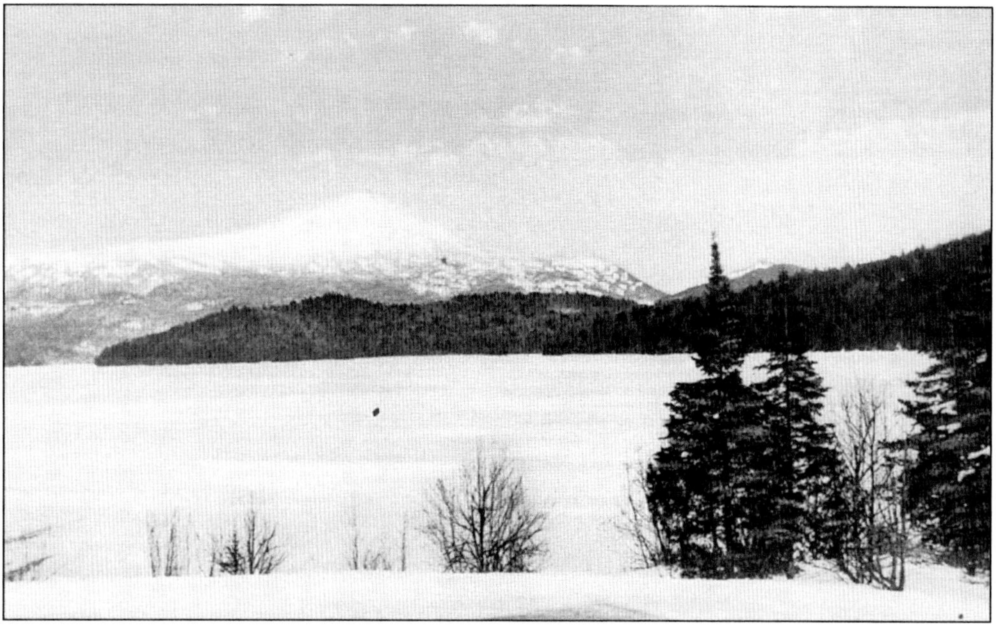

A winter scene of Whiteface Interval with Whiteface Mountain in the distance, Sandwich, NH. (alt. 4,007 feet). "His grandeur and grace so interfuse; And when his angels leave him unawares, A sullen rock, his brow to heaven he bares." —From Lucy Larcom's *An Idyl of Work.*

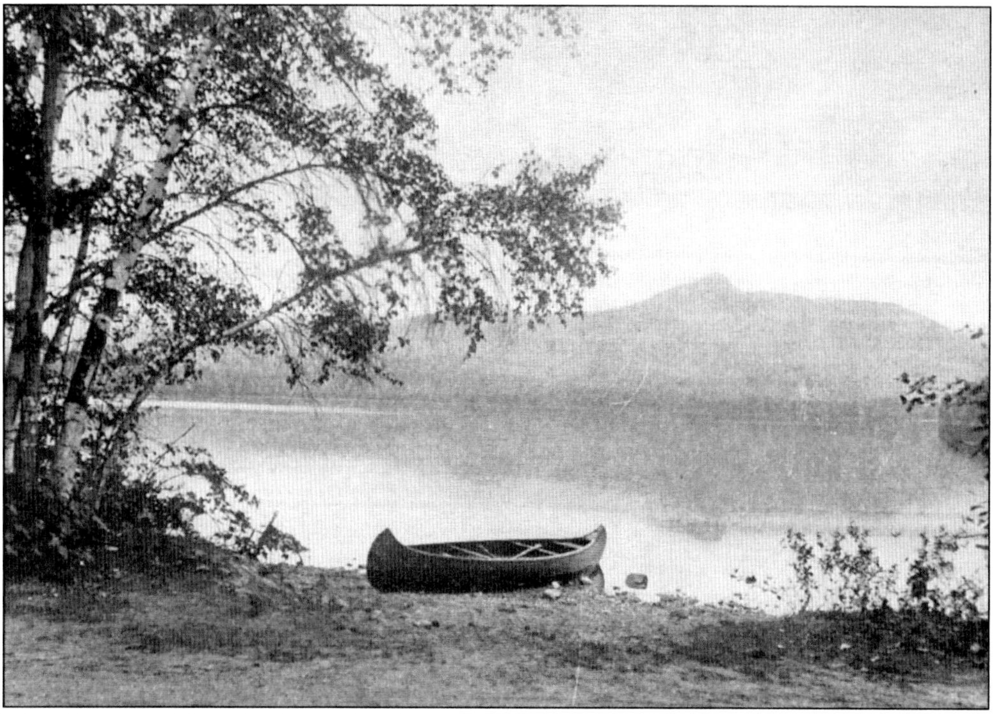

Lake Chocorua. This lake, located in the town of Tamworth at the base of Mount Chocorua, is more than one mile long and is divided into two parts, connected by a narrow strait over which a bridge has been built. The shores are partly formed by curving sandy beaches, overhung by shadowy trees.

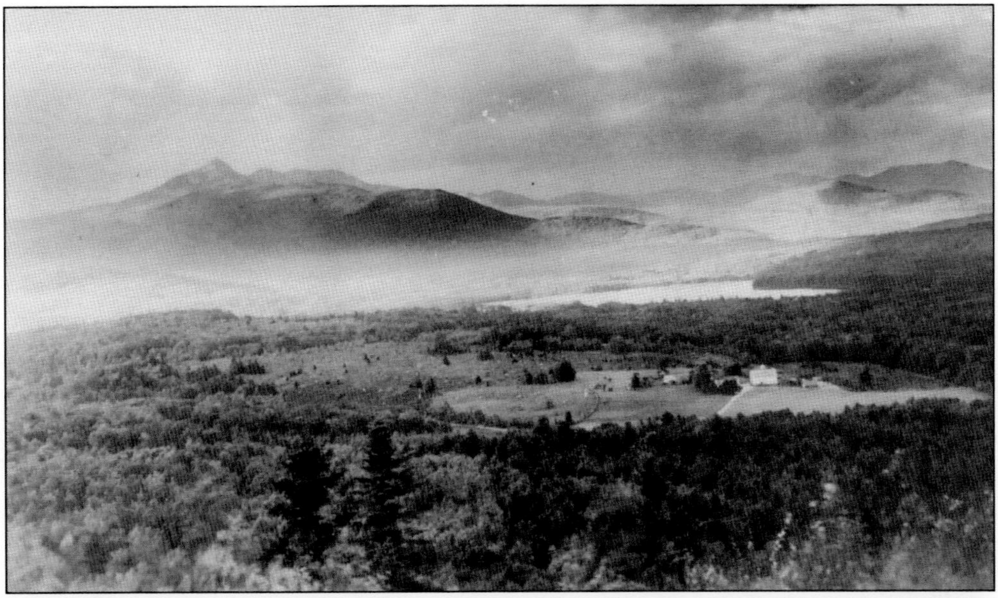

Mount Chocorua and Chocorua Lake from Page Hill in Tamworth, NH (alt. 3,540 feet). The main peak is surrounded by steep cliffs, in many places impassable, and has a long pile of rocks on its crest, under which shelter may be gained from north and west winds. This mountain is probably the most beautiful of the mountains of New England. It can be seen from the border towns of Maine and New Hampshire, and from the west borders of the Lakes Region, always presenting to view the same blanched peaks, sharp in outline and unique in form.

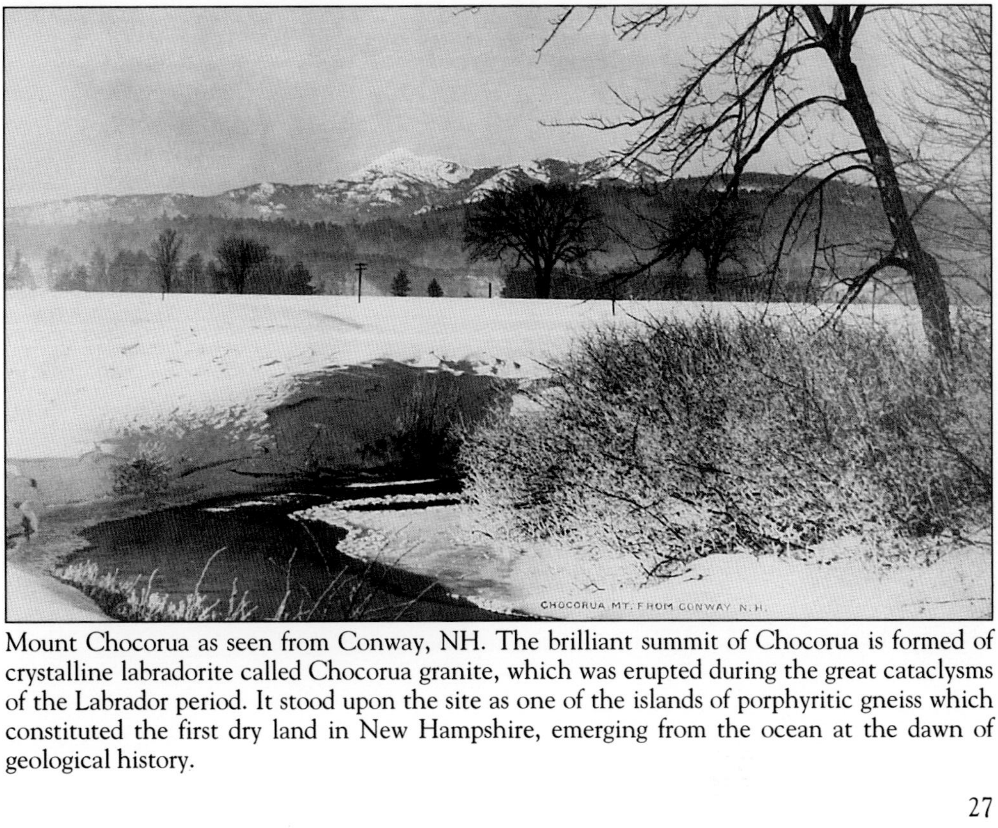

Mount Chocorua as seen from Conway, NH. The brilliant summit of Chocorua is formed of crystalline labradorite called Chocorua granite, which was erupted during the great cataclysms of the Labrador period. It stood upon the site as one of the islands of porphyritic gneiss which constituted the first dry land in New Hampshire, emerging from the ocean at the dawn of geological history.

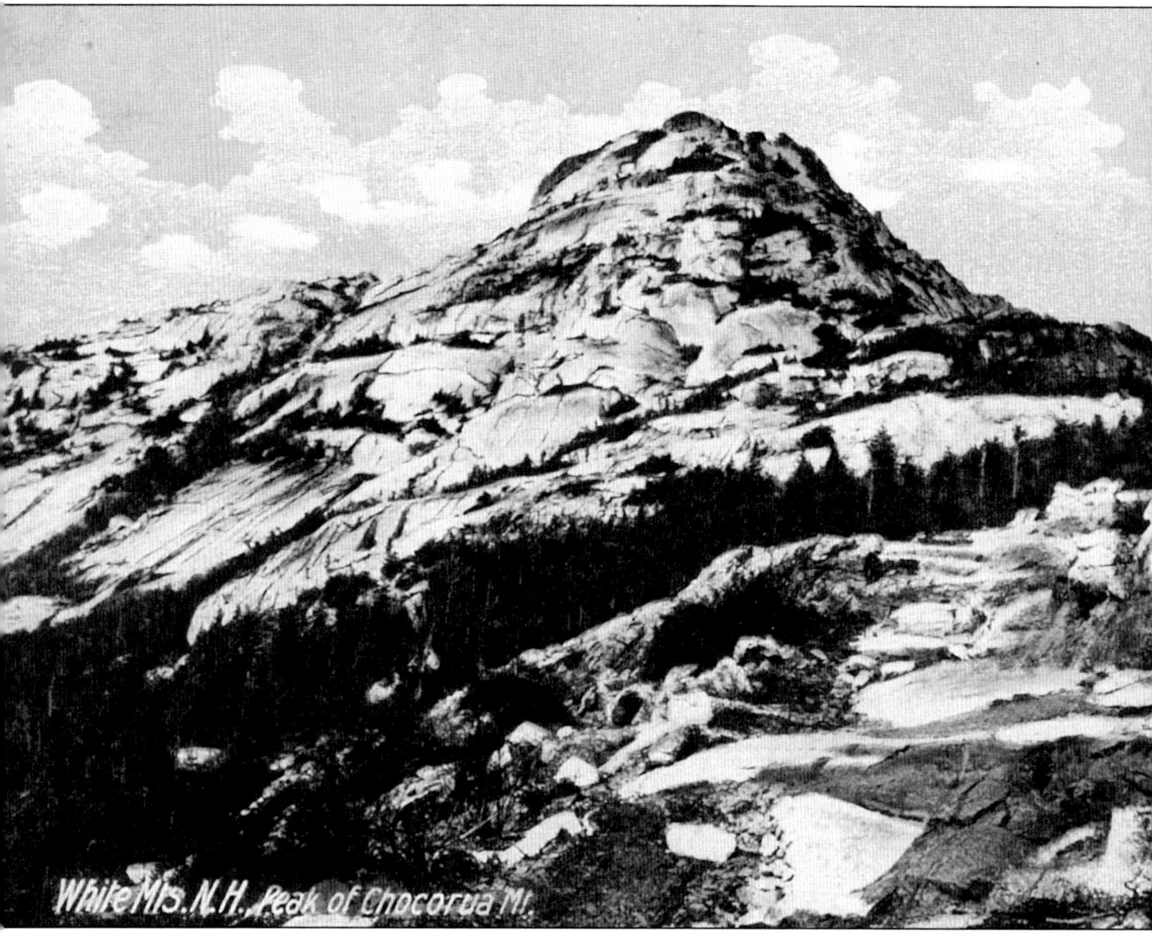

The peak of Mount Chocorua.

The pioneer of a great company
That wait behind him, gazing toward the east,
Mighty ones all, down to the nameless least,
Though after him none dares to press, where he
With bent head listens to the minstrelsy
Of far waves chanting to the moon, their priest.

What phantom rises up from winds deceased?
What whiteness of the unapproachable sea?
Hoary Chocorua guards his mystery well:
He pushes back his fellows, lest they hear
The haunting secret he apart must tell
To his lone self, in the sky-silence clear.
A shadowy cloud-cloaked wraith, with shoulders bowed,
He steals, conspicuous, from the mountain-crowd.

—From Lucy Larcom's *An Idyl of Work*.

Two

Village Scenes and Landmarks

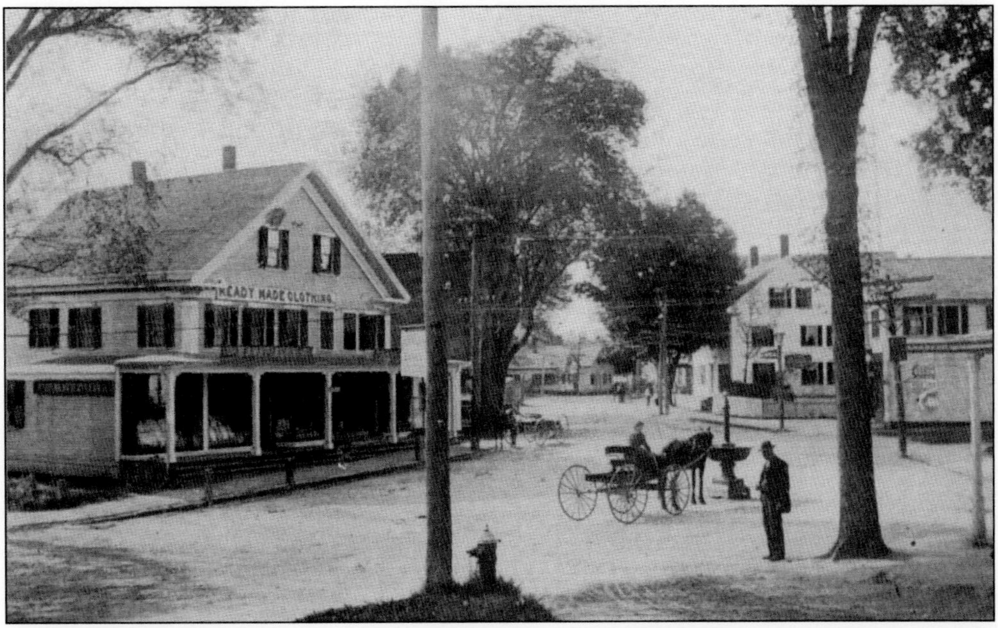

A view of Post Office Square in Meredith, NH, 1880s. Meredith's early history is closely associated with that of Laconia. The original territory of 6 square miles was granted in 1748, but it soon found that the indentations of the bays made less acreage, and that a line 7 miles from the northwest corner would not reach the big lake. In 1754, the Portsmouth proprietors increased the grant by calling the northern boundary 12 miles instead of 7; this is presently known as Meredith Neck.

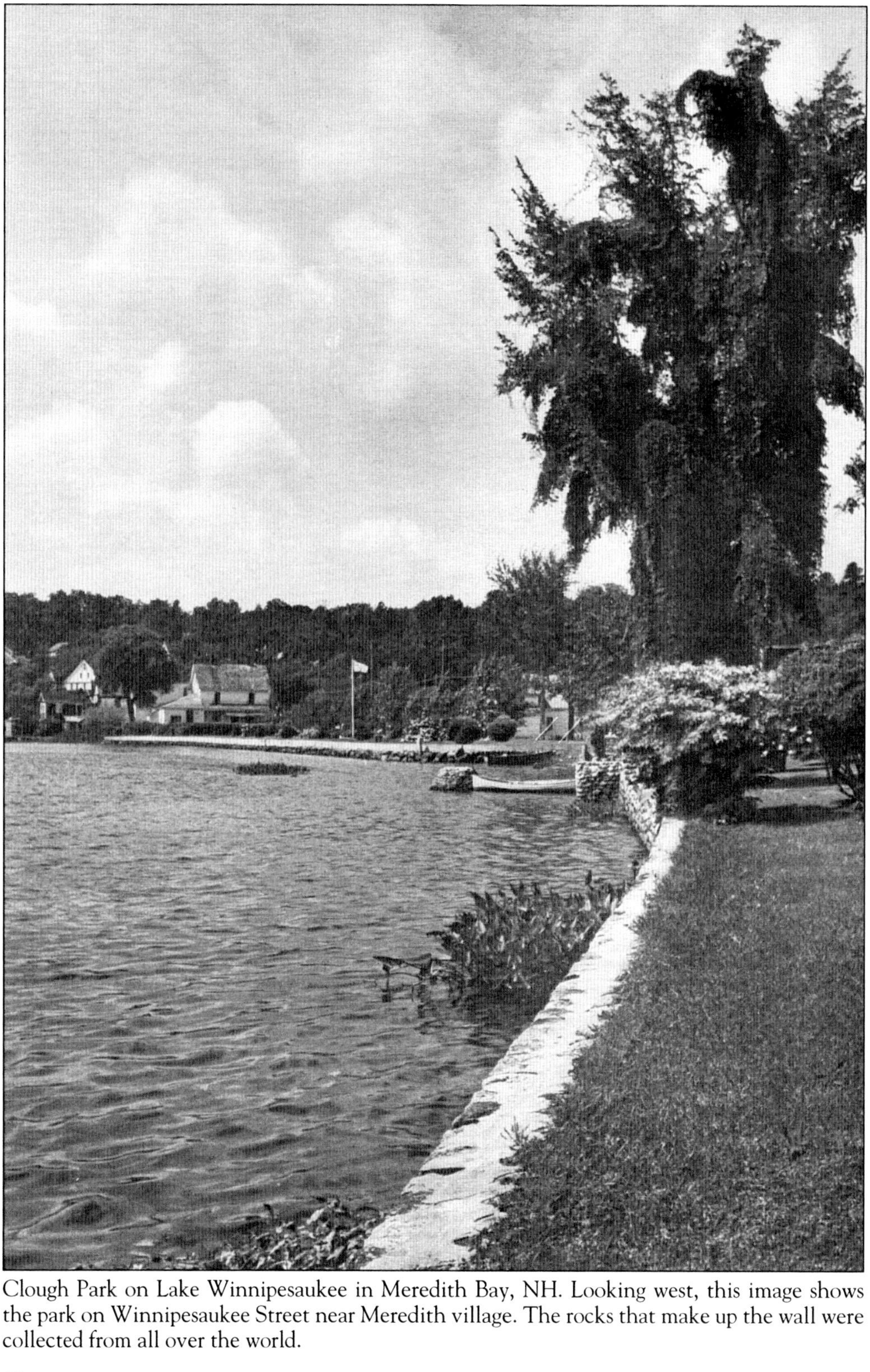

Clough Park on Lake Winnipesaukee in Meredith Bay, NH. Looking west, this image shows the park on Winnipesaukee Street near Meredith village. The rocks that make up the wall were collected from all over the world.

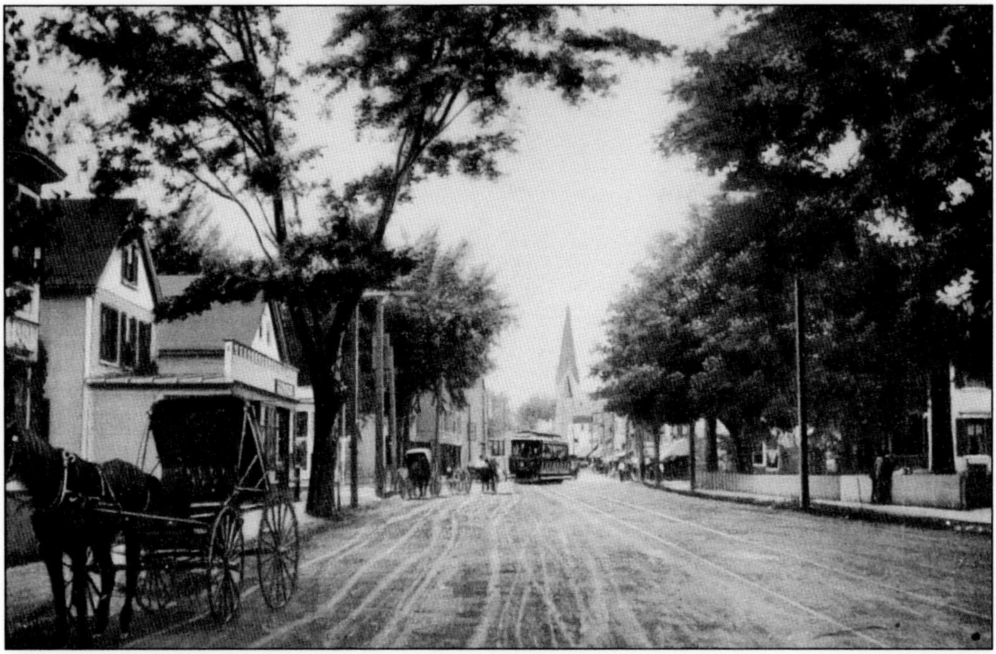

Main Street looking north, Laconia, NH, 1908. Laconia is a compact city of houses and businesses which line the slow-moving but clear waters of the Winnipesaukee River. The city has a choice water setting: three lakes extend into its limits, thus it may well put on its seal, "The City of the Lakes." It carries an air of prosperity, reflected in its business section and in the various factories and tourist industries throughout the city. During the summer, vacationists from all over the country are found enjoying this resort area.

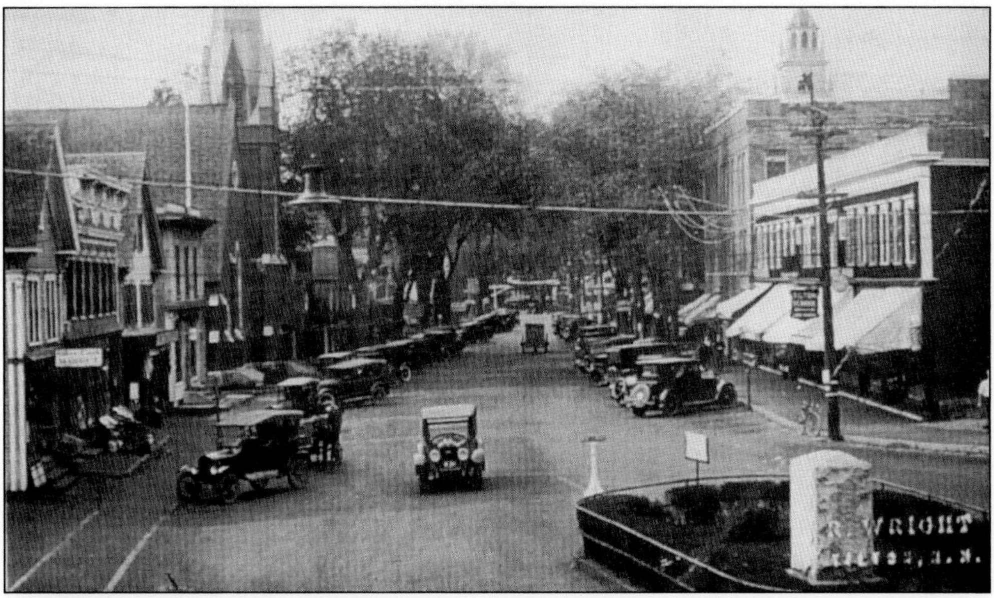

Main Street in Tilton, NH, 1920s. Tilton is a small community with few industries, but rather accents on tourism and the Tilton School, a very prominent and successful private school. The town is united industrially, commercially, and residentially with Northfield, located to the south of it, across the Winnipesaukee River.

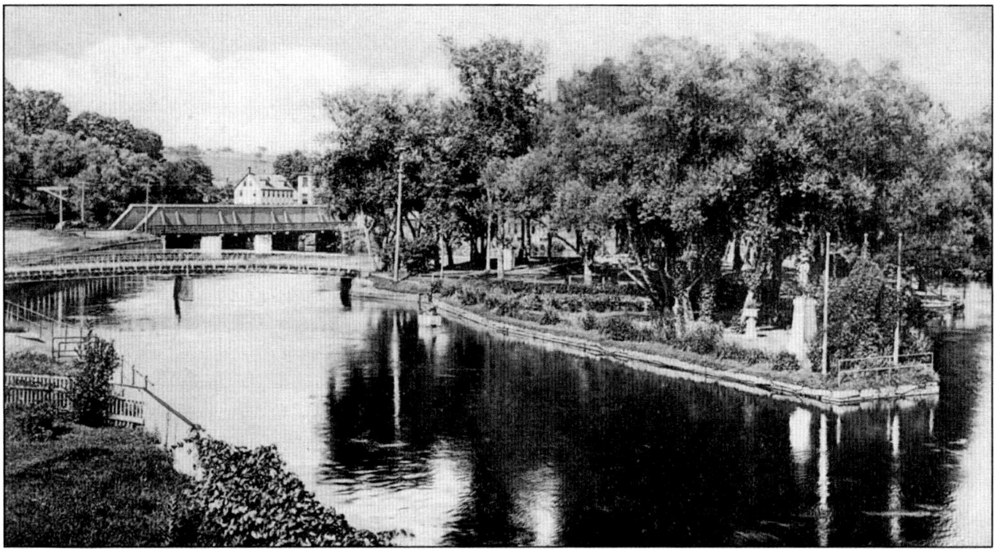

The Winnipesaukee River in Tilton, NH, with a railroad bridge and island in the center, 1908. Originally, this town was settled as a part of Sanbornton. Tilton Township was not incorporated until 1869, when it took its name in honor of Nathaniel Tilton, the first settler in 1768.

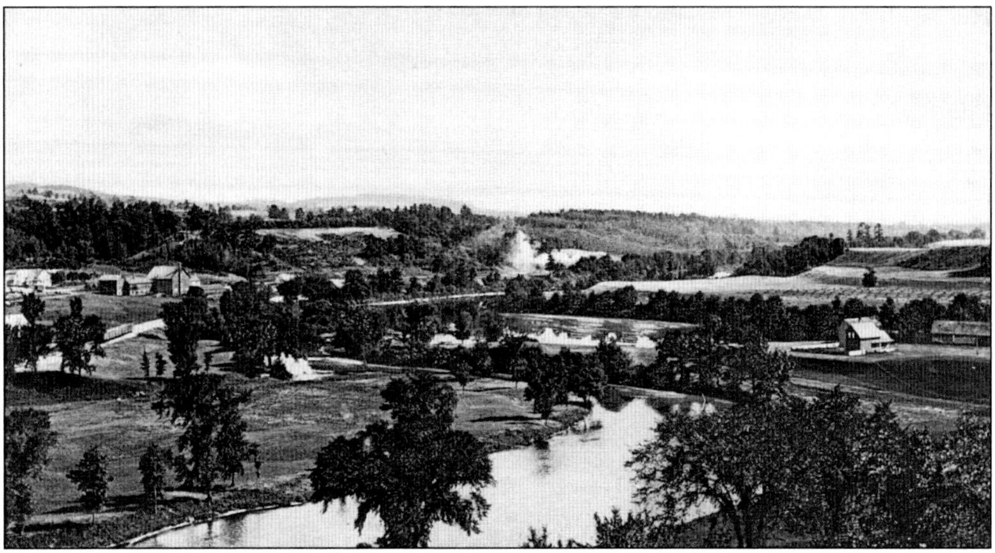

The head of the Merrimack River in Franklin Falls, NH, 1900. This is the meeting place of the Pemigewasset and Winnipesaukee Rivers, which unite to form the Merrimack River in Franklin, NH.

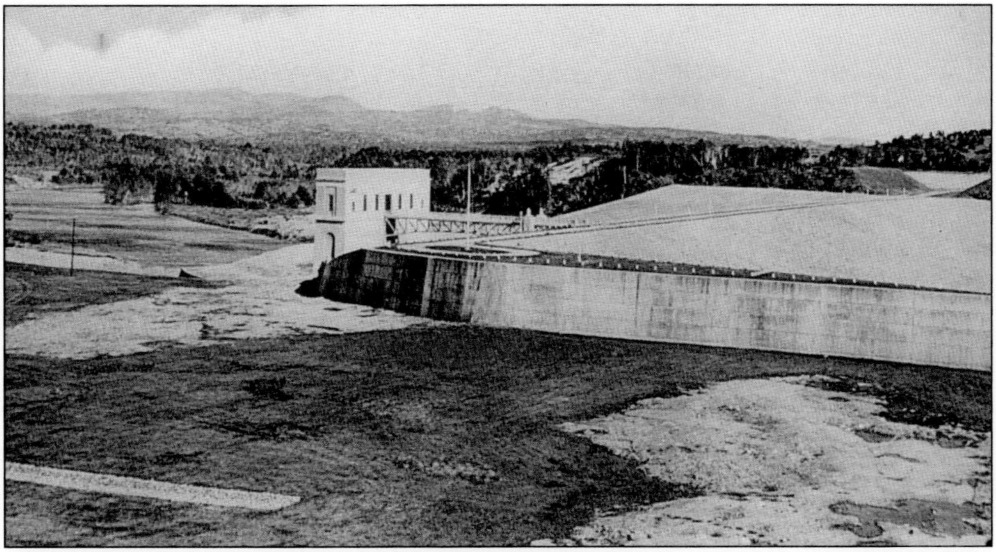

A view of the Franklin Falls Flood Control Dam across the Spillway Channel up the Pemigewasset River Valley. This dam, constructed under the supervision of the Boston District, Corps of Engineers, U.S. Army, provides flood control for the Merrimack Valley. Construction of the $4.9 million dam was commenced in November 1939, and was completed in October 1942.

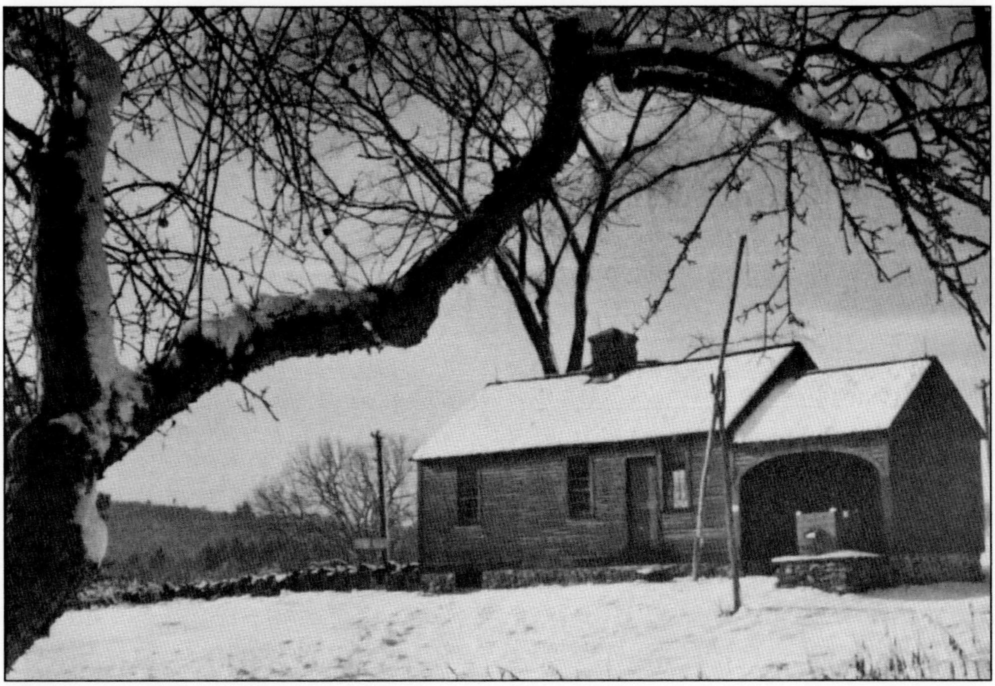

The Daniel Webster birthplace facing the mill. This small, two-room frame house, located off Route 127, is the spot where the famous attorney spent his boyhood years. The structure was built about 1780; it was restored in 1913.

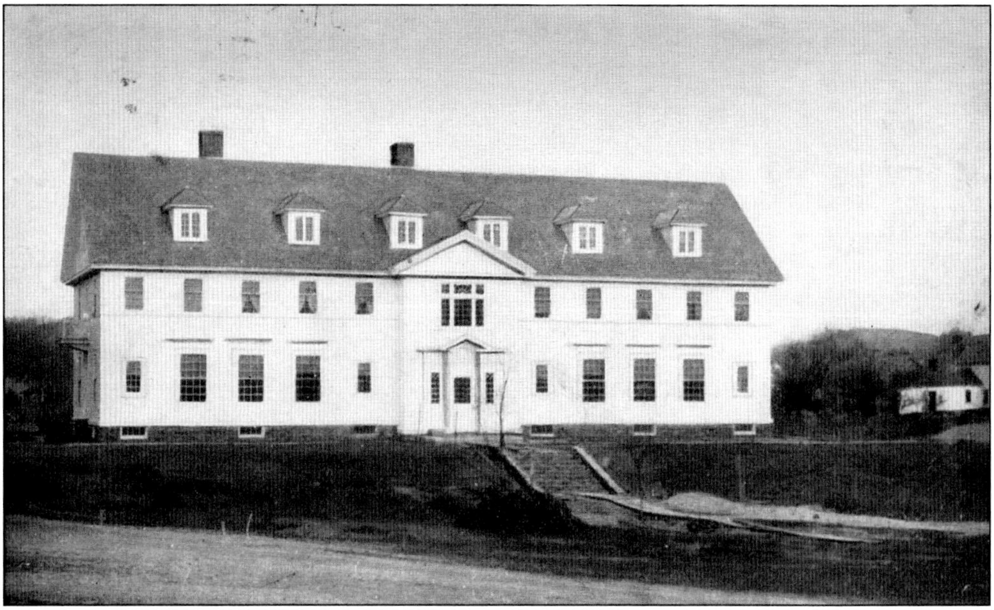

The Carey House, dormitory for girls, Proctor Academy, Andover, NH, 1910. This academy was founded in the Unitarian Church in 1848. In 1856, the trustees turned over the property to the New England Christian Conference, which formed a new school, the New England Christian Literary and Biblical Institute, which was moved to Wolfeboro (1865), where it operated until 1874. A move was then made to return the academy back to Andover. With new financial backing and building renovations, the school was once again incorporated (1879), and renamed, this time in honor of John Proctor, a liberal contributor to the school.

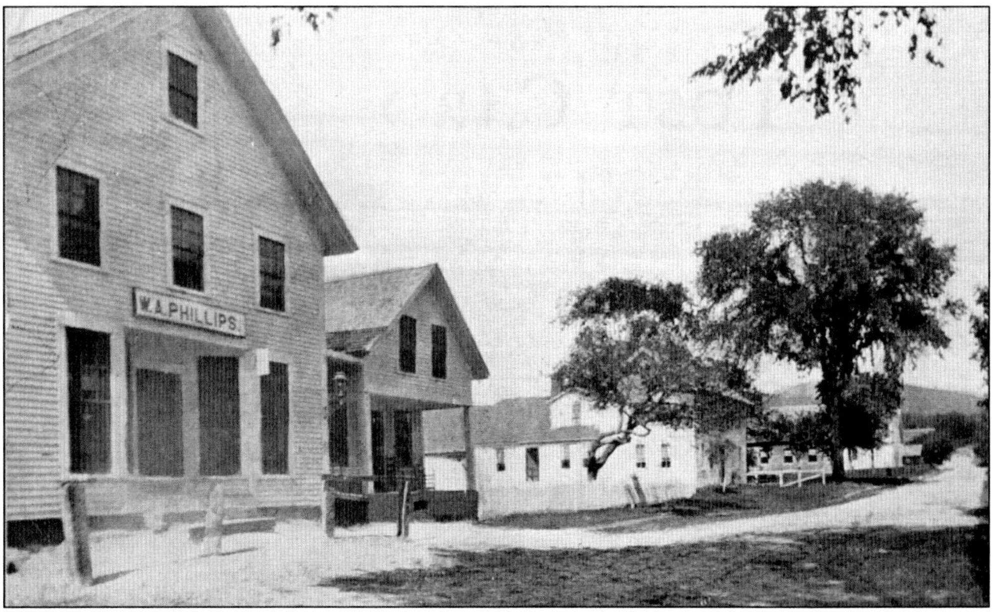

The business district of Alexandria, NH. Originally, this town was a part of the Masonian Grant of New Chester. Many acres of valuable land in the intervale of the Fowler River attracted settlers as early as 1769, although the town was not incorporated until 1782.

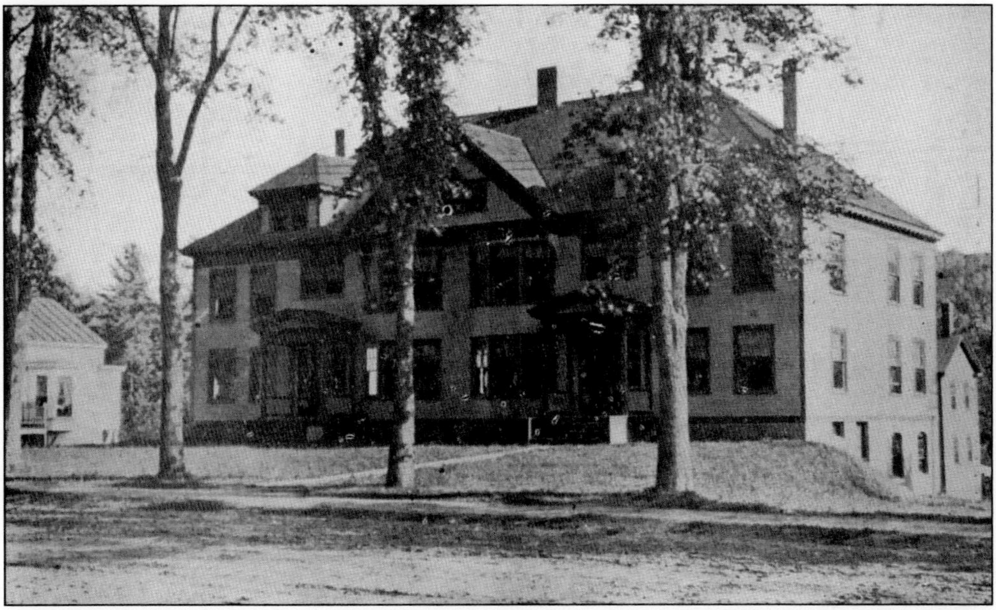

Draper Hall, New Hampton Academy, New Hampton, NH, 1912. This academy, located in the village and housed in a row of brick buildings of the American Georgian type, was founded in 1812 by William B. Kelley and Nathaniel Norris. Today it is considered one of the finest private preparatory institutions in New England.

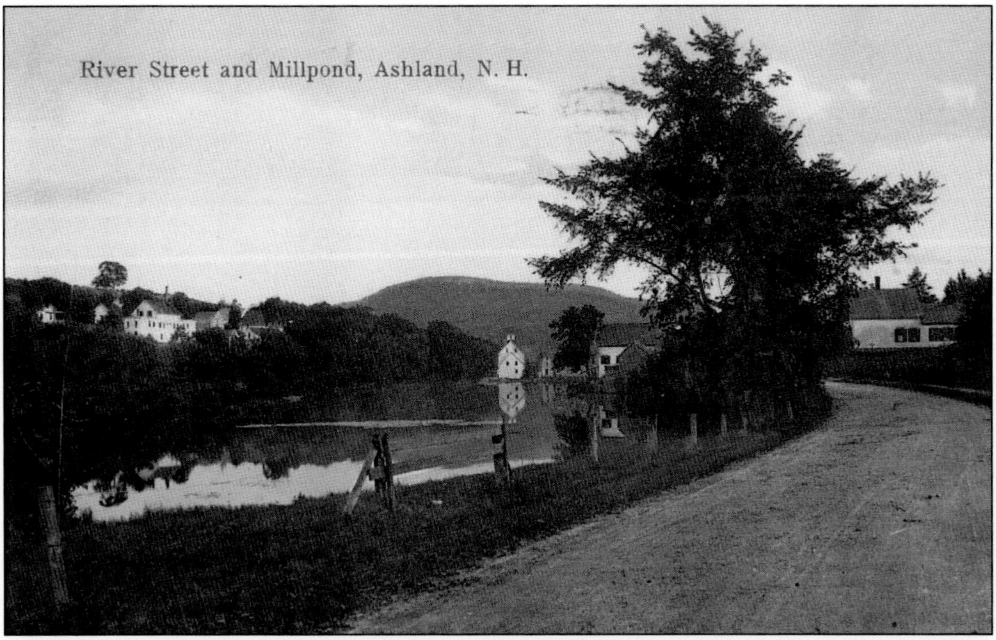

River Street and Millpond in Ashland, NH, 1910. During its early days of settlement, Ashland was part of Holderness; it was incorporated independently in 1868. Gristmills and sawmills were operated here in 1770. Today, this thriving community's chief industries are paper and textile goods, as well as tourism. It is located in the geographical center of the state.

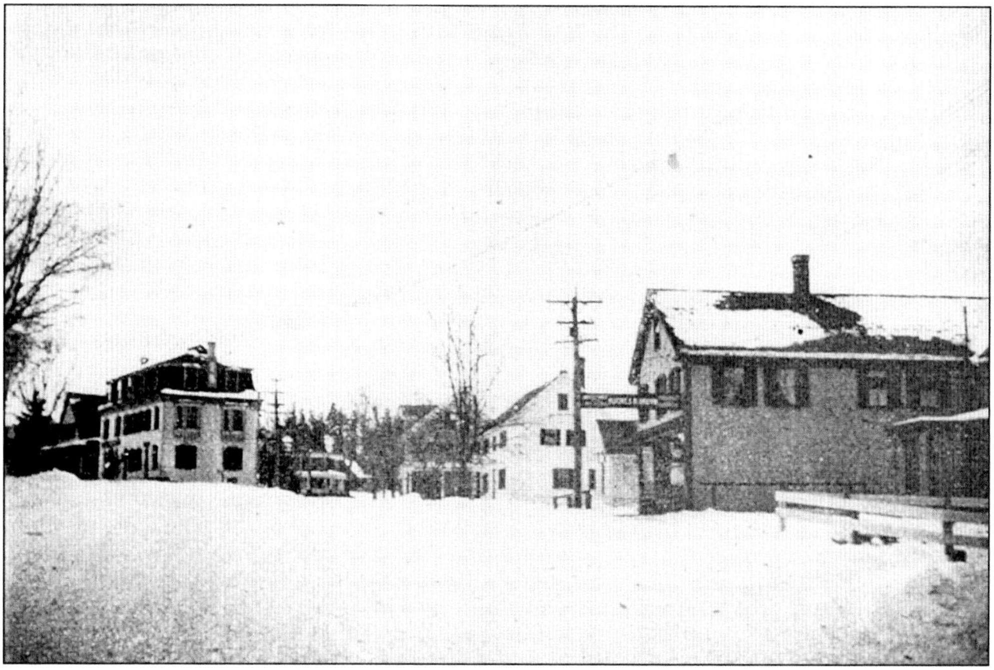

Ashland's Main Street, showing the post office and the Hughes & Brown Store (on the right).

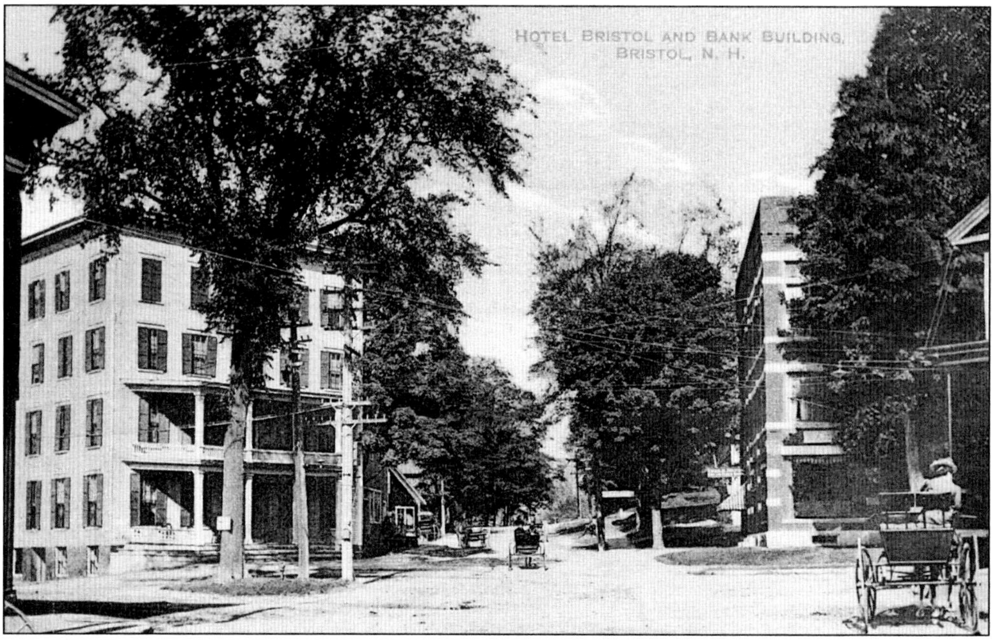

Bristol Village, with the Hotel Bristol on the left and a bank building on the right, late 1800s. Bristol was granted in 1753 as a part of New Chester, and was later set off and incorporated in 1819, taking the name of Bristol, England. At first a farming community, it was spurred to industrial activity by the opening of a railroad from Franklin in 1848.

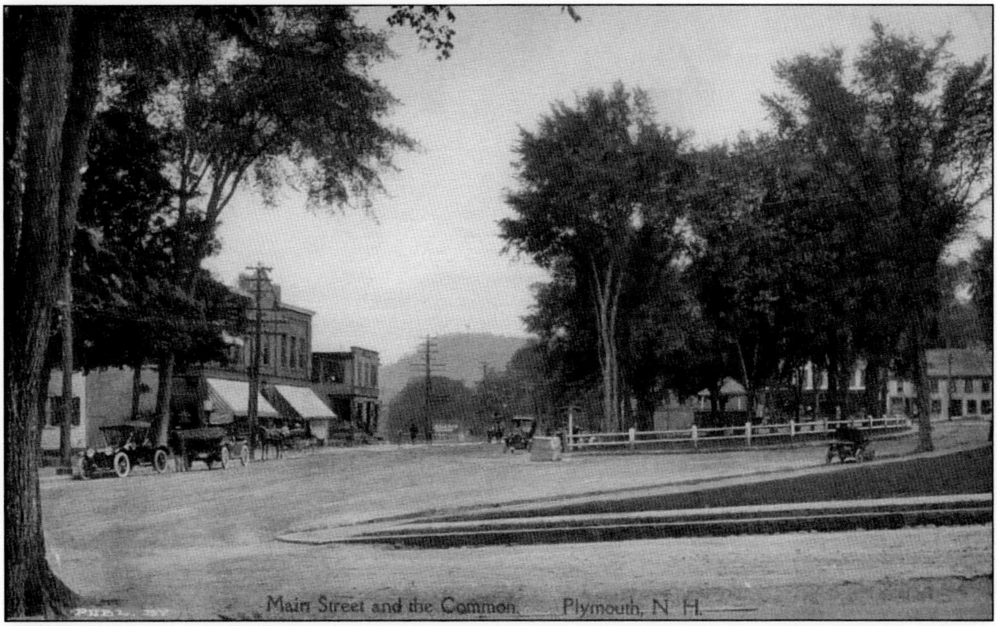

The Main Street and Common in Plymouth, NH, 1918. This town was granted to Joseph Blanchard and others on July 15, 1763. Located on the Pemigewasset River and on the line of the Boston, Concord & Montreal Railroad, it is the home of the State Normal School, presently known as Plymouth State College.

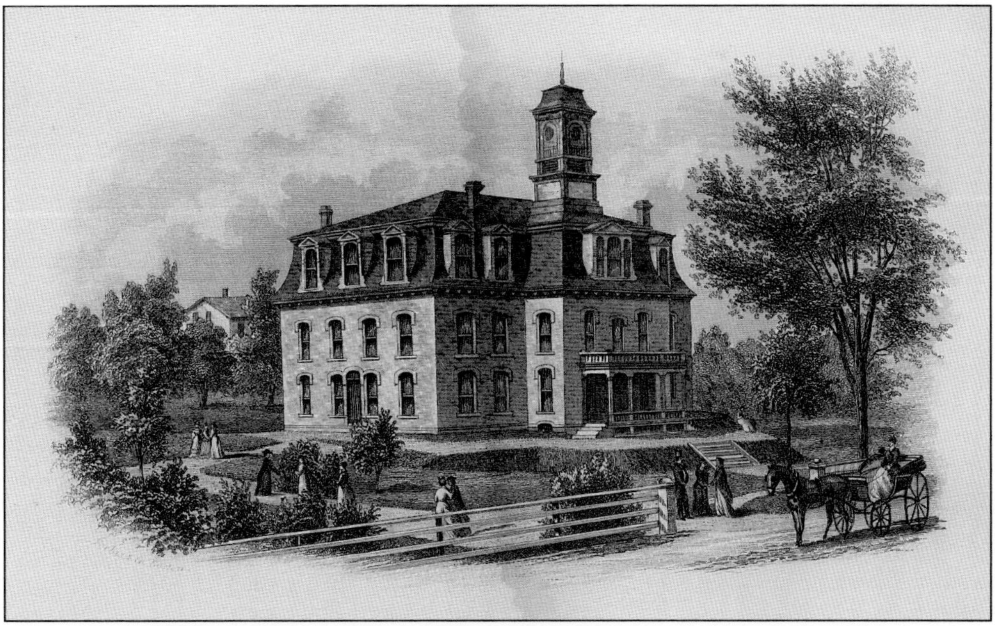

The original Plymouth Normal School. This school was the first teacher's college in New Hampshire, called a Normal School after the French "Ecole Normal" to distinguish it, presumably, from a medical or other specific type of school.

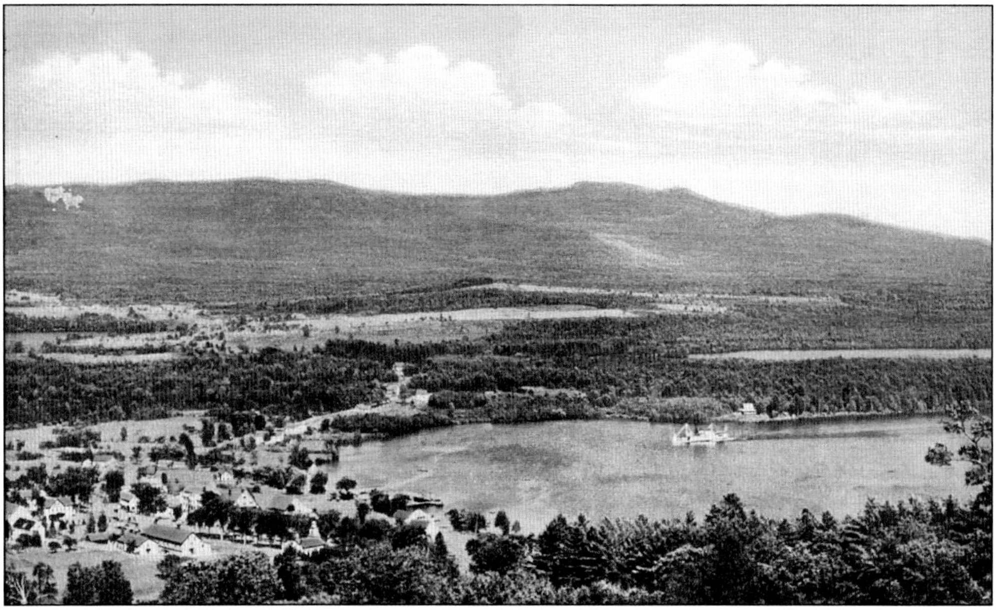

An early 1930s view of Center Harbor and Lake Winnipesaukee, as seen from Sunset Hill, Center Harbor, NH. In the harbor can be seen the sidewheeler *Mount Washington* approaching the town dock.

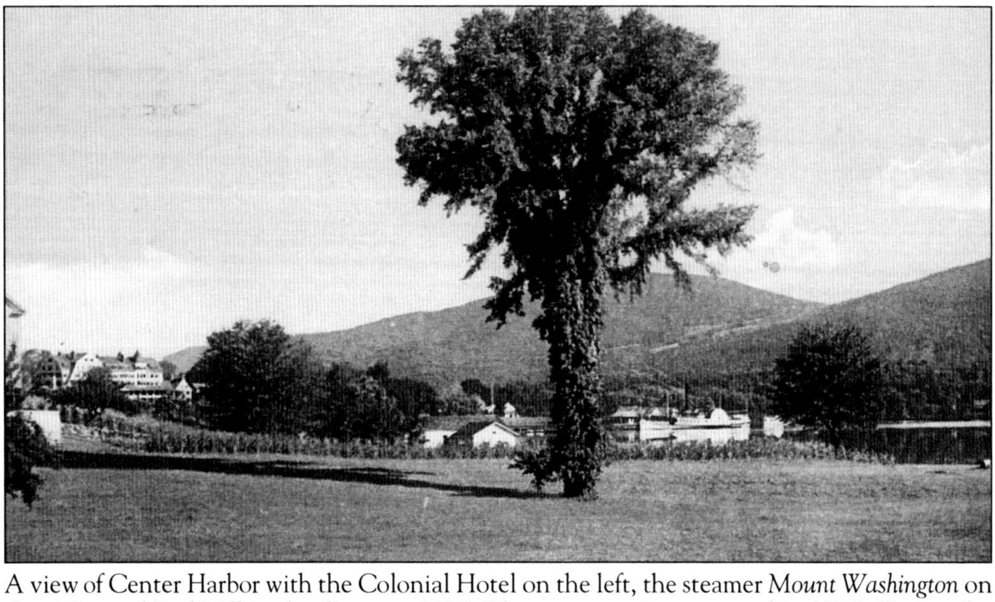

A view of Center Harbor with the Colonial Hotel on the left, the steamer *Mount Washington* on the right, and Red Hill in the distance, 1906. The town was incorporated in 1797. During the early years, the village was an important halfway station between Concord and Fryeburg. The early hotels and taverns located in the town were popular stopping-places for travelers en route to the mountains in the days when two-thirds of the travel to them came from this direction.

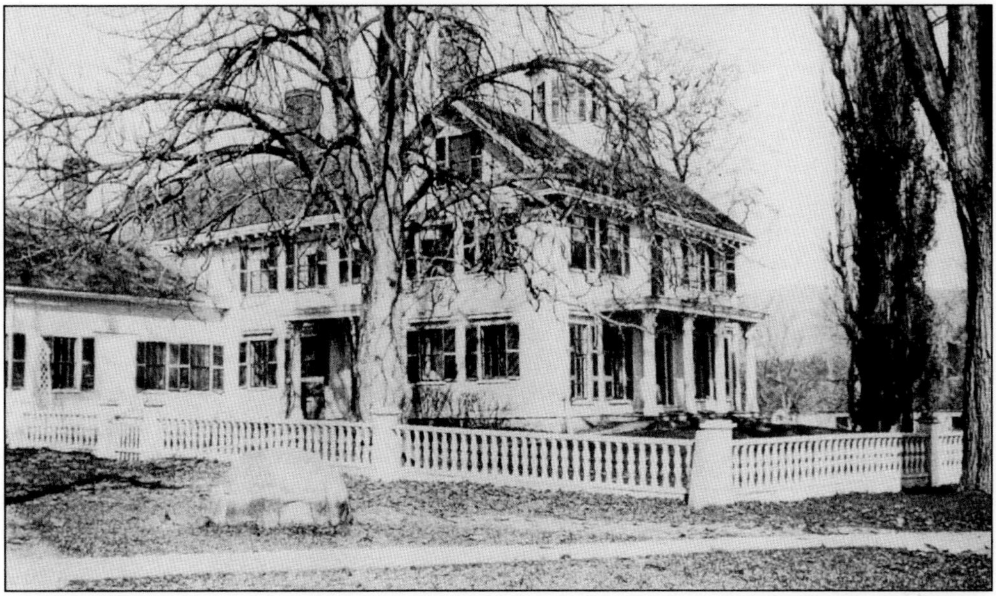

The Coe Mansion in Center Harbor, NH. Conspicuous on the north side of the main street is the Coe Mansion, a large white frame house surmounted by a hexagonal, windowed tower. The house was built about 1820 by John Coe Sr.

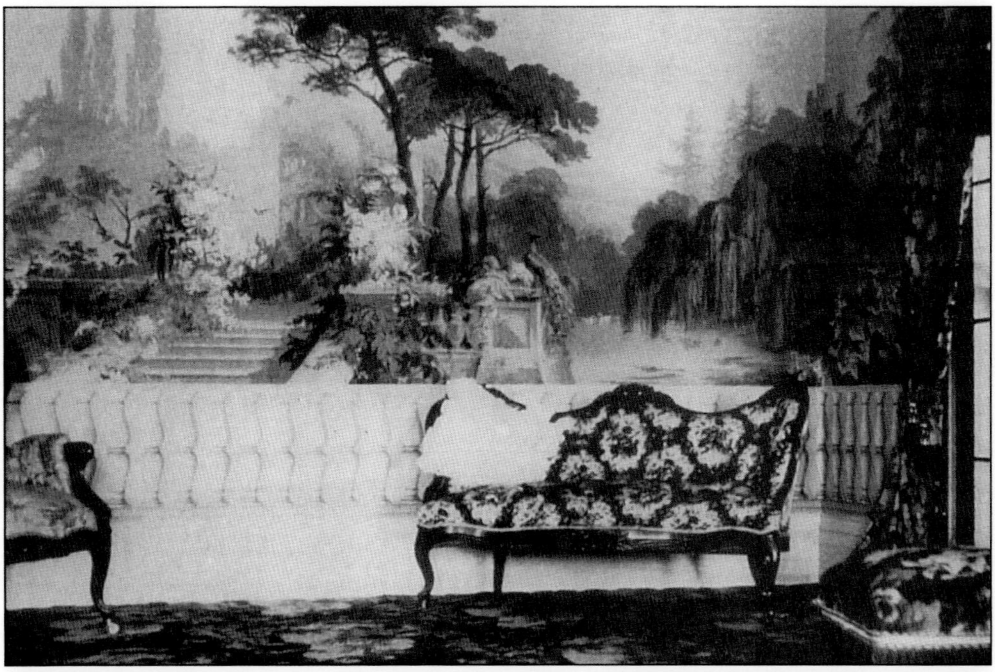

The French wallpaper found in the living room of the Coe House in Center Harbor, NH. This parlor was furnished in the style of the Boston parlors more than a century ago. Its walls were decorated with landscaped paper imported from Alsace-Lorraine, in brilliant colors portraying scenes on the Nile and in Italy. In this parlor were entertained the poets John Greenleaf Whittier and Lucy Larcom, and Presidents Franklin Pierce and Grover Cleveland.

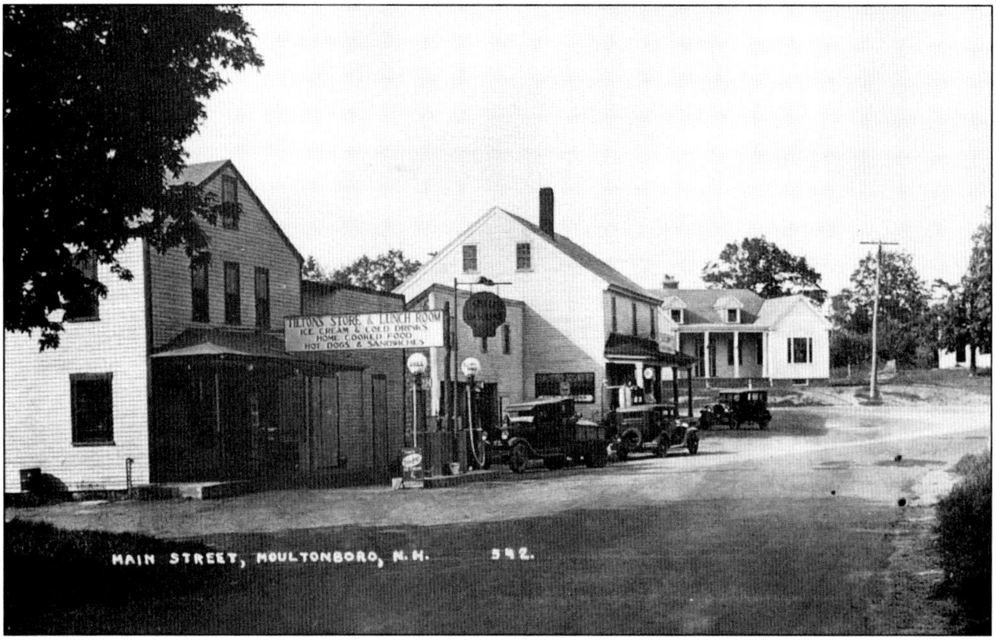

The village of Moultonboro, NH, looking east with Tilton's General Store, The Olde Country Store, and the town library on the left and center of the picture, 1920s. This town was granted in 1763 by the Masonian Proprietors to a group headed by Colonel Jonathan Moulton, whose name was given to the settlement. It was incorporated in 1777.

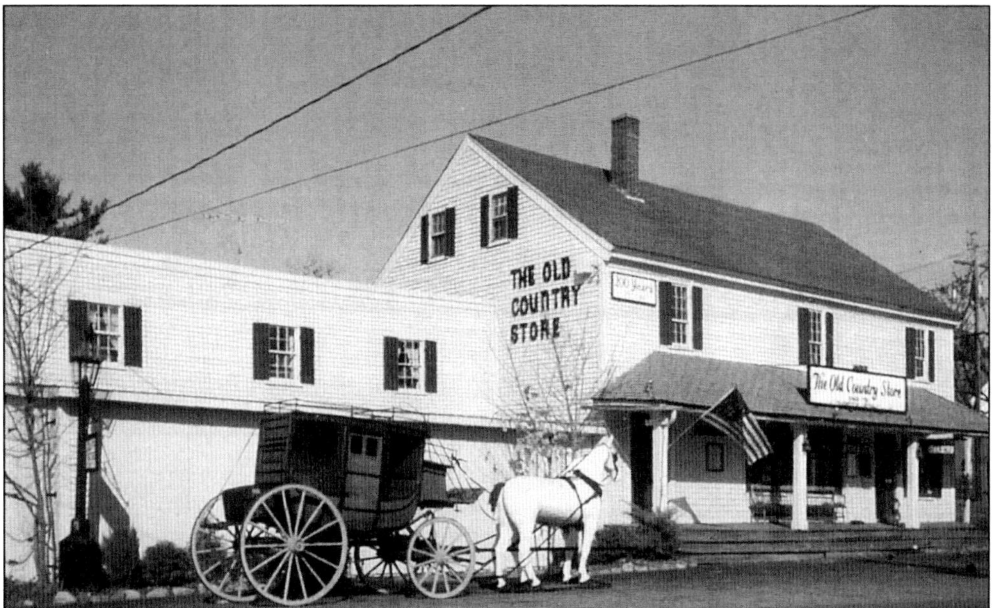

The Olde Country Store in Moultonboro, NH. This store, presently listed on the National Register of Historic Places, has turn-of-the-century store fixtures and houses an original Concord Coach. Its wares include cheddar cheese, aged on the premises, pickles, penny candy, and other interesting items.

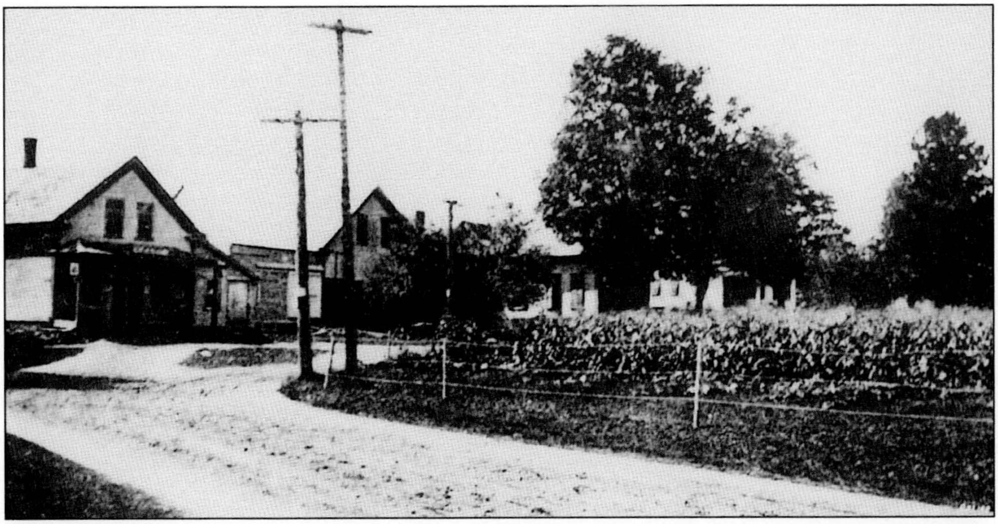

A view of North Sandwich with the general store on the left, 1920s. About 1760, a party headed by Colonel Jacob Smith visited Sandwich to hunt and trap. Upon arrival, they discovered a small river, which they called Bearcamp, a name closely associated with this region ever since. Three years later a charter was granted by Gov. Benning Wentworth to grantees who were largely relatives and friends of the governor. This quiet village sits in a basin surrounded by mountains—the Ossipee, Red Hill, Squam Range, and Sandwich Range forming the rim. Industry in Sandwich was mainly confined to farming; however, it is now largely a summer resort.

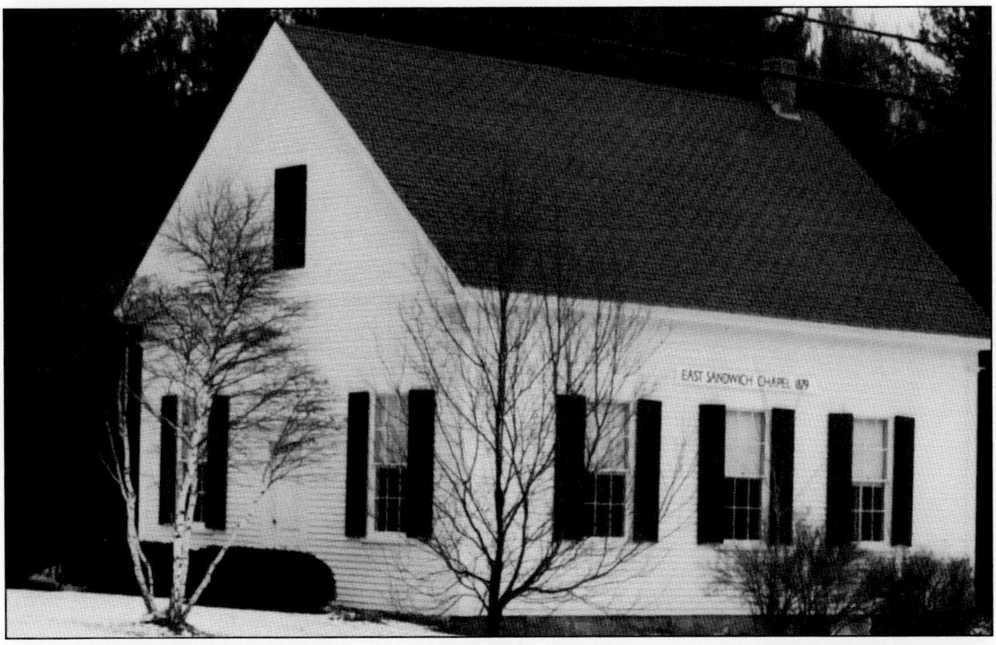

The East Sandwich Chapel, 1879. This chapel became the headquarters of the local Temperance Movement, where weekly meeting were held on Sunday evenings for 20 years. In January 1886, the Carroll County Temperance Convention was held at the chapel. The enthusiasm for the cause joined men and women from all churches throughout the town and caused Sandwich to become a dry town in 1895.

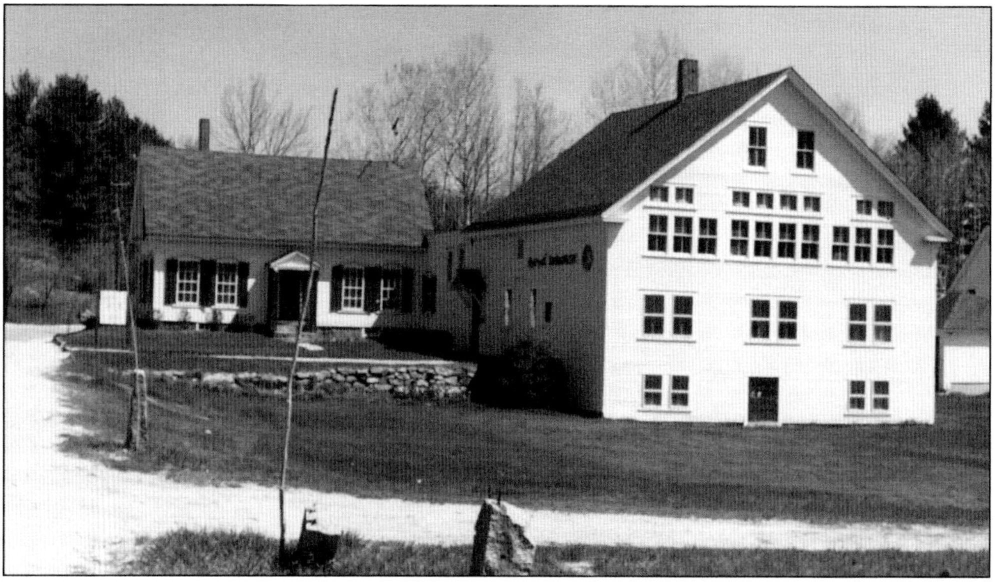

The Quimby School, Center Sandwich, NH. The Quimby School was originally founded in 1923 and endowed by Alfred E. Quimby of Manchester to train the young people and keep them in town by teaching agriculture to the boys and home economics to the girls. In 1963 the school ceased operation and closed its doors. In 1966, Robert and Roberta Ayotte bought the old Quimby School and marketed their talents in weaving and design, teaching their craft to others, both in an innovative series of mail-order lessons and in the Sandwich Shop.

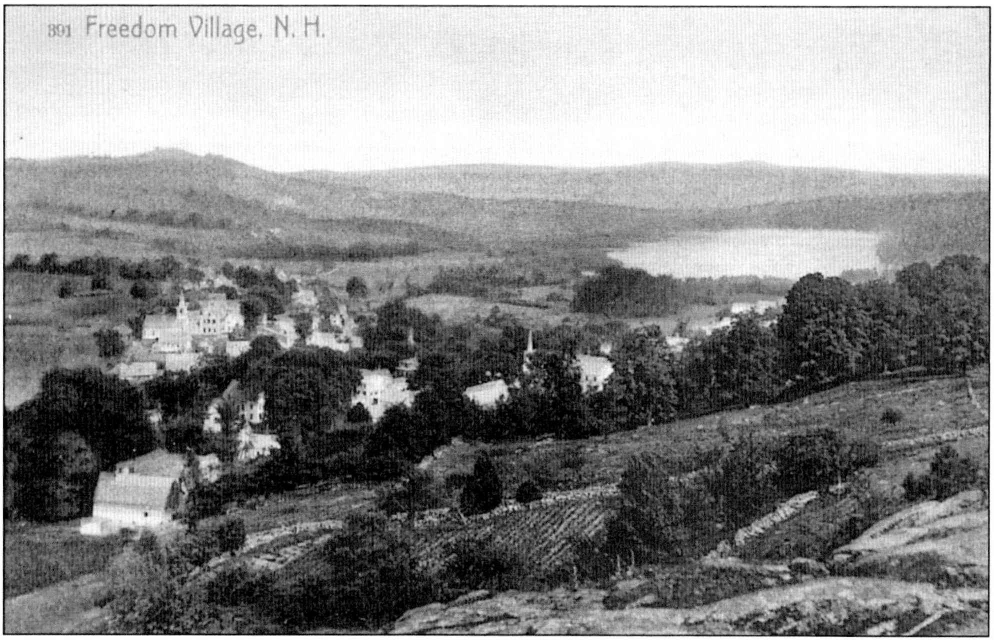

A view of Freedom, NH, during the early 1920s. Freedom is an angular sort of village with the point at the bridge over Cold Brook. The residential section is on the eastern leg of the angle, while the western leg spreads out along the side of the brook at the base of a low hill. The village was once known as Leavitt's Town. The town was originally an agricultural community, but today its varied scenic attractions draw many summer residents.

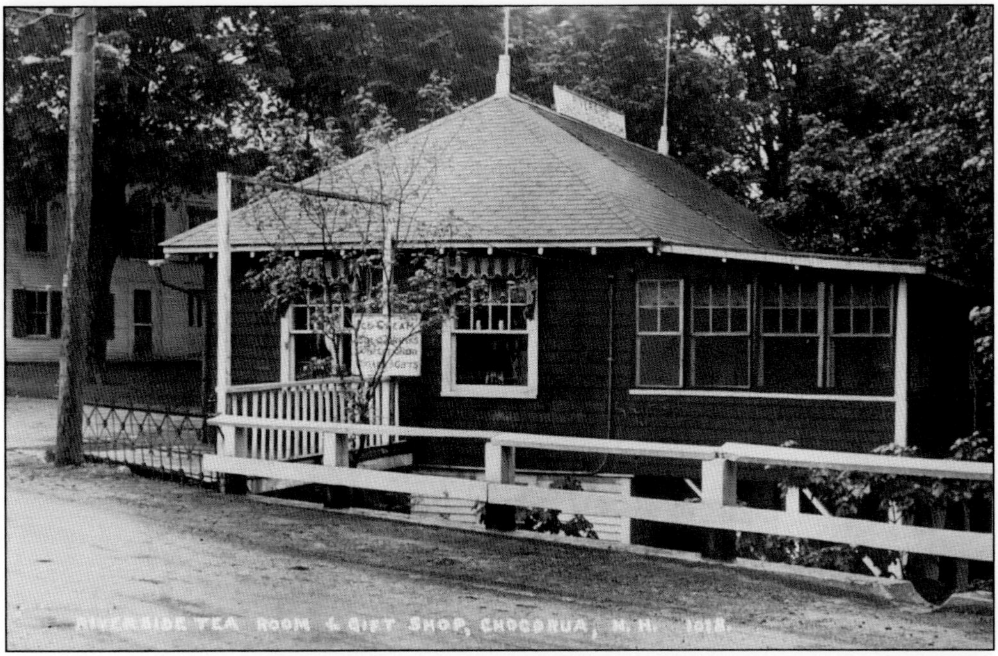

The Riverside Tea Room & Gift Shop in Chocorua Village, NH, 1918. This village in Tamworth Township, formerly called Tamworth Iron Works, is a little settlement of tourist homes, gift shops, small stores, and a few small houses on both banks of the Swift River.

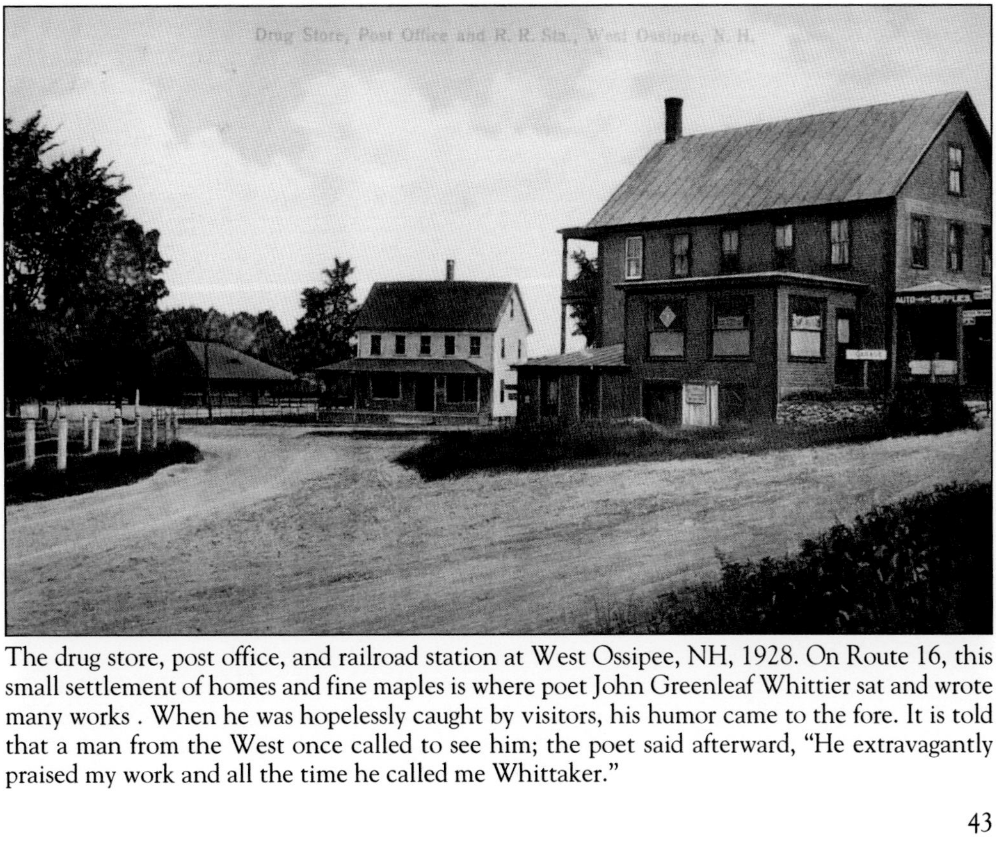

The drug store, post office, and railroad station at West Ossipee, NH, 1928. On Route 16, this small settlement of homes and fine maples is where poet John Greenleaf Whittier sat and wrote many works . When he was hopelessly caught by visitors, his humor came to the fore. It is told that a man from the West once called to see him; the poet said afterward, "He extravagantly praised my work and all the time he called me Whittaker."

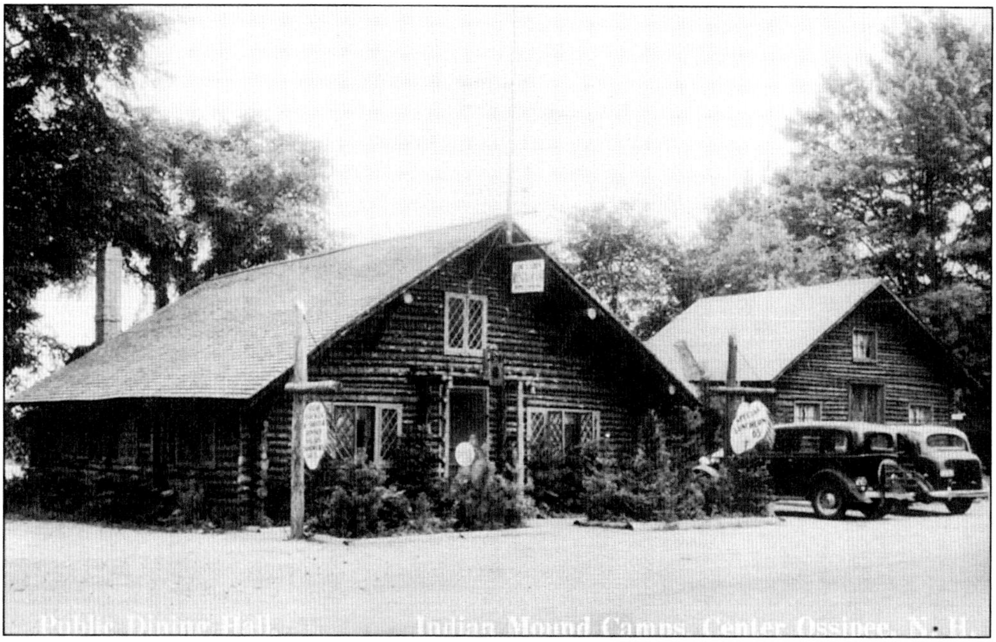

The public dining hall at the Indian Mound Camps in Center Ossipee, NH, 1939.

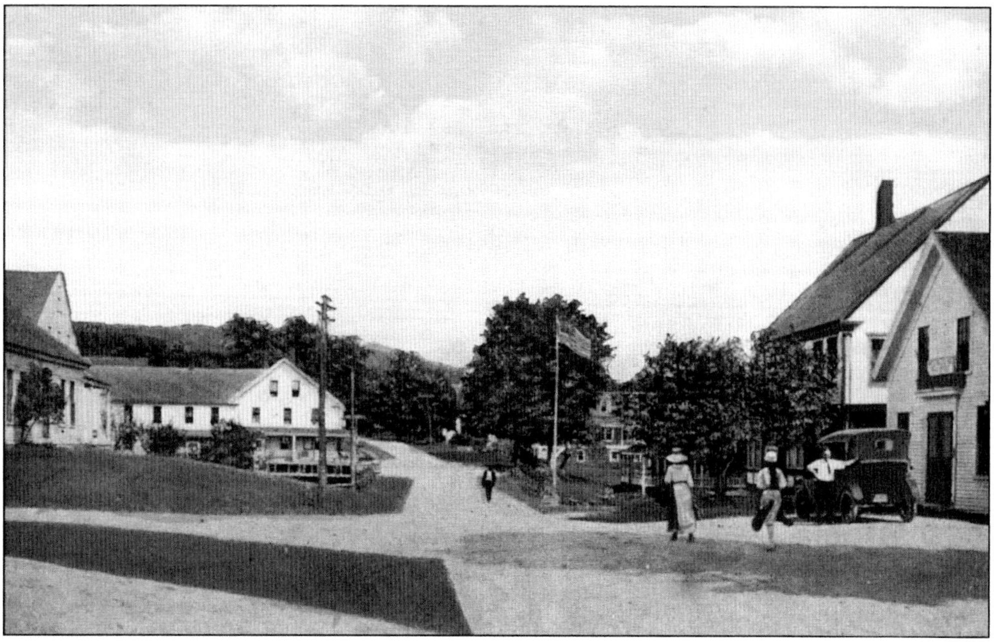
Main Street, the post office, and the general store in Melvin Village, NH, 1931. This village is part of Tuftonboro, NH. The name Melvin was given in honor of David and Eleazer Melvin, who fought in the French and Indian War. Tuftonboro has the distinction of being the only town once having been owned entirely by one man, John Tufton Mason, after whom it was named in 1750.

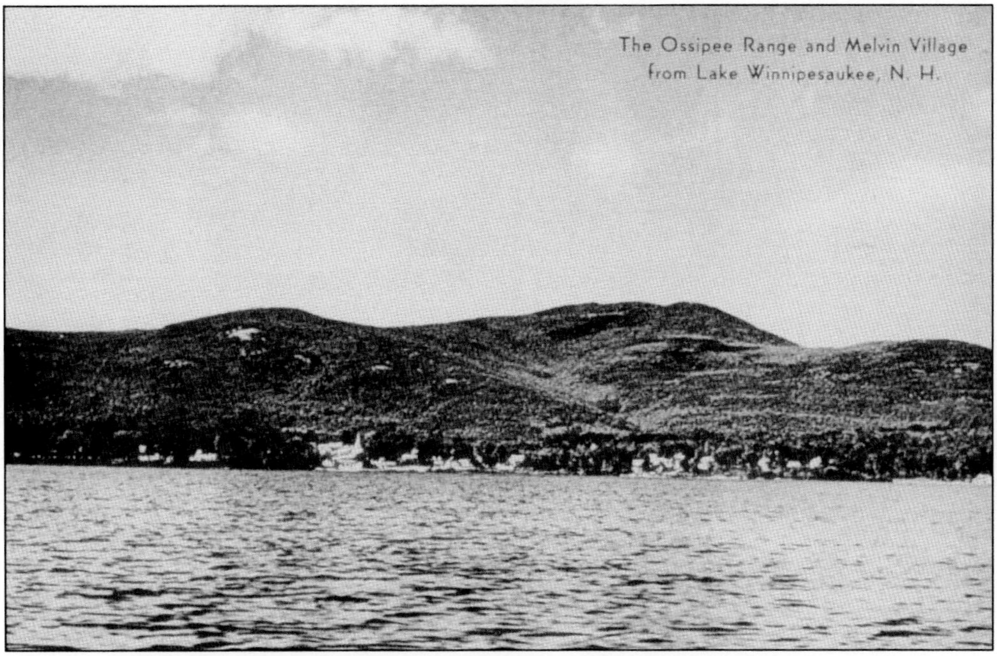

The Ossipee Mountain Range and Melvin Village from Lake Winnipesaukee, 1946.

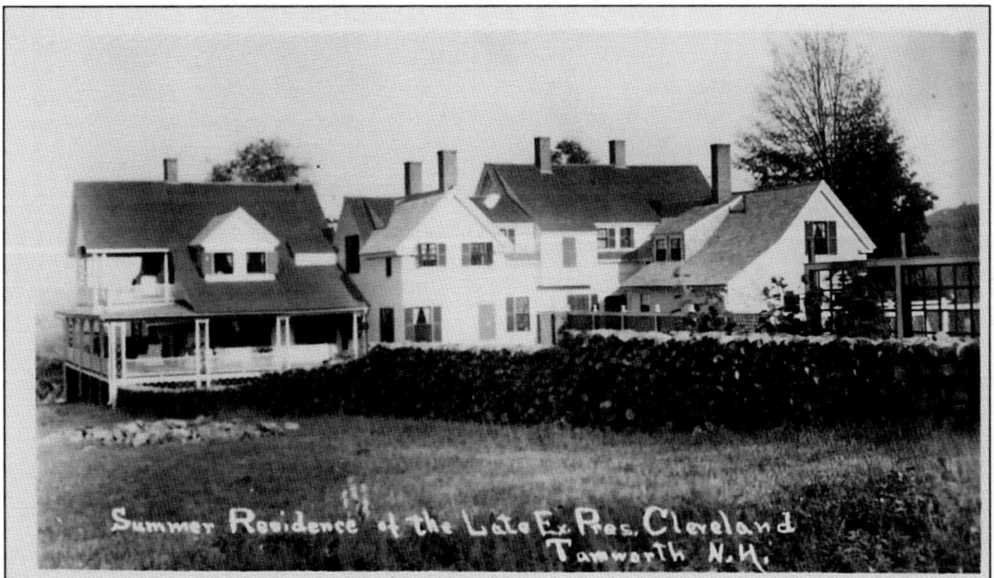

The summer residence of the former-President Grover Cleveland, Tamworth, NH, early 1900s. The town of Tamworth had the proud distinction of having been selected by Mr. Cleveland, twice President of the United States, as his summer home during the last years of his life. He loved the out-of-doors and quiet stillness of the countryside. From his cottage he enjoyed the beautiful landscape of the majestic White Mountains.

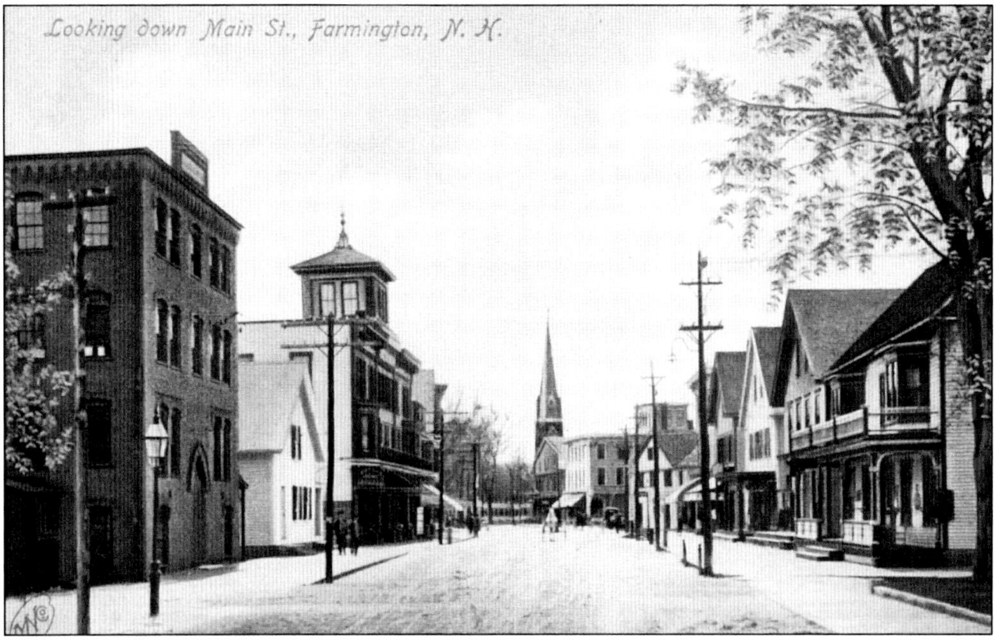

Main Street in Farmington, NH, 1908. Farmington was originally part of Rochester, but was incorporated as a town in December 1798. During the turn of the century, the inhabitants were extensively engaged in the manufacture of shoes, and the number of pairs made exceeded that of any made in the state.

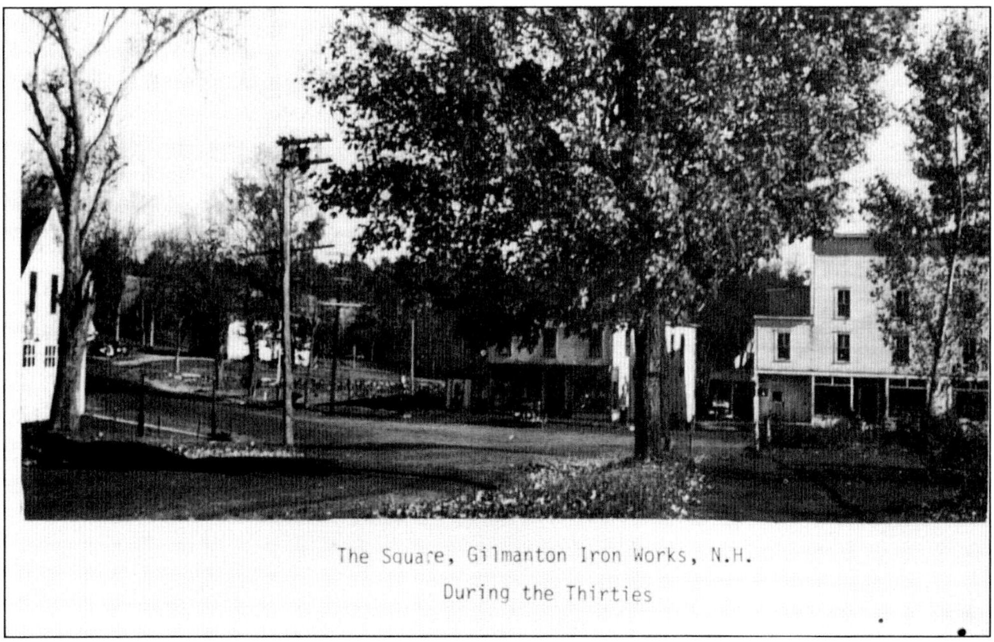

The square, Gilmanton Iron Works, NH, 1930s. Gilmanton was considered one of the best farming towns in the county, and before Belmont disannexed from it, the value of agricultural products exceeded that of any town in the state. Gilmanton was granted in May 20, 1727. This settlement was delayed several times by frequent depredations of the Native Americans. Belmont was taken from this town on June 28, 1859.

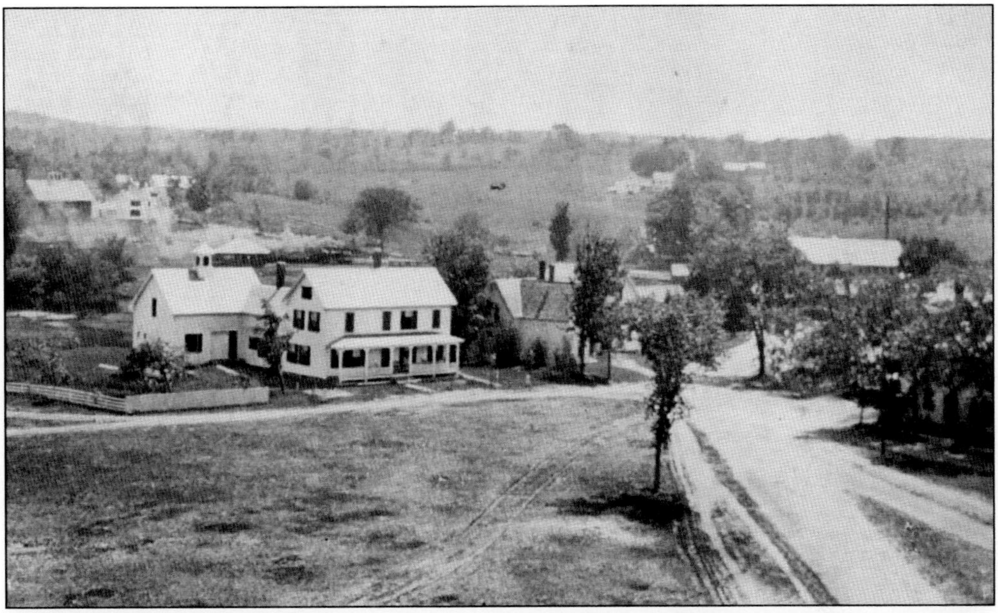

Barnstead Village, 1921. This is a compact little settlement which was granted to the Rev. Joseph Adams, uncle of President John Adams, and others of Newington in 1727; settlement began in 1768. Among the early settlers was Colonel Richard Sinclair, whose wife frequently brought hay 30 miles from Newington on a hand sled. Barnstead profited by the building of the Province Road in 1770.

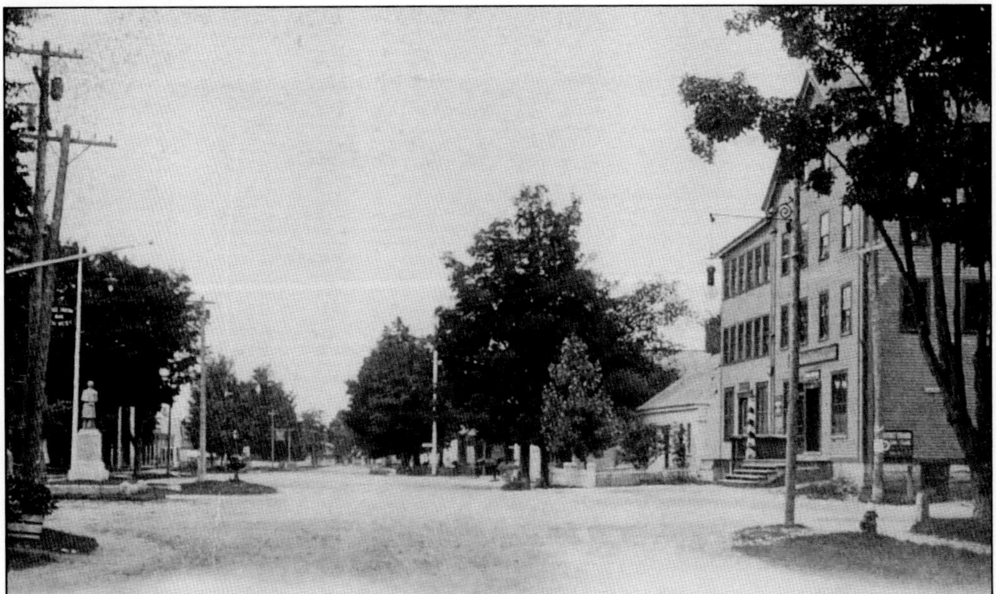

Alton's Main Street looking south, early 1900s. Once called New Durham Gore, Alton was settled in 1770. When it was incorporated in 1796, the citizens requested that it be called Roxbury, but Gov. Wentworth gave it the name of an English town. Alton is situated in the bed of a river that was once the outlet of Lake Winnipesaukee toward the sea. Geologists have demonstrated that the Merrymeeting River once flowed in the opposite direction of what it currently does. Note the Alton Shoe Co. on the right.

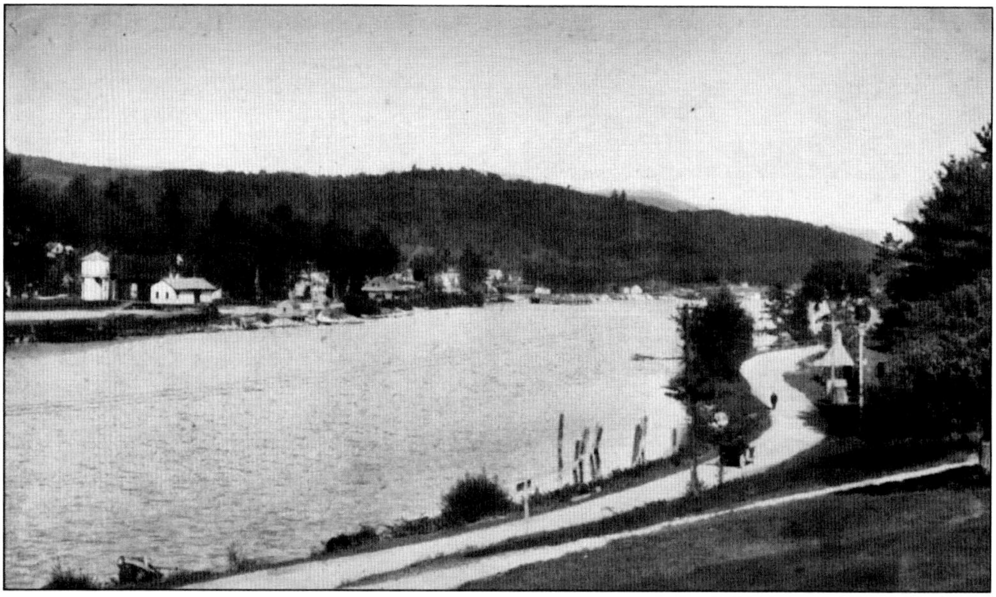

A view of Alton Bay, looking northwest, early 1920s. The settlement is largely a summer resort and a port for the steamer *Mount Washington*. It was here that she was built by the Boston & Maine Railroad Co., and launched in 1872.

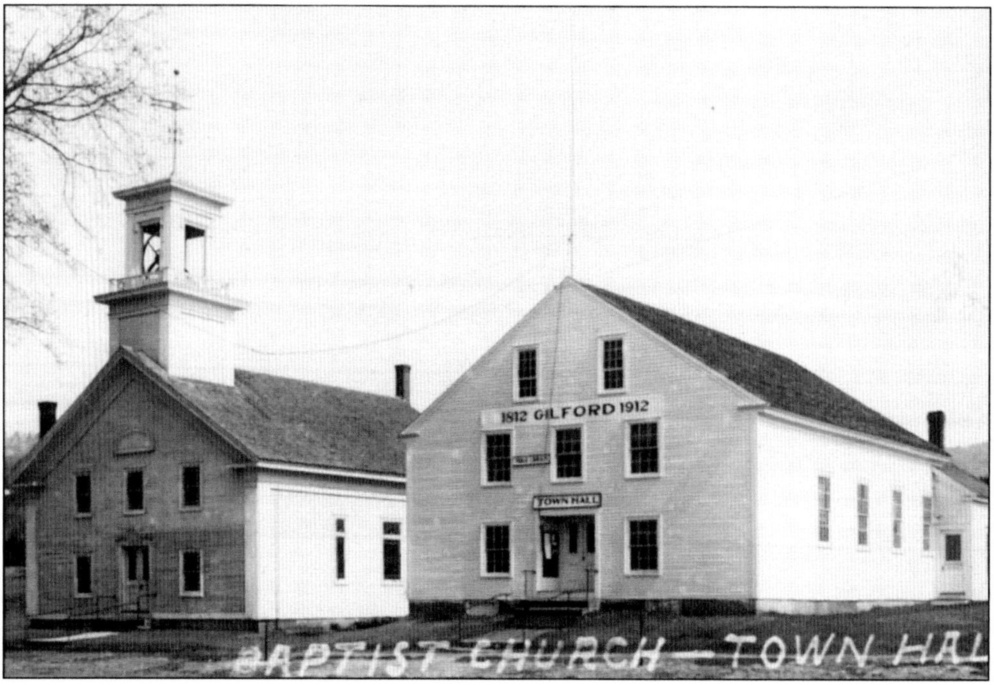

The Baptist church and town hall, Gilford, NH, 1914. The first settlement of this area is said to have taken place in 1777, the year James Ames and Captain Samuel F. Gilman took up land in the "Upper Parish," the northern part of Gilmanton. On June 5, 1811, the inhabitants of the "Upper Parish" presented a petition to the General Court of New Hampshire in order to form their own township. On June 16, 1812, the New Hampshire Senate passed the bill separating the "Upper Parish" from Gilmanton.

Three

Railroad Stations, Depots, and Whistle Stops

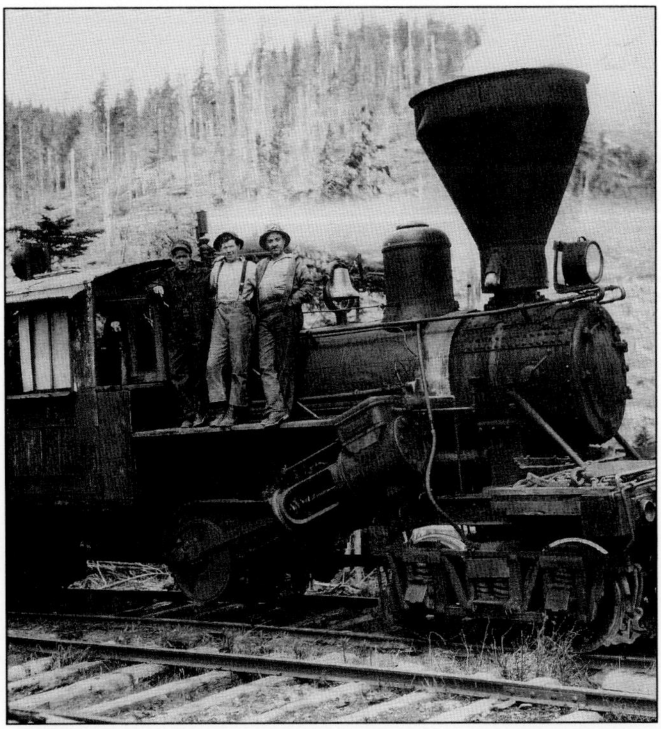

The Sandwich Notch logging train. The logging railroad was in full operation by 1920 in Sandwich Notch with 12 camps and a huge imported labor force of 408 men. This manpower consisted mostly of the new immigrants, including 95 Russians and 65 French Canadians who worked as choppers, teamsters, loaders, landing rollers, sled tenders, saw filers, blacksmiths, carpenters, and cooks. These trains ran five times a day, seven days a week, and needed a dispatcher's telephone line from the Beebe River mill to each camp. On July 12, 1923, however, the entire operation came to a virtual halt.

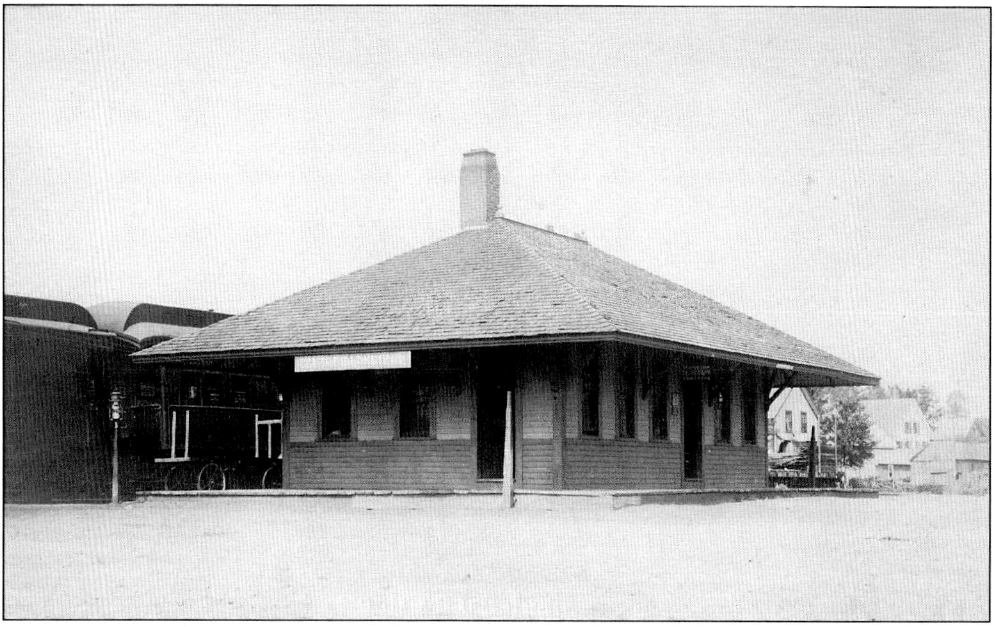

Center Barnstead Station, Barnstead, NH. This was a single line from Pittsfield to Center Barnstead, 4.46 miles long. The line was opened in 1889 and the 765 shares of stock issued were bought by the Concord & Montreal Railroad for $76,577. It was operated since September 28, 1924, by the Suncook Valley Railroad.

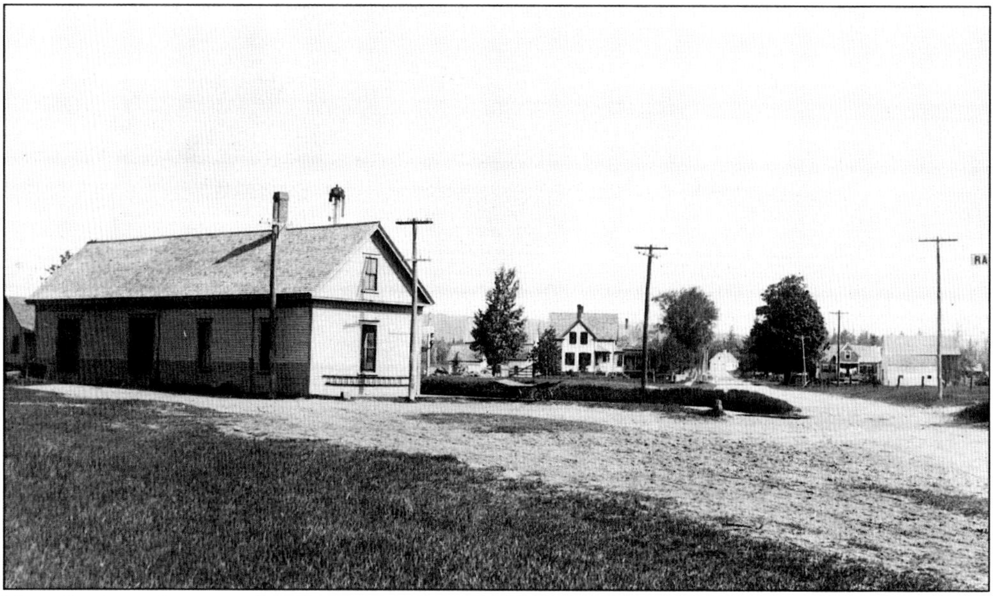

New Durham Station, New Durham, NH, 1900. The Dover & Winnipesaukee Railroad was a single-track line from Dover to Alton Bay, 29 miles. The first charter was granted in 1839. This charter lapsed and a second charter was granted in 1847, under the name of the Cocheco Railroad Company. The road was completed in 1851. In 1861 the interest on the bonds was defaulted and the property was surrendered to the trustees under the mortgage.

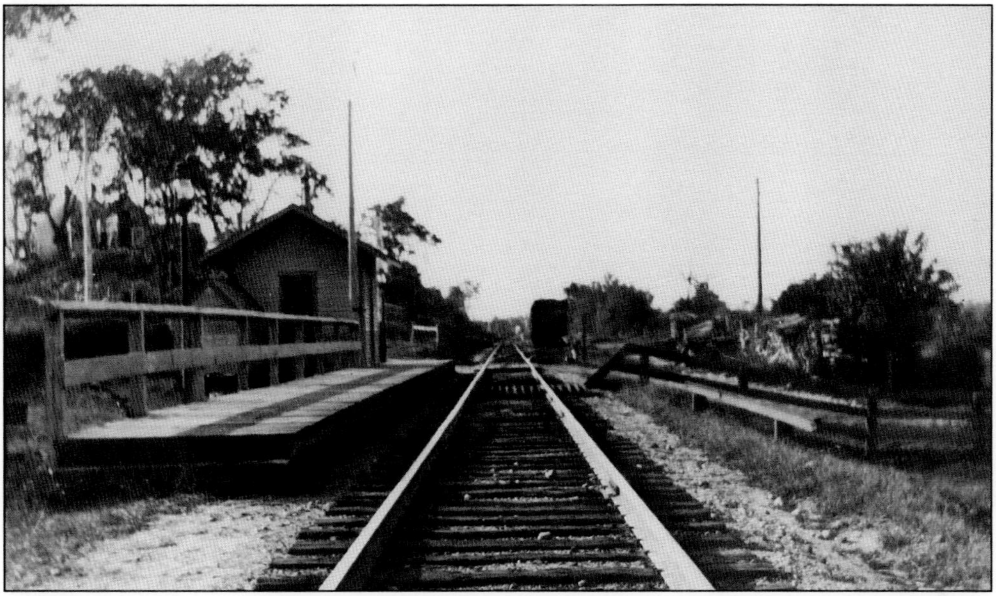

The Davis Station in Farmington, NH, 1910. In 1863 the company was reorganized as the Dover & Winnipiseogee Railroad. The road was then leased to the Boston & Maine Railroad for a term of 50 years.

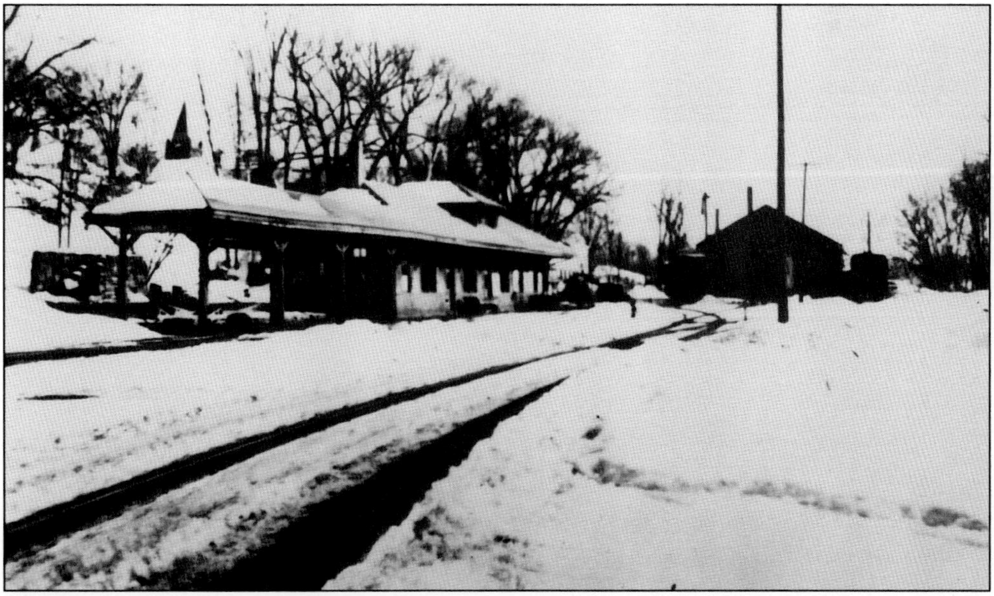

The Farmington Station, 1910 (second station). In 1892 the road was purchased by the Boston & Maine Railroad and consolidated with that system. The price paid was three-fourths of the share of Boston & Maine for each share of the Dover & Winnipiseogee stock.

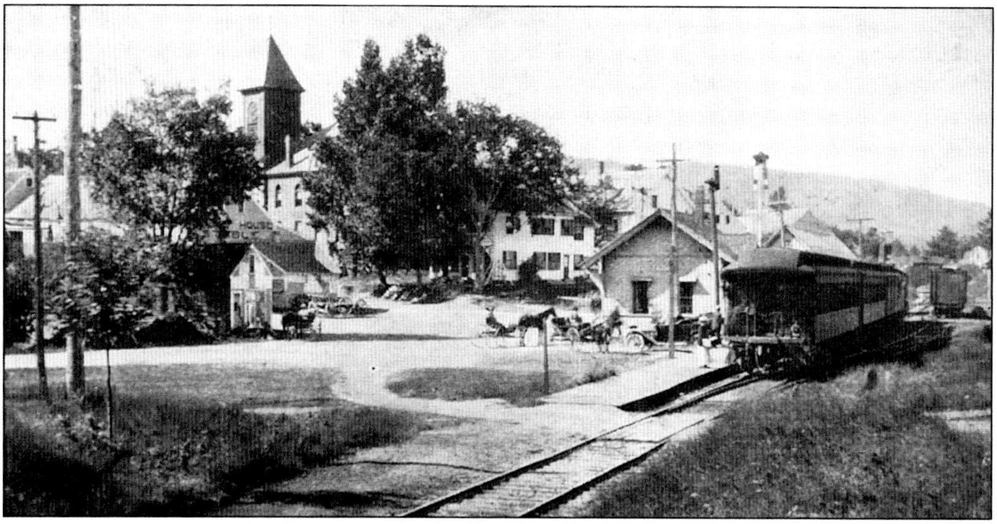

The Alton Station, Boston & Maine Railroad, 1920.

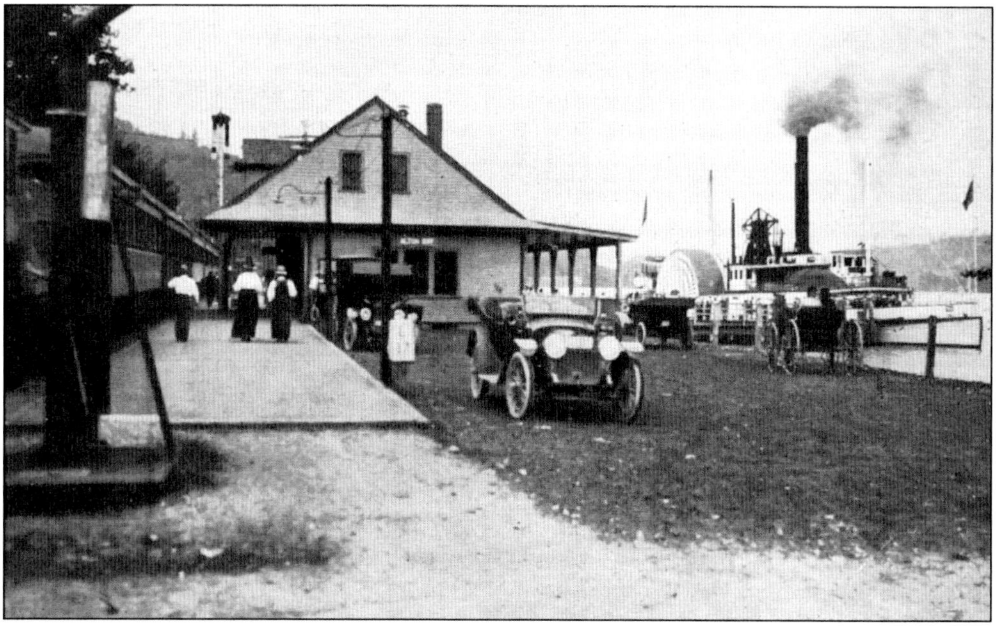

The Alton Bay Station with the steamer *Mount Washington* on the right in Alton Bay, NH, 1920s. This was a single-track line from Alton Bay to Lakeport, 17.28 miles. The line was basically established so to connect the Cocheco Road, on the eastern side of the lake, with the Boston, Concord & Montreal Railroad in Meredith Bridge (Laconia). In 1872 the Boston & Maine Railroad built the steamer *Mount Washington* at Alton Bay as an extension of the passenger services in the Lakes Region and to the White Mountains.

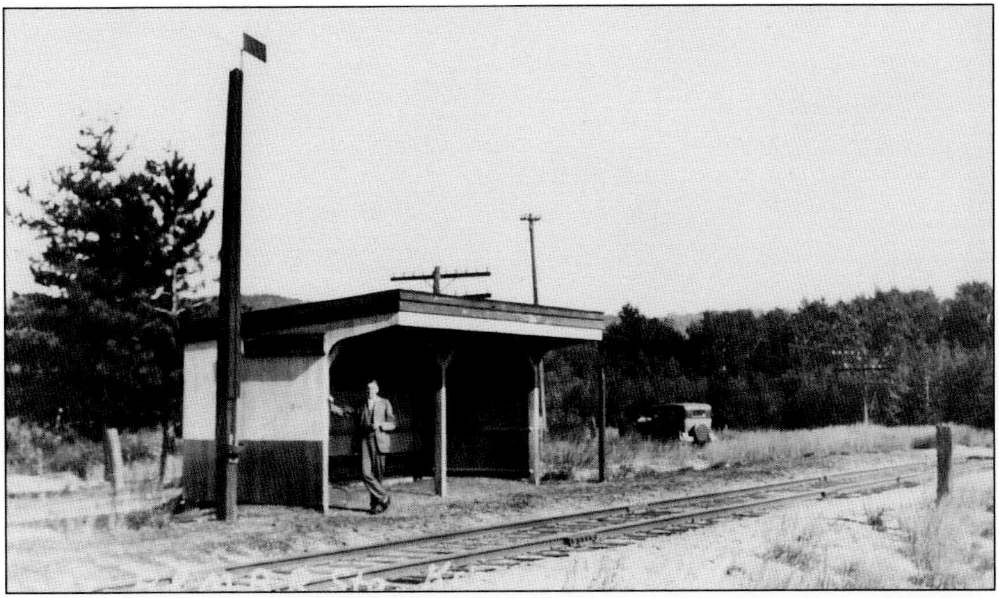

The Keewaydin Station, 1930. The Lake Shore line was opened in 1890, and the 2,752 shares of stock issued were bought by the Concord & Montreal Railroad for $279,913.

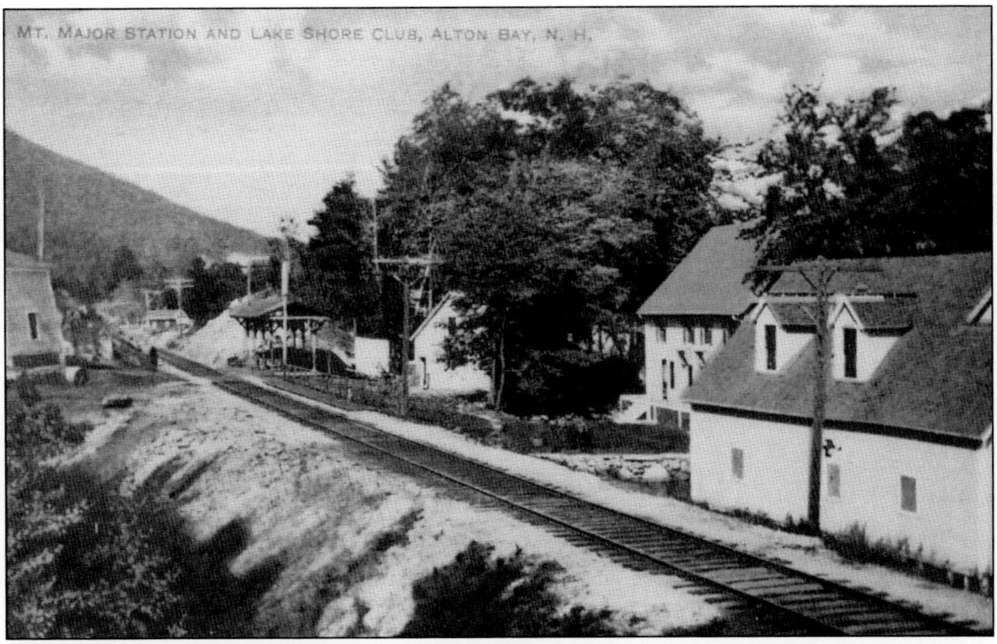

Mount Major and the Lake Shore Club, West Alton, NH, 1910.

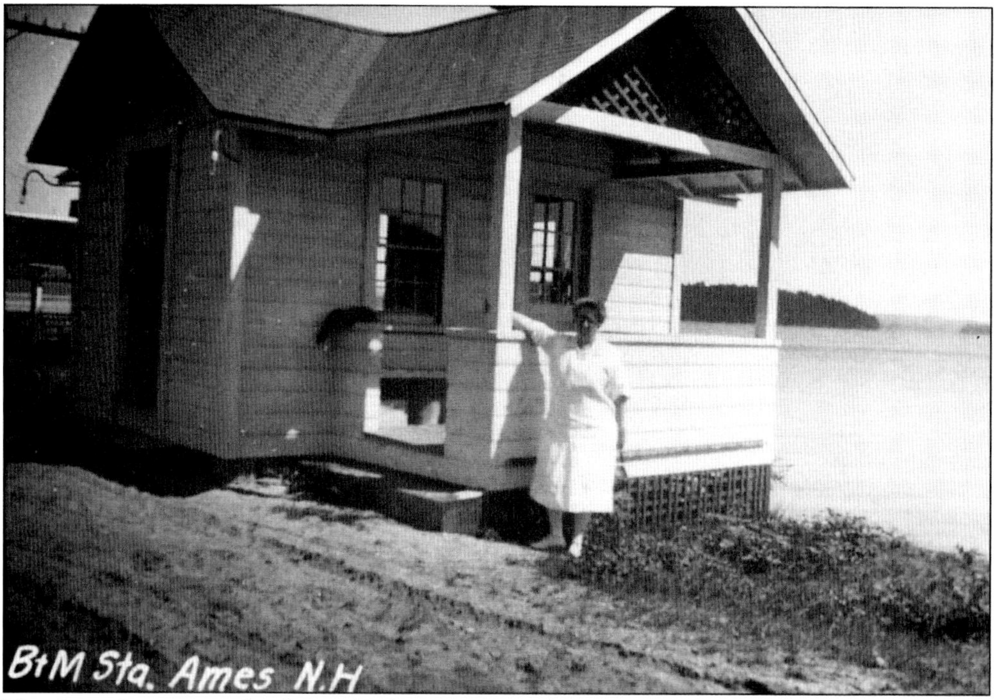

The Ames Station on the shore of Lake Winnipesaukee in Gilford, NH, 1935.

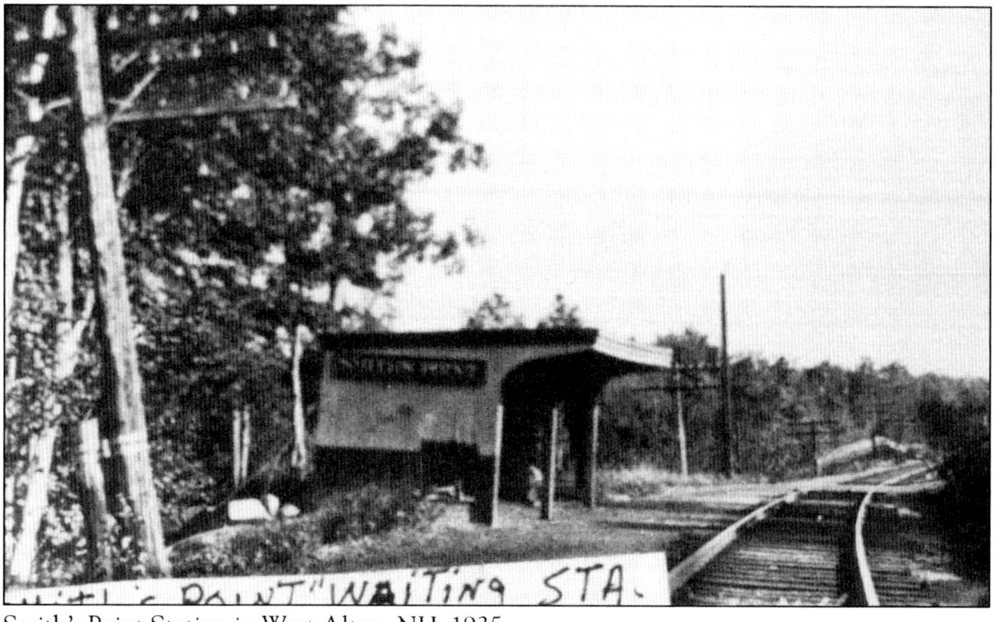

Smith's Point Station in West Alton, NH, 1935.

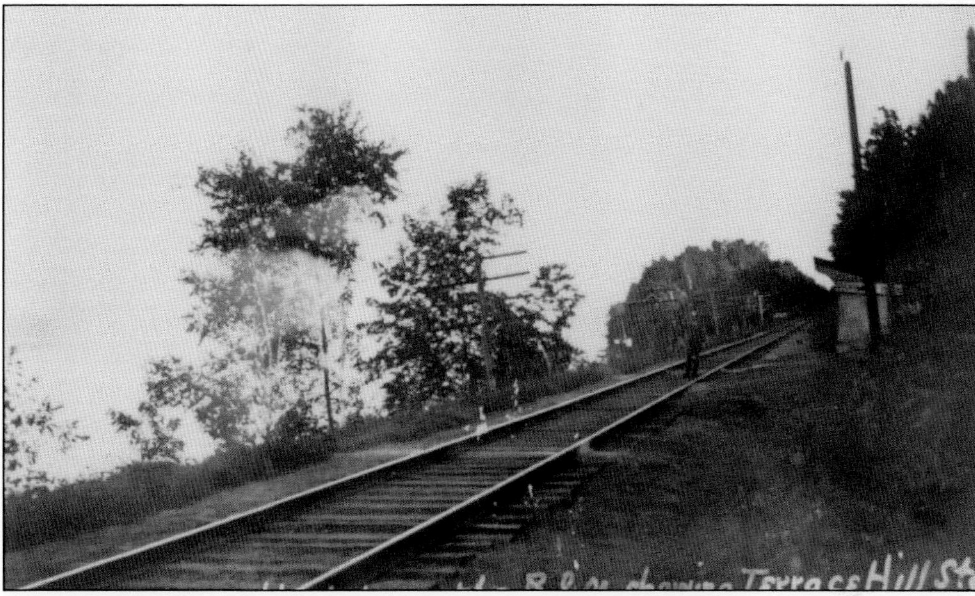

The Terrace Hill Stop on Lake Winnipesaukee in Gilford, NH, 1930.

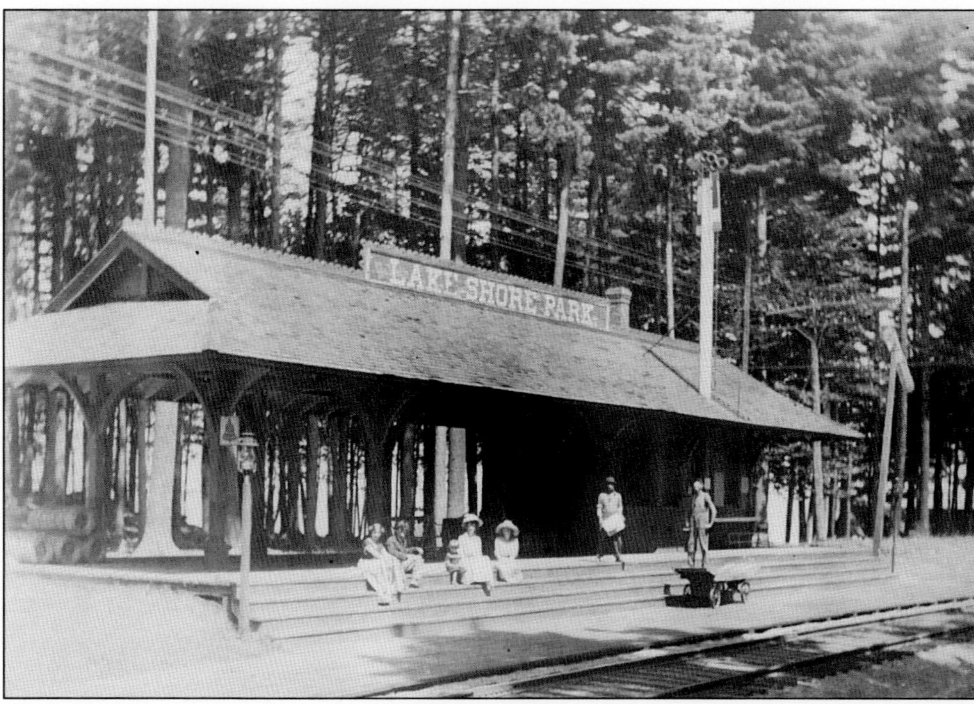

The Lake Shore Park Station in Gilford, NH, 1919.

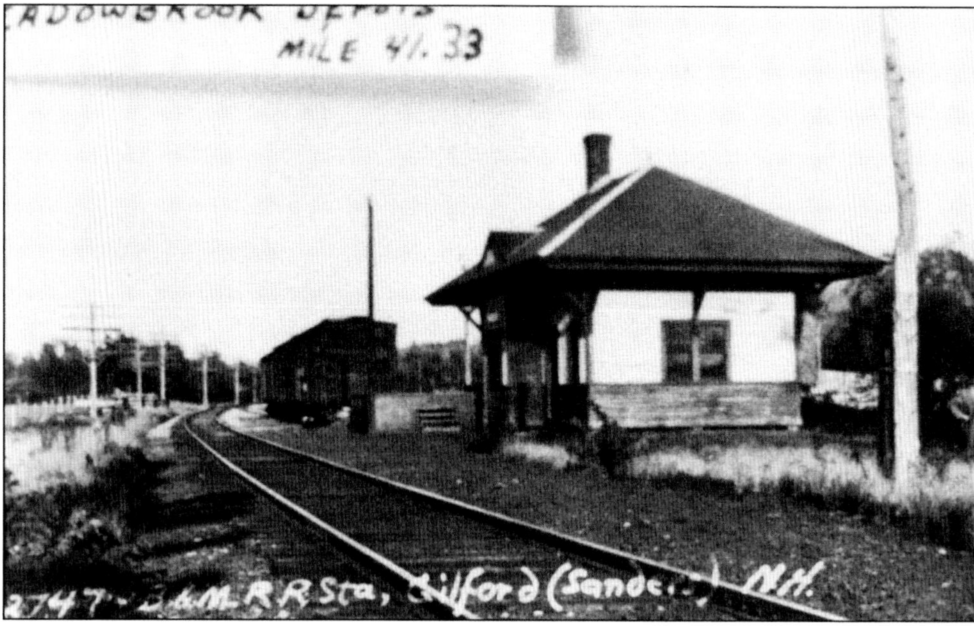

The Sander's Bay Station in Gilford, NH, 1933.

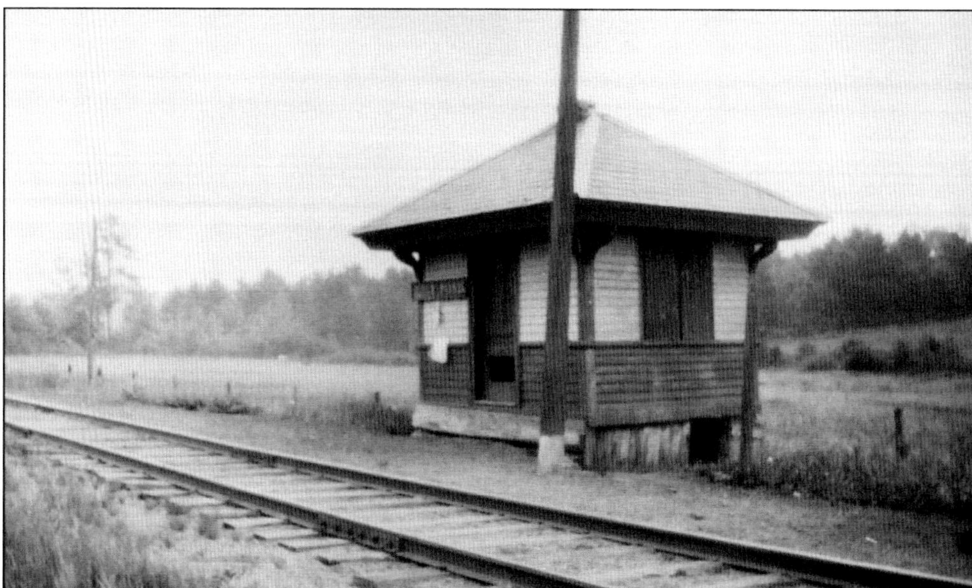

The Lily Pond Station in Gilford, NH, 1930.

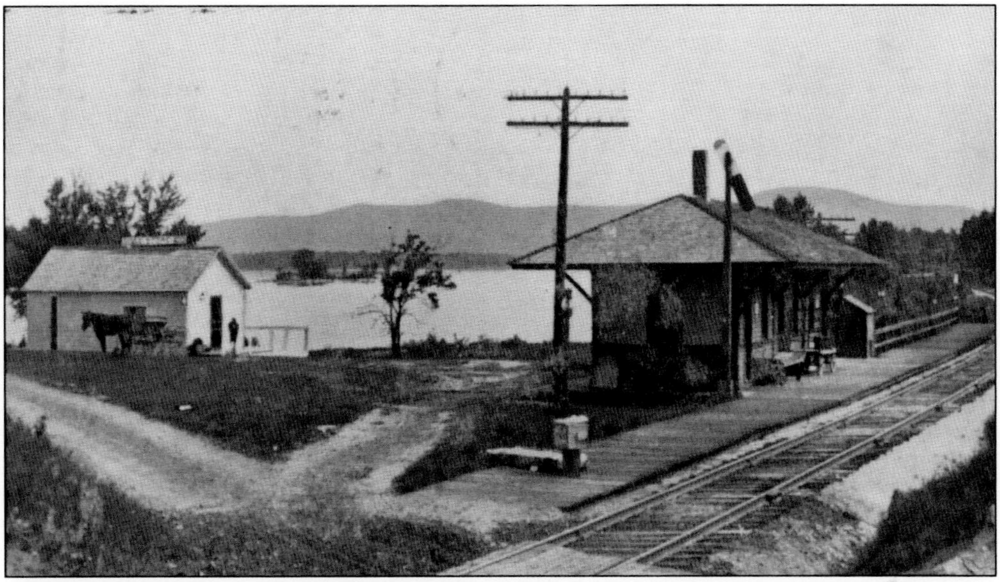

The Glendale Station on Lake Winnipesaukee, 1880.

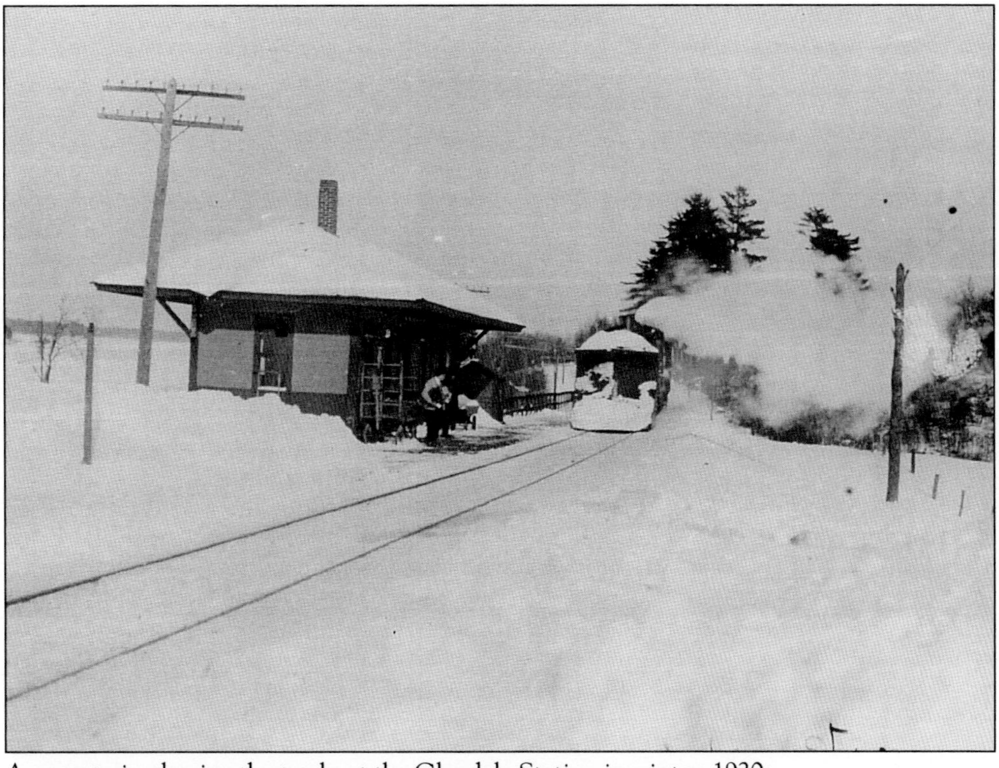

A snow train clearing the tracks at the Glendale Station in winter, 1920s.

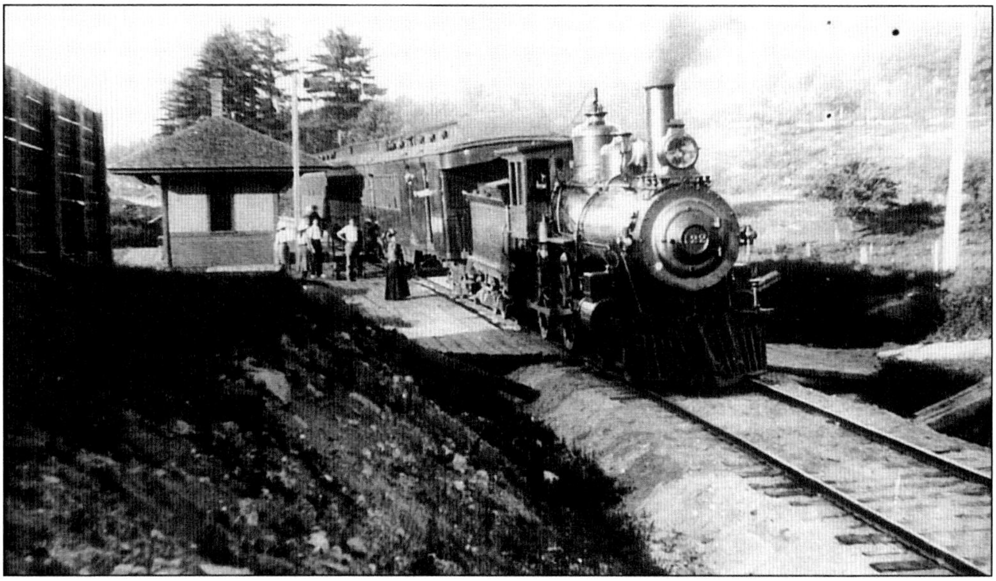

The steam train No. 122 of the Lake Shore Railroad at the Glendale Station in the summer of 1897. The railroad ended its service in 1930. In 1933 the tracks were removed.

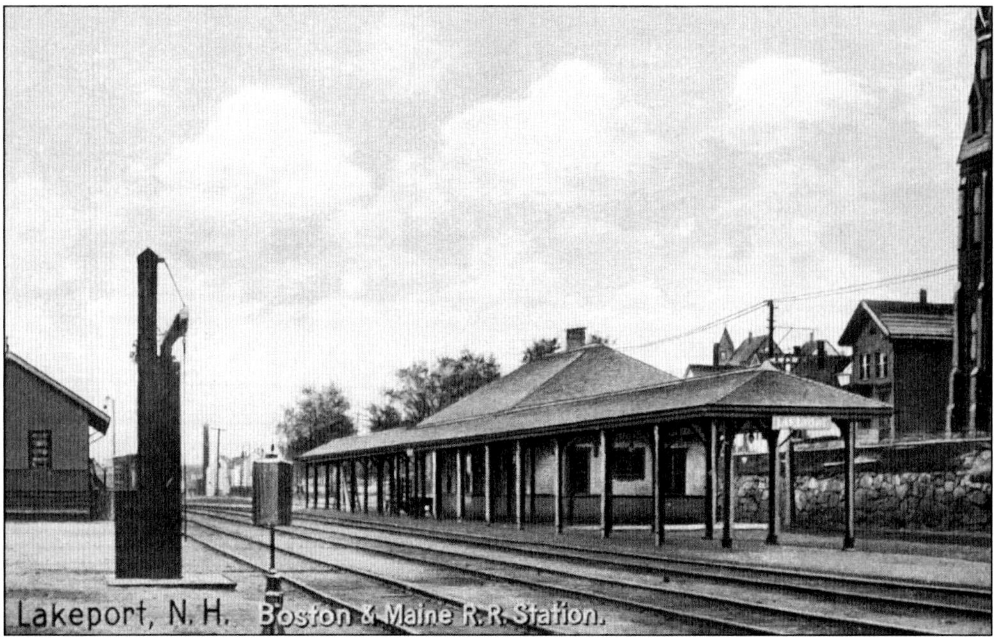

The Lakeport (Lakeville) Station, the Boston & Maine Railroad Station, Lakeport, NH, 1911. In 1848, the Boston, Concord & Montreal Railroad opened a single-track line from Concord to Tilton and Laconia, and the following year it was extended to Lakeport (Lake Village). This event marked one of the largest celebrations the town had ever seen. In 1890 the Lake Shore, Tilton & Belmont, and the Suncook Valley Extension were designed to be branches of the Concord & Montreal Railroad, though they were chartered as independent roads, and they had been operated as a part of that system. In 1895 the Boston & Maine leased the railroad service from the Concord & Montreal Railroad.

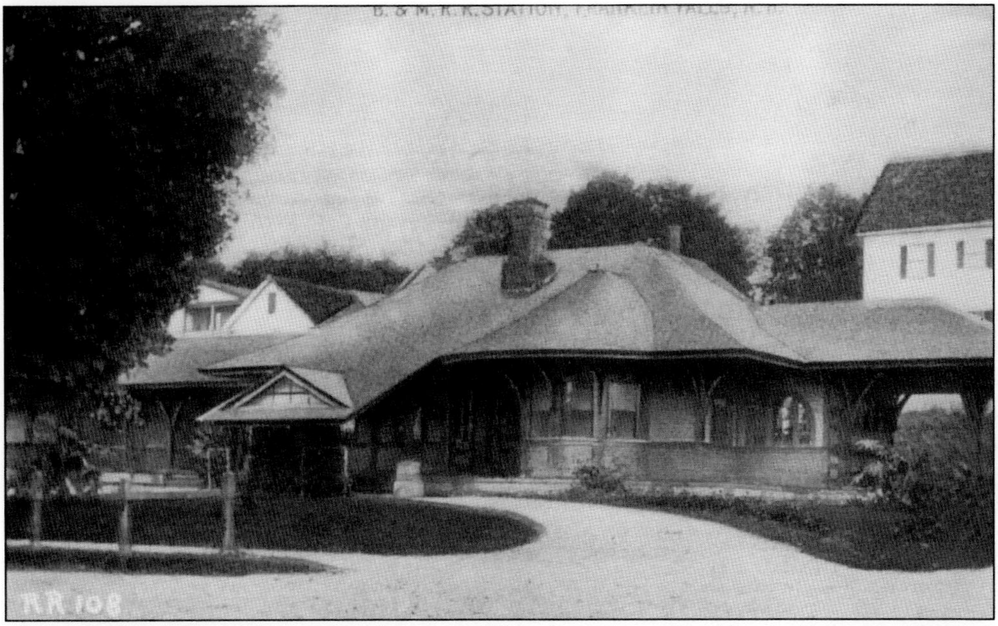

The Franklin Falls Depot, originally part of the old Tilton, Franklin & Belmont Railroad, Franklin, NH, 1900.

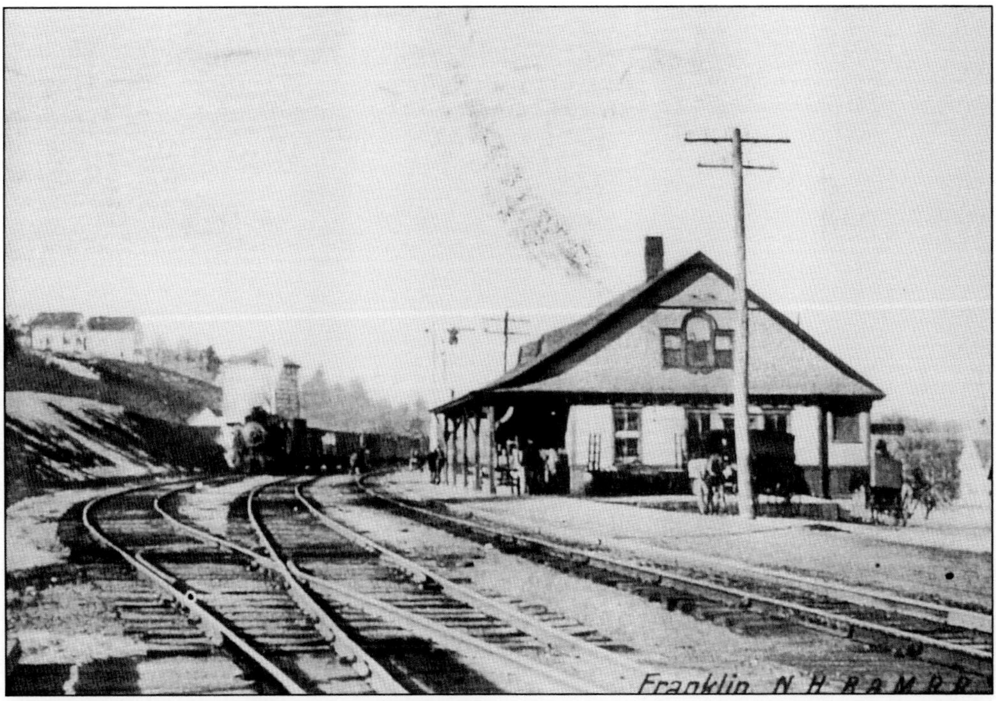

The Boston & Maine Railroad Station in West Franklin looking north, 1910. This is where the Pemigewasset and Winnipesaukee Rivers unite to form the Merrimack River, from whence some say it derived its name, signifying in the Algonquin tongue, "the meeting of the waters." The rivers furnished the power for numerous large manufactories.

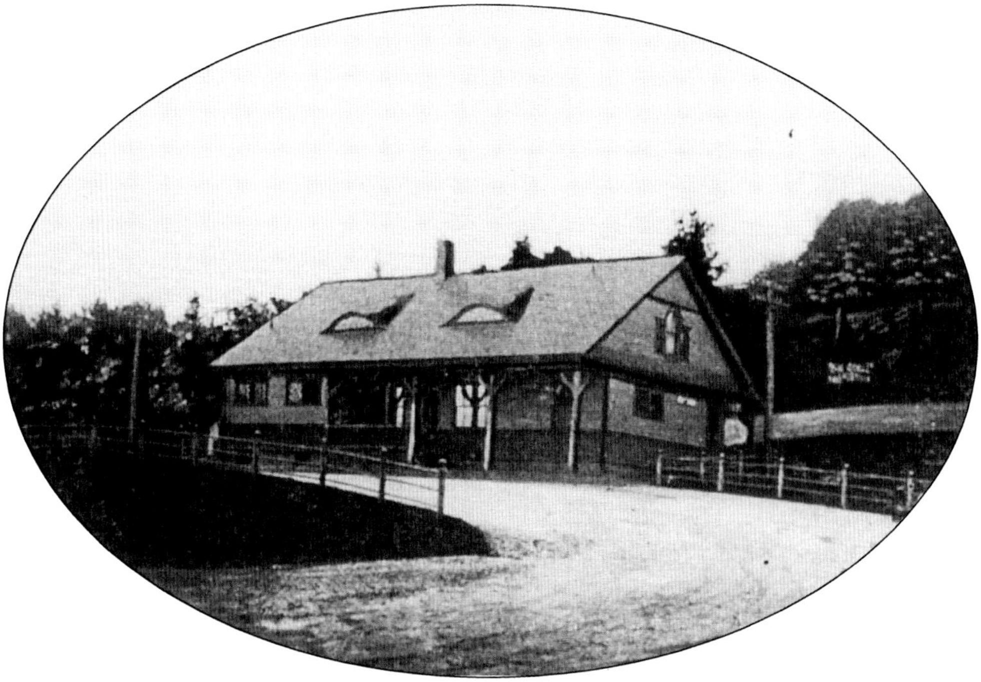

The Boston & Maine Railroad Station, Franklin, early 1900s. In 1895 the Concord & Montreal system was leased to the Boston & Maine Railroad. Previous to this time, the Boston & Maine had also acquired 51 percent of the capital stock of the Maine Central Railroad. This brought under Boston & Maine the control of 1,122 of the 1,174 miles of railroad in New Hampshire.

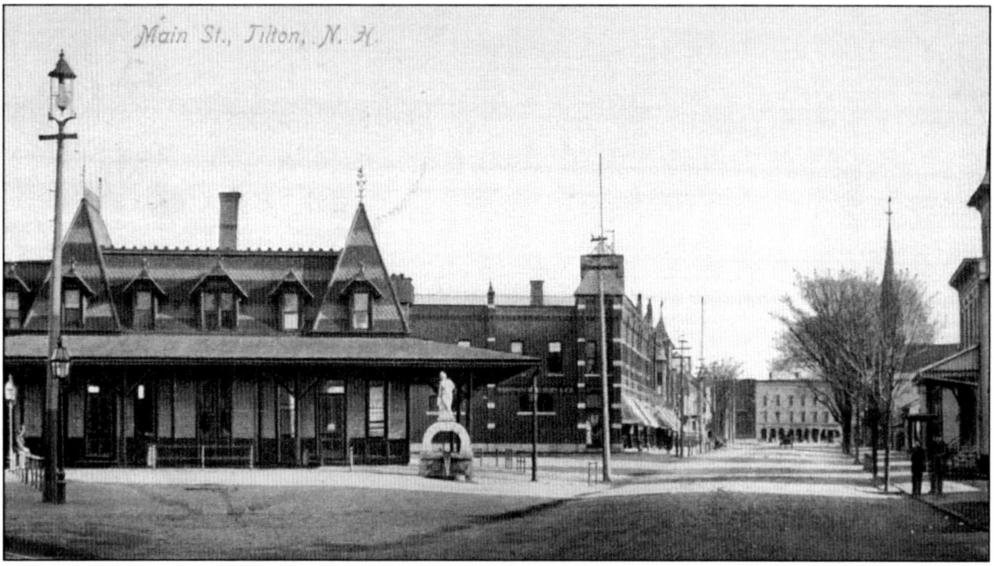

The Tilton Station in Tilton, NH, 1908. This is a single-track line from Franklin to Tilton, 4.95 miles long. The line was built in 1890 at the joint expense of the Northern and the Concord & Montreal Railroad. It was operated by the Concord & Montreal Railroad, to which it was leased in 1895 for the term of 91 years, at the nominal rental of $1 annually, with such additional sums as may be necessary to keep up the organization of the lesser. On the same date, this lease was assigned to the Boston & Maine Railroad.

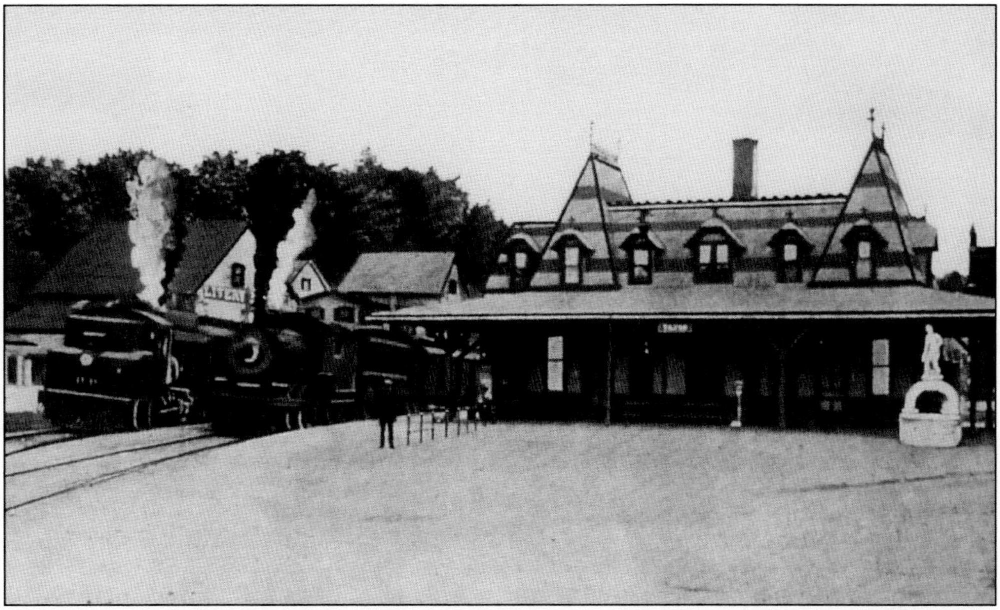

The Boston & Maine Railroad station looking east from Main Street in Tilton. The train on the left is the Tilton, Franklin & Belmont Branch Line which shows part of the B & M main line to Tilton and Belmont Junction from Tilton, c. 1912. In referring to the building of this line the report of the railroad commissioners in 1891 says, "We know of no other case in which so much money has been spent to so little purpose in a railroad project."

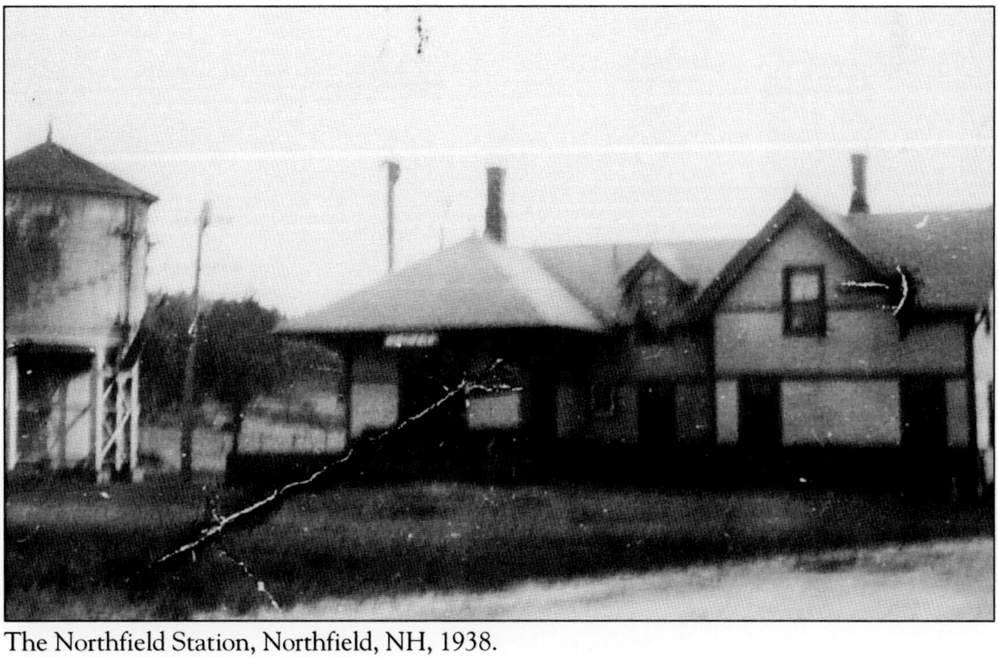

The Northfield Station, Northfield, NH, 1938.

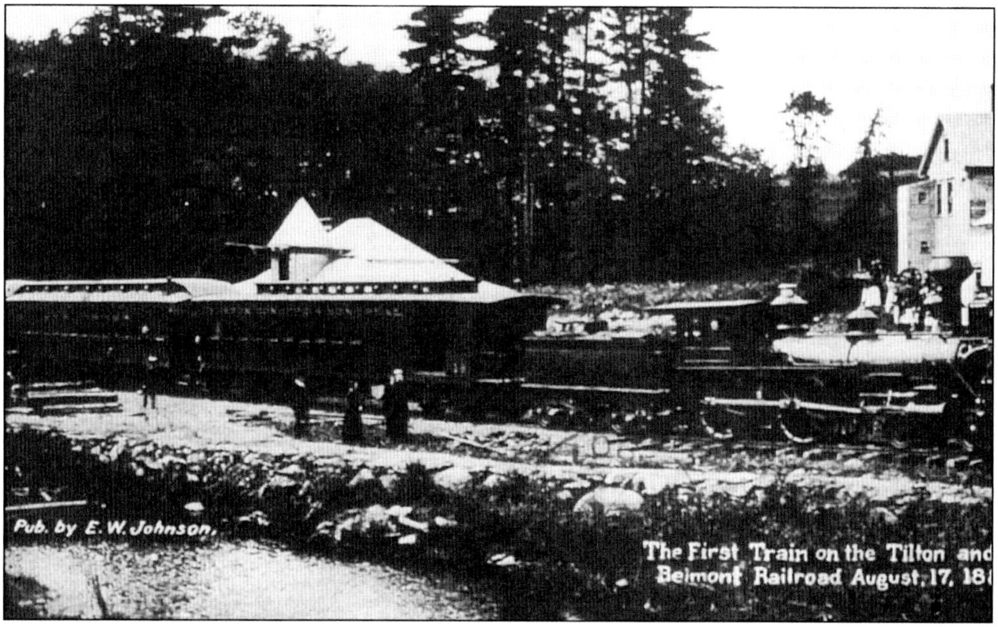

The first train on the Tilton and Belmont Railroad, 1889. This is a single-track line from Belmont Junction to Belmont, 4.17 miles long. The line was opened on August 17, 1889, and the 472 shares of stock issued were all bought by the Concord & Montreal Railroad for $48,550.

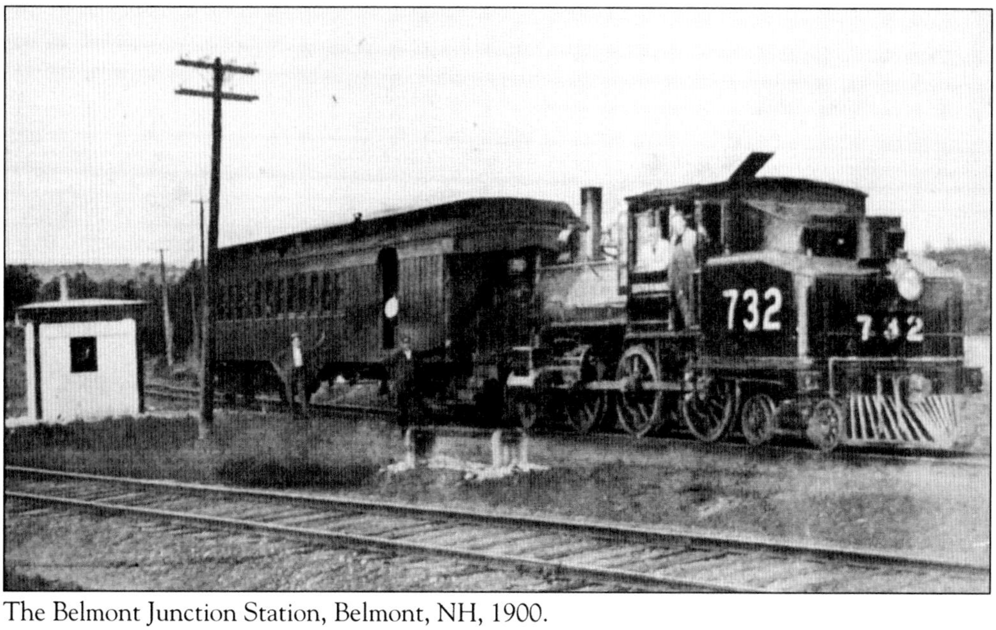

The Belmont Junction Station, Belmont, NH, 1900.

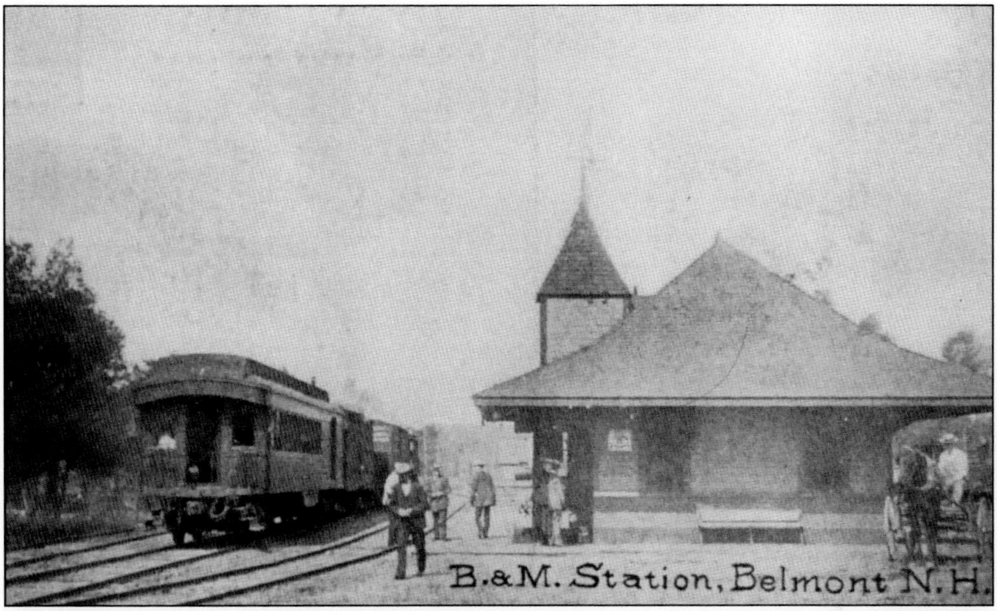

The Belmont Station, Belmont Branch, Belmont, NH, with a mix train heading west to the main line in Tilton, early 1890. On December 22, 1924, the Boston & Maine entered a petition with the Interstate Commerce Commission to abandon the Belmont branch. It was stated that the road had been built through the influence of the Concord & Montreal, and that it was merged with the Concord & Montreal in 1901. The commission at first granted the petition of the railroad to abandon this branch, but a rehearing was secured and this decision was reversed in July 1926.

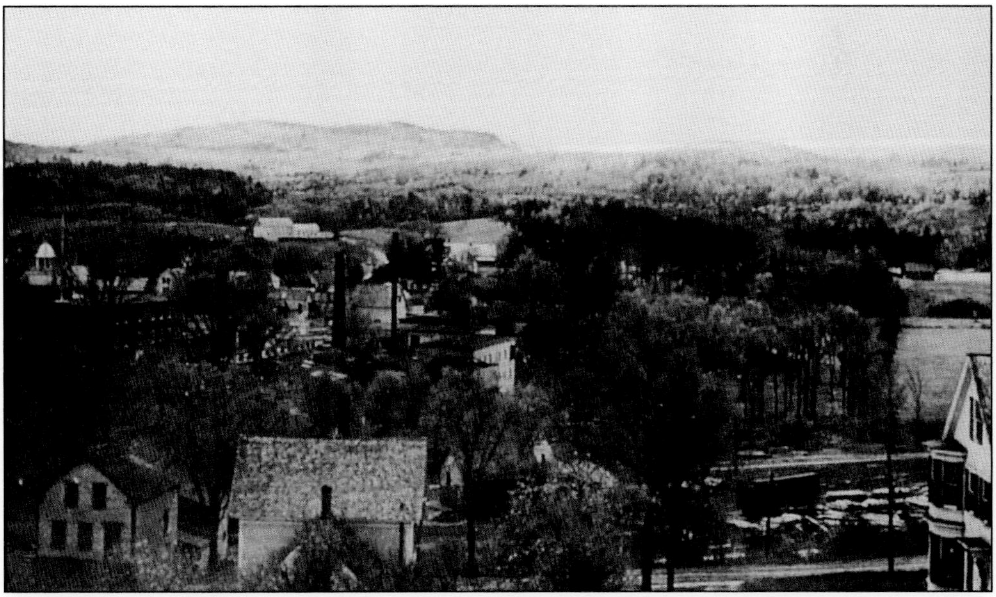

The Belmont and Tilton Railroad yard at the millyard complex on Depot Street, Belmont, NH, *c.* 1900. Between the years 1920 and 1925, passenger traffic declined 50 percent.

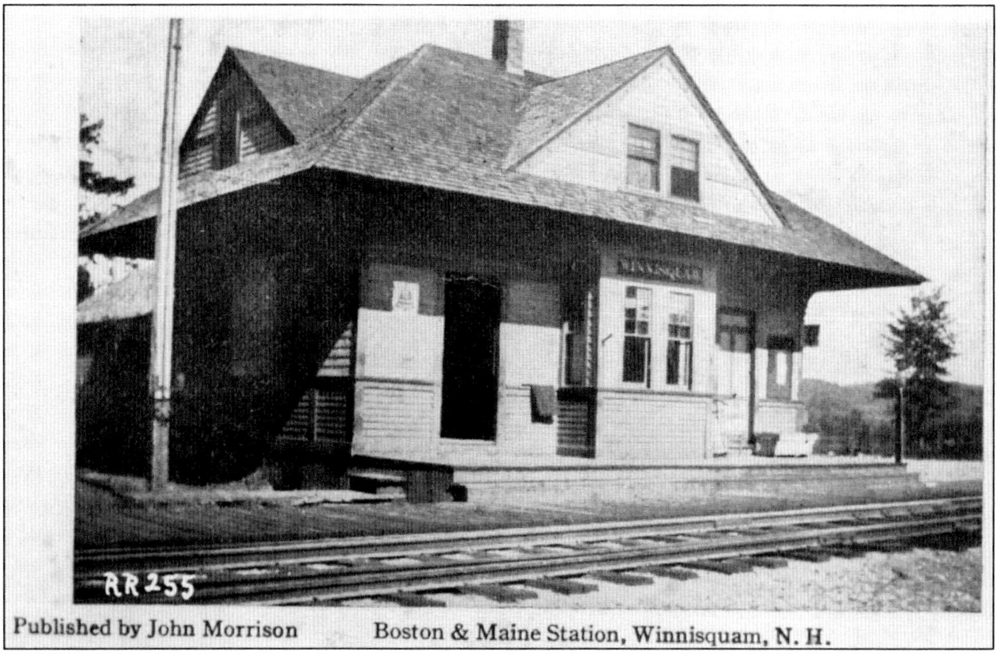

The Winnisquam Station, Winnisquam, NH, 1900.

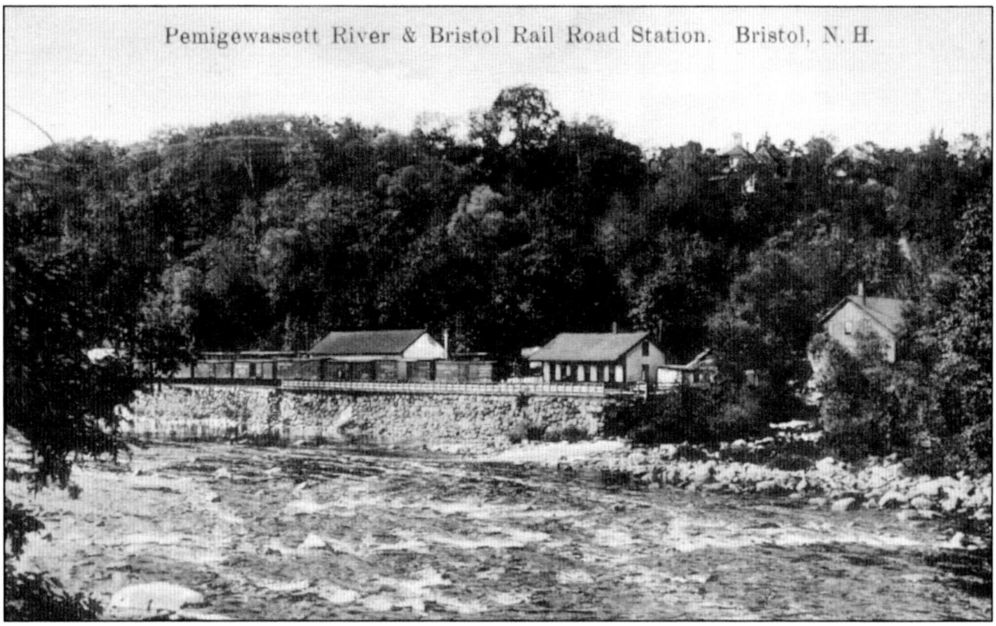

The Pemigewasset River and Bristol Railroad Station, Bristol, NH, 1909. The Bristol branch was charted as the Franklin & Bristol Railroad in 1846, and was completed in 1848. By authority of an act of the state legislature, the Franklin & Bristol Railroad Corporation was united with the Northern on January 31, 1849. In the report of May 1, 1849, the cost of construction of roads, depots, and equipment for the main line and branch together was given as $2,672,791.97. The Northern Railroad was operated independently to January 1, 1888, and then operated by the Boston & Maine Railroad until leased to the Boston & Lowell. In 1890 the Northern was leased to the Boston & Lowell for 99 years.

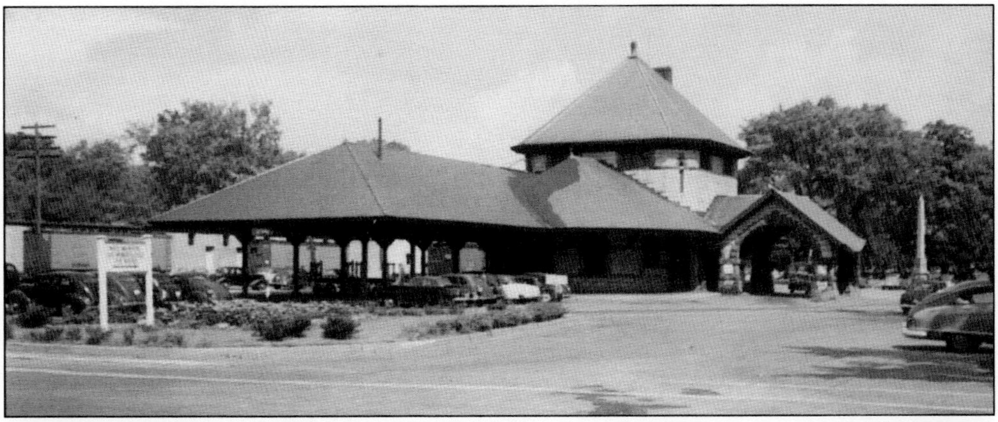

The Laconia Depot at Veterans Square, 1917. On August 8, 1848, the opening of the Boston, Concord & Montreal Railroad between Concord and Meredith Bridge was established and marked an important development to the growth of what is now Laconia. After the merge of the Boston, Concord & Montreal Railroad and the Concord Railroad, to form the Concord & Montreal Railroad in 1889, the new railroad company immediately proceeded to modernize its many railroad stations.

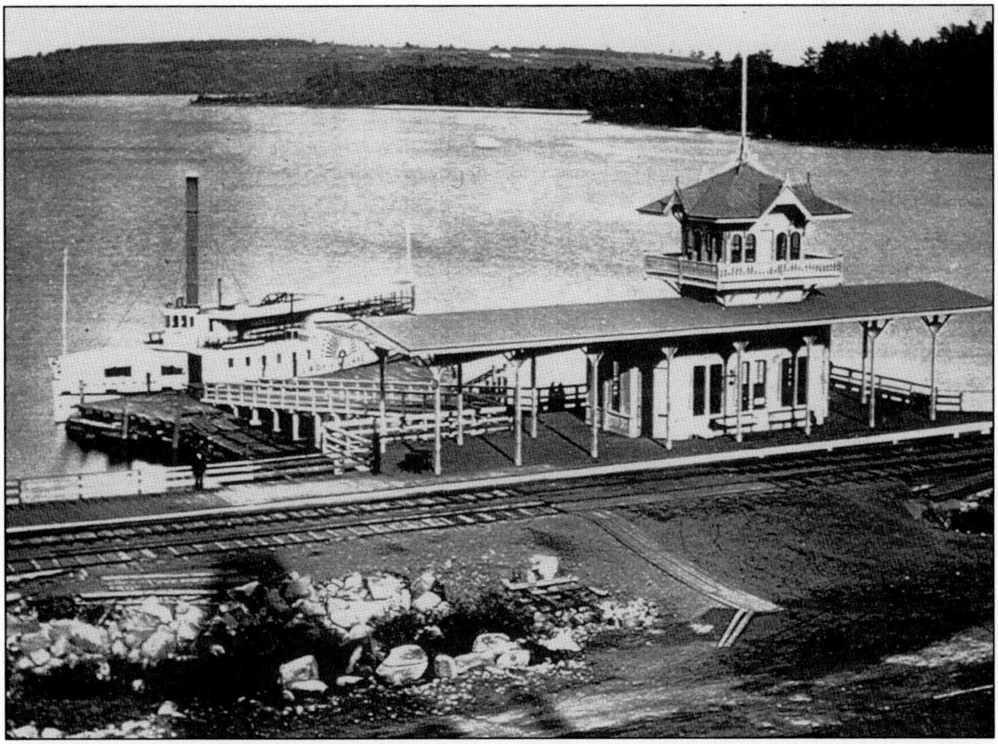

The Weirs Station on Lake Winnipesaukee with the *Lady of the Lake* docked at the station and Governor's Island in the distance, 1880s. In 1848–49, the Boston, Concord & Montreal continued the line to The Weirs, and established a station on the west shore of Lake Winnipesaukee. During the second half of the 19th century, it was customary for the railroad companies to build and own their own steamboats so as to transfer their passengers from trail to boat on their trek to the grand hotels in the Lakes Region and the White Mountains of New Hampshire.

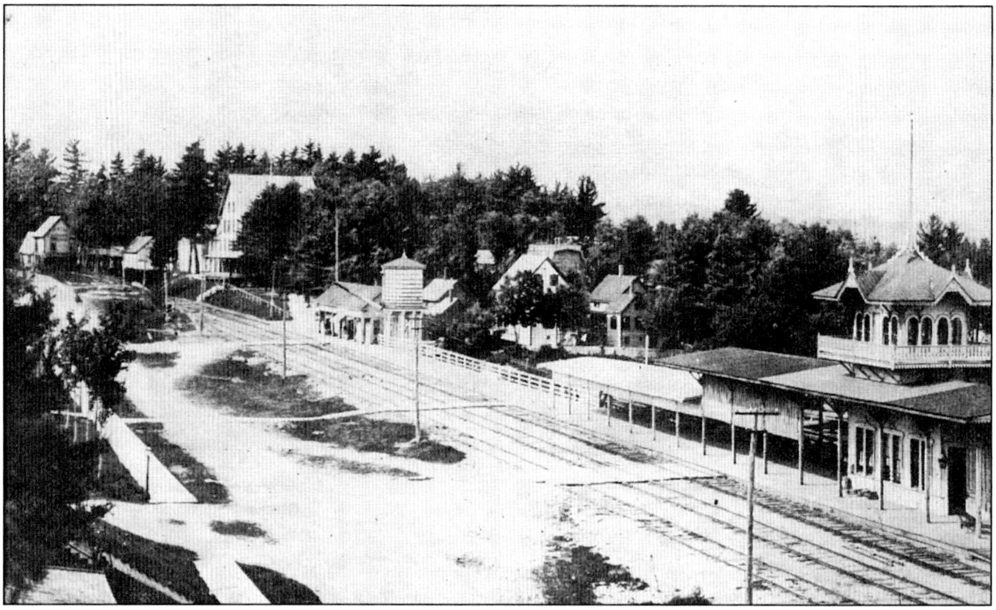

The Weirs Station looking northeast, 1880s.

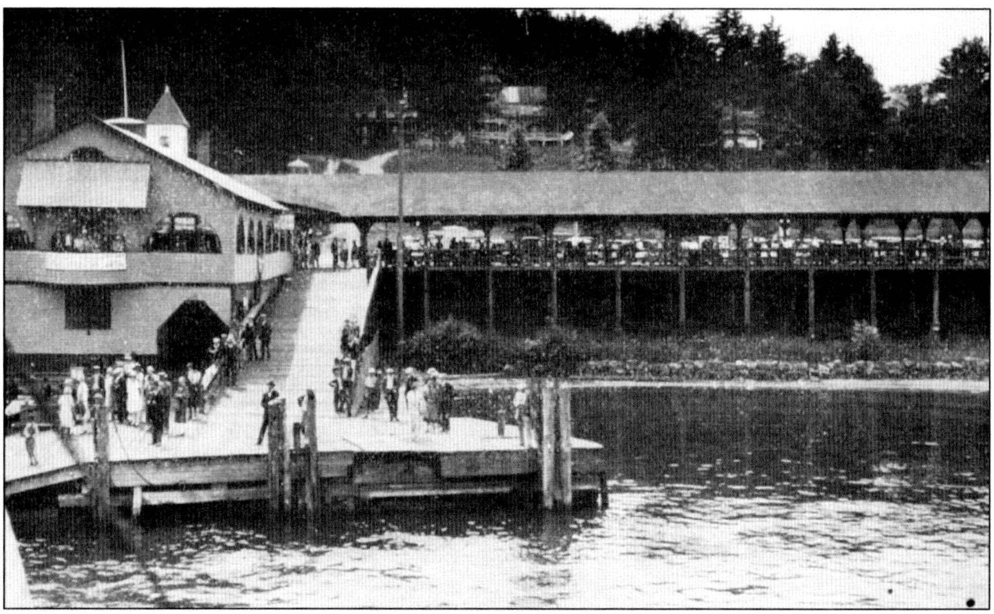

The Weirs Station, as seen from the deck of the steamer *Mount Washington*, 1920s. In the distance is seen the New Hampshire Veterans Association Campground.

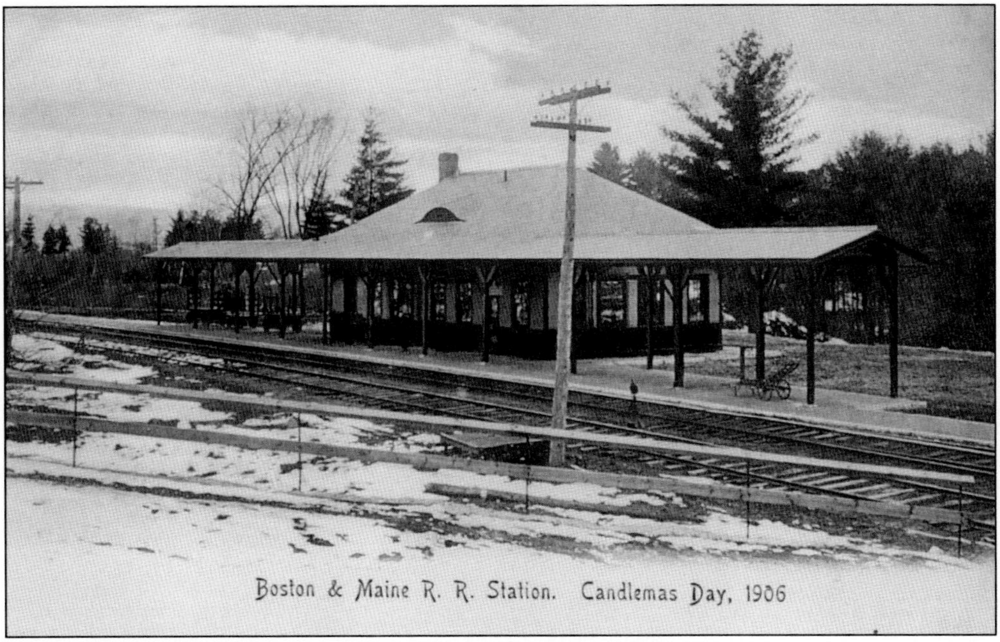

The Boston & Maine Railroad Station in Meredith, NH, 1906.

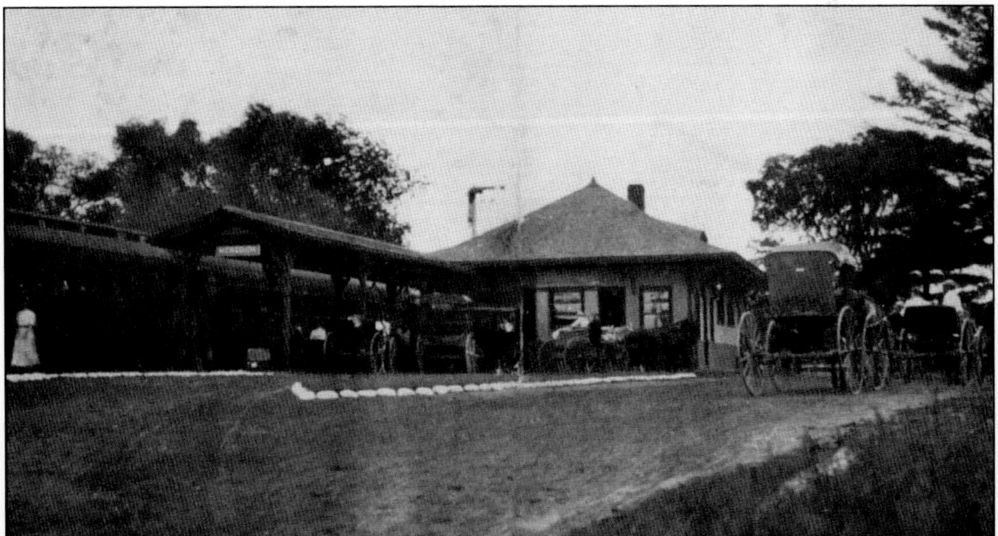

The Boston & Maine Railroad Station in Meredith, NH, with a passenger train en route to the White Mountains, c. 1900s.

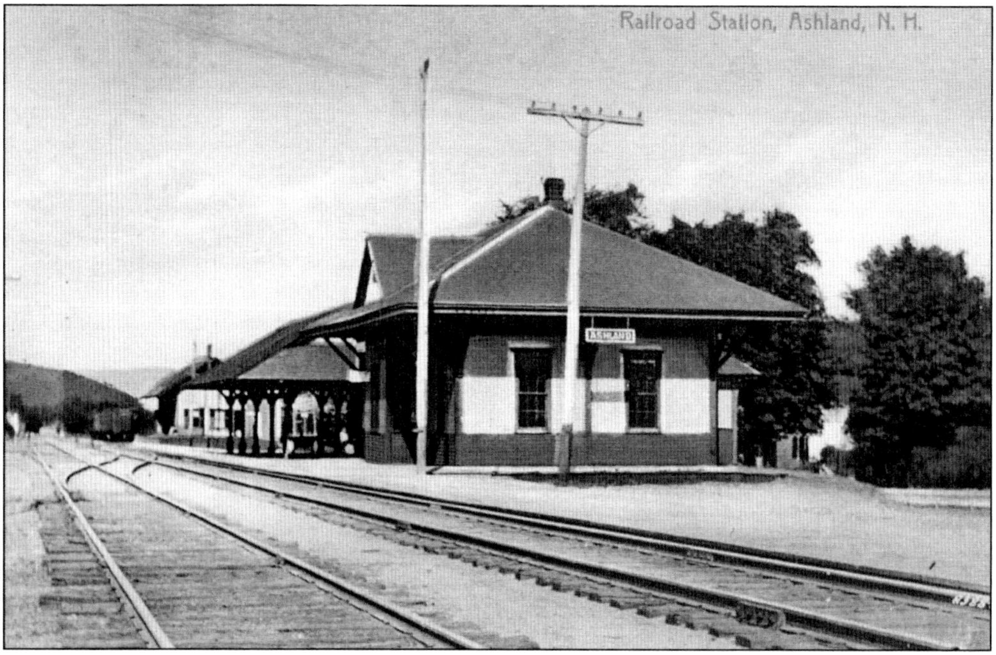

The Ashland Station in Ashland, NH, early 1900s. The Boston, Concord & Montreal Railroad ran the first train from Concord to Plymouth on Friday, January 18, 1850.

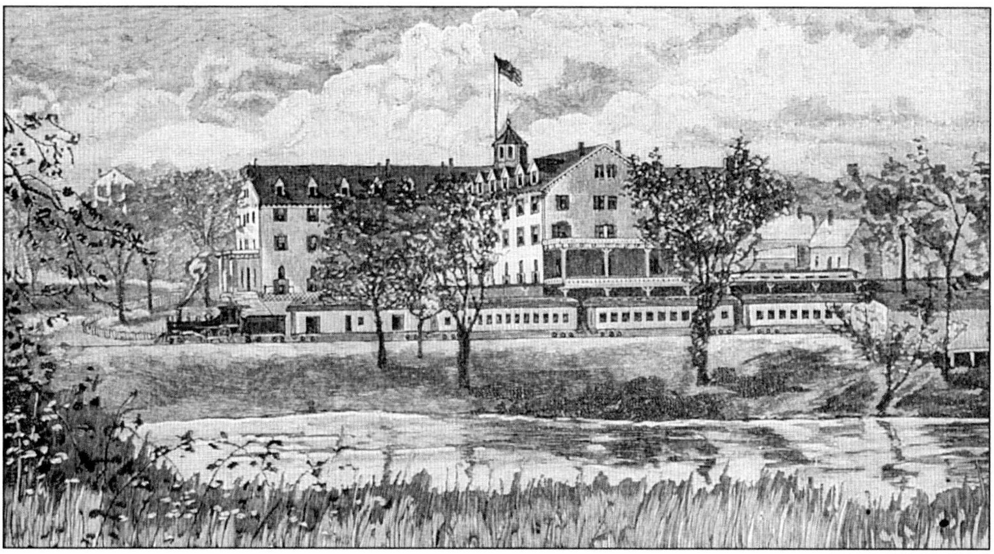

The Plymouth Station for the Boston, Concord & Montreal Railroad, and the Pemigewasset House, Plymouth, NH, 1877. In 1850 the Boston, Concord & Montreal Railroad completed the line to Plymouth from Concord. In 1858 the BC&M leased the White Mountain Railroad, which continued the line from Plymouth to Littleton. In 1869 the construction of an extension of the White Mountain Railroad beyond Littleton was undertaken, and in 1872 the road from Wing Road toward the base of Mount Washington was begun.

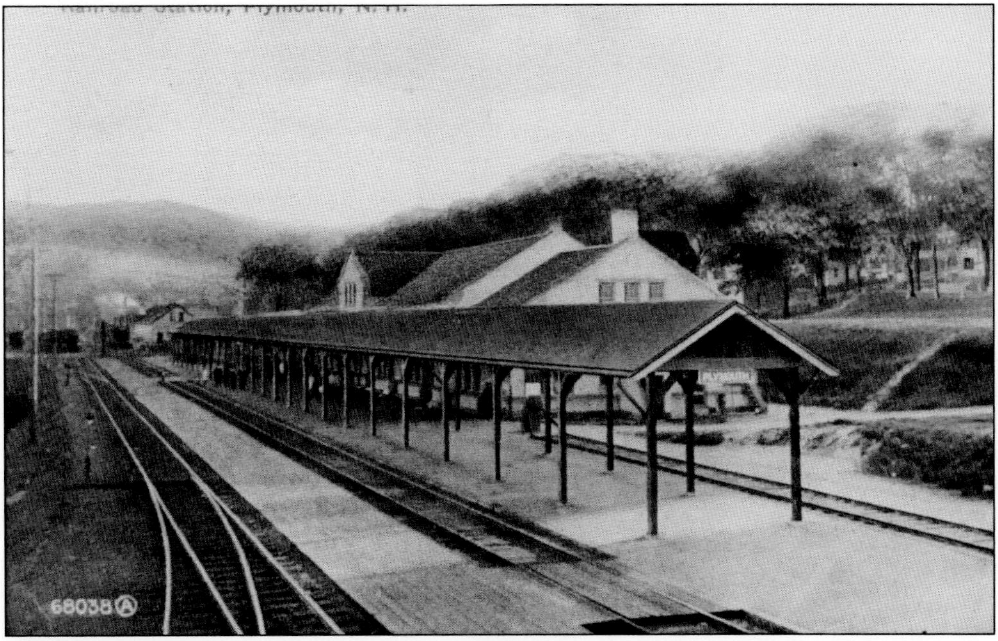

The Plymouth Station, Plymouth, NH, *c.* 1900s. This station was situated a little above the Pemigewasset River, while the village was located upon a terrace reached by a sharp grade from the railroad station.

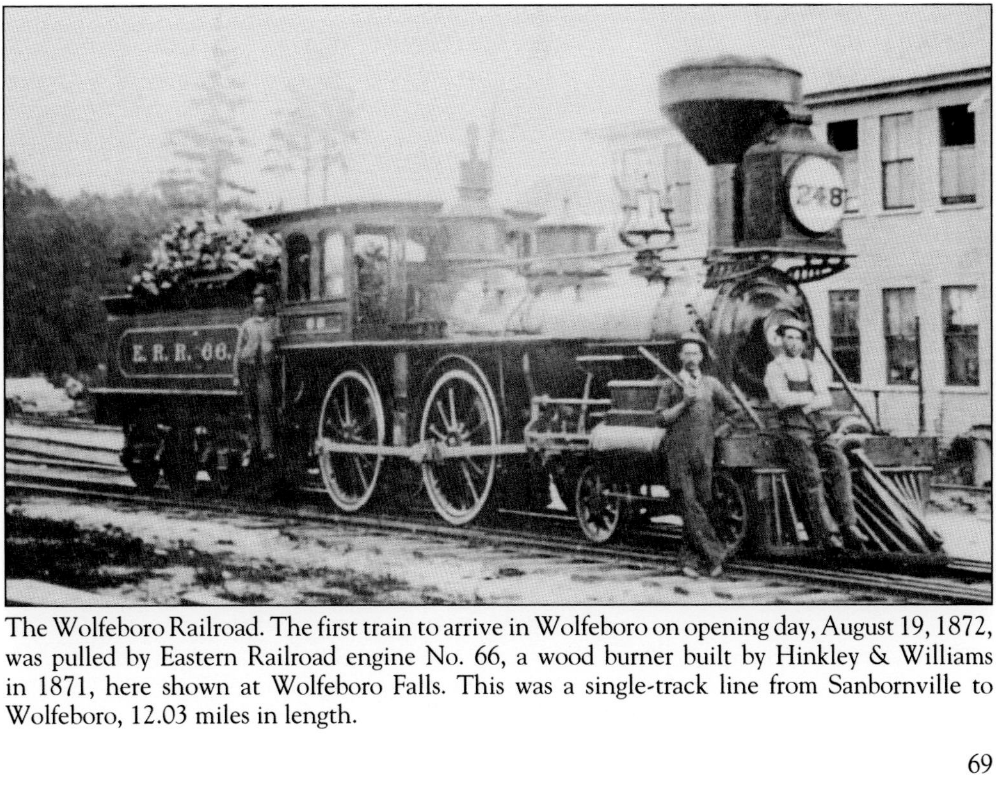

The Wolfeboro Railroad. The first train to arrive in Wolfeboro on opening day, August 19, 1872, was pulled by Eastern Railroad engine No. 66, a wood burner built by Hinkley & Williams in 1871, here shown at Wolfeboro Falls. This was a single-track line from Sanbornville to Wolfeboro, 12.03 miles in length.

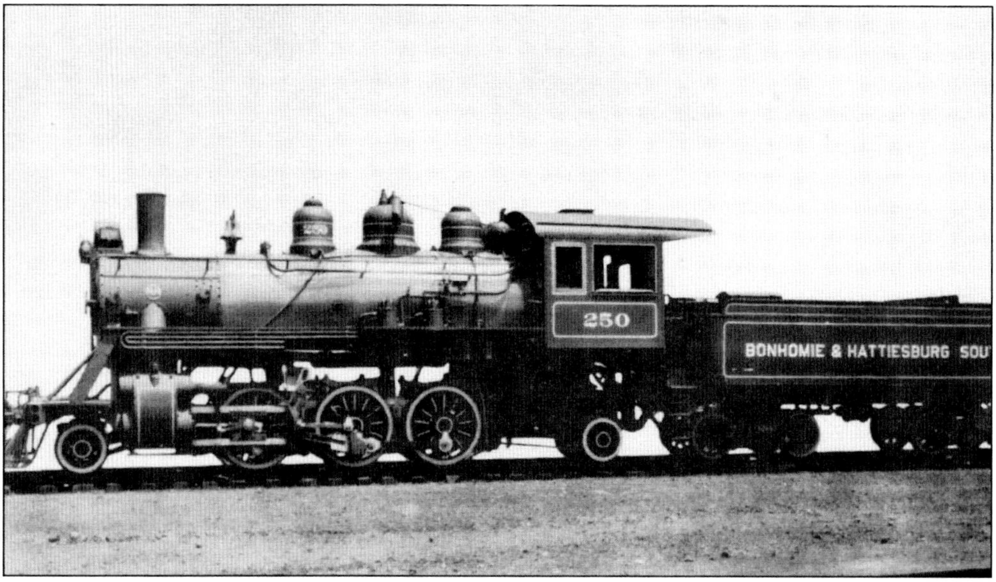

Wolfeboro Railroad Locomotive No. 250, shown as it was originally built in 1926. This line was chartered in 1868 and opened in 1872. In 1878 the cost was given as $386,500. Upon its completion it was leased to the Eastern Railroad. The lease was on the basis of 6 percent on the capital stock for a term of 68 years from the time of completion of the road.

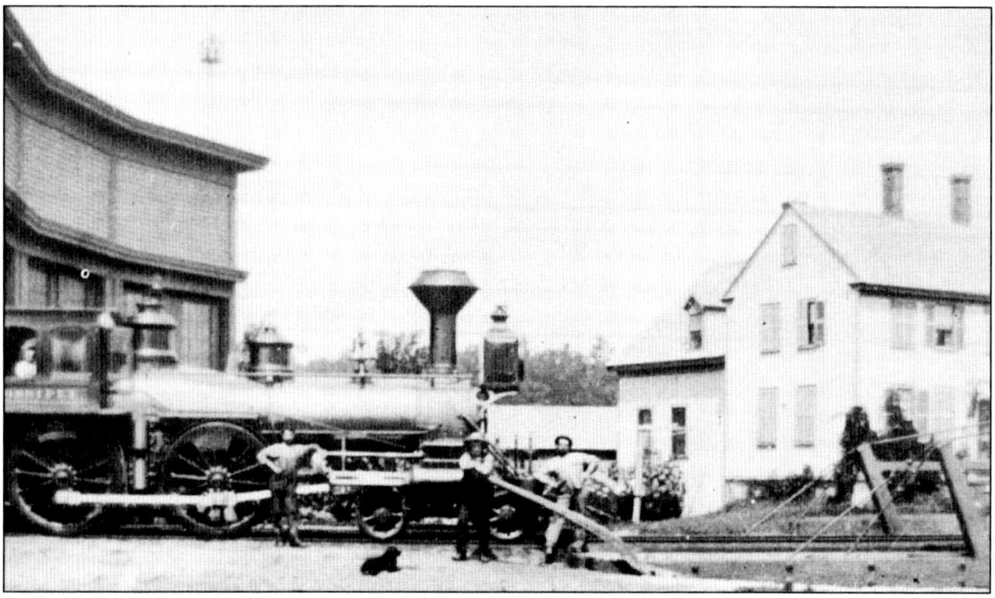

The Wolfeboro Roundhouse with the wood-burning locomotive *Ossipee* on the turntable, 1890. The house in the rear was owned by the railroad company.

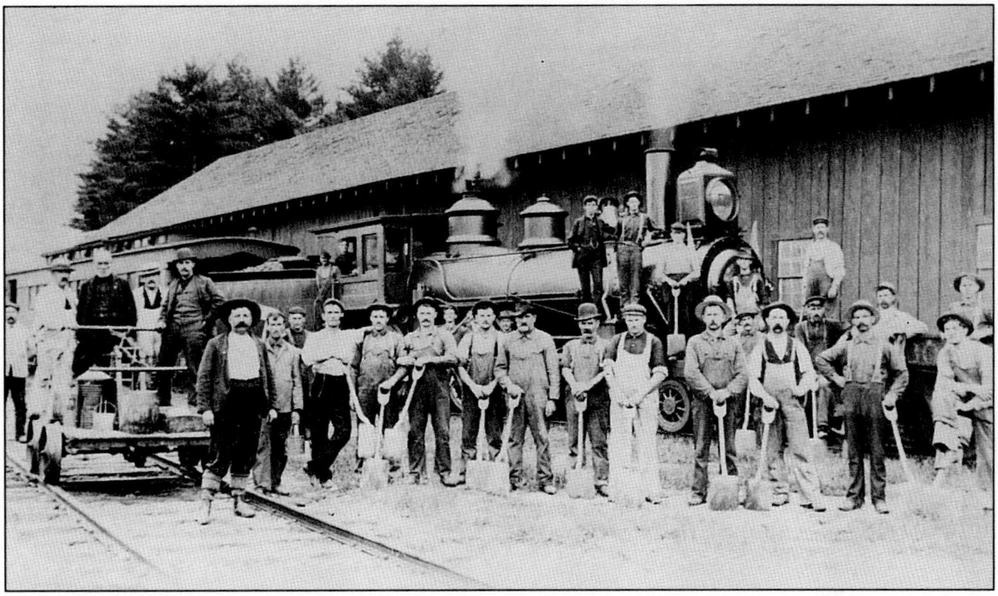

The Sanbornville Car and Paint Shop in the early days of the century, with the track gang posing for a picture. These shops employed approximately 60 men.

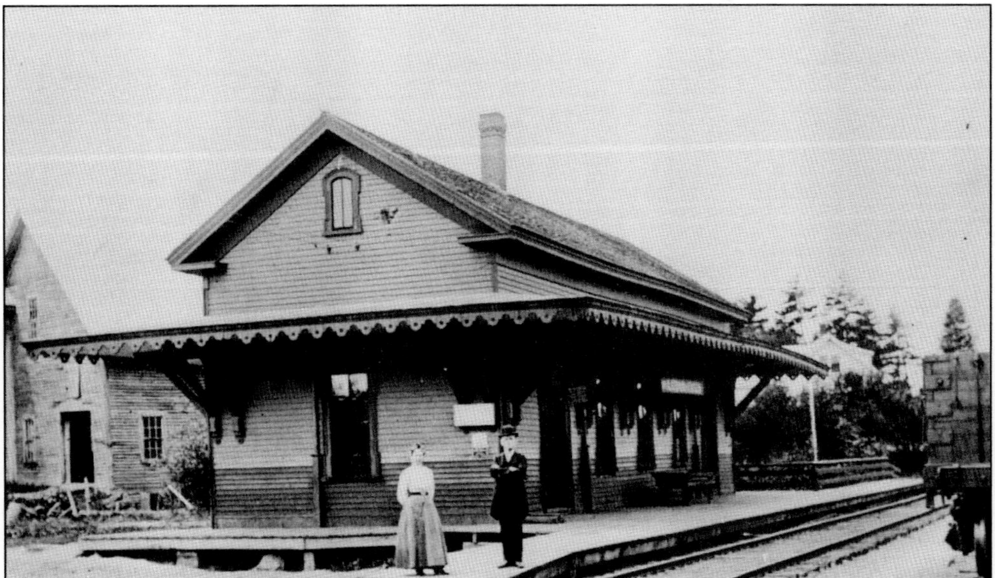

The Wolfeboro Falls Station, .6 miles from Wolfeboro, had a full-time agent and a freight house. This station was originally called "Mill Village," 1910.

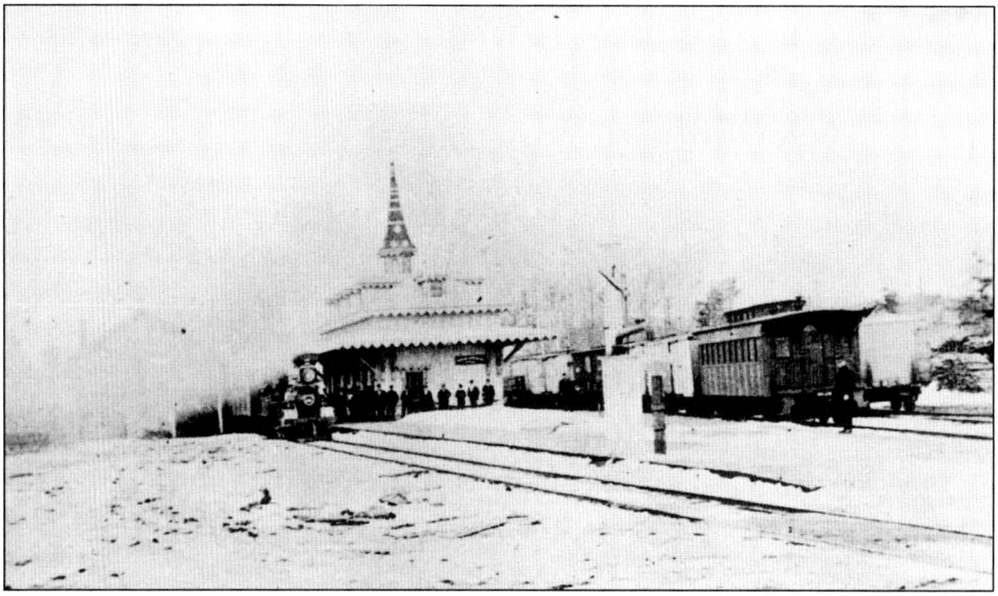

The Sanbornville Station with a wood-burning train en route to the Conways. The cars at right are on the Wolfeboro track, which was to the west of the building, *c*. 1875.

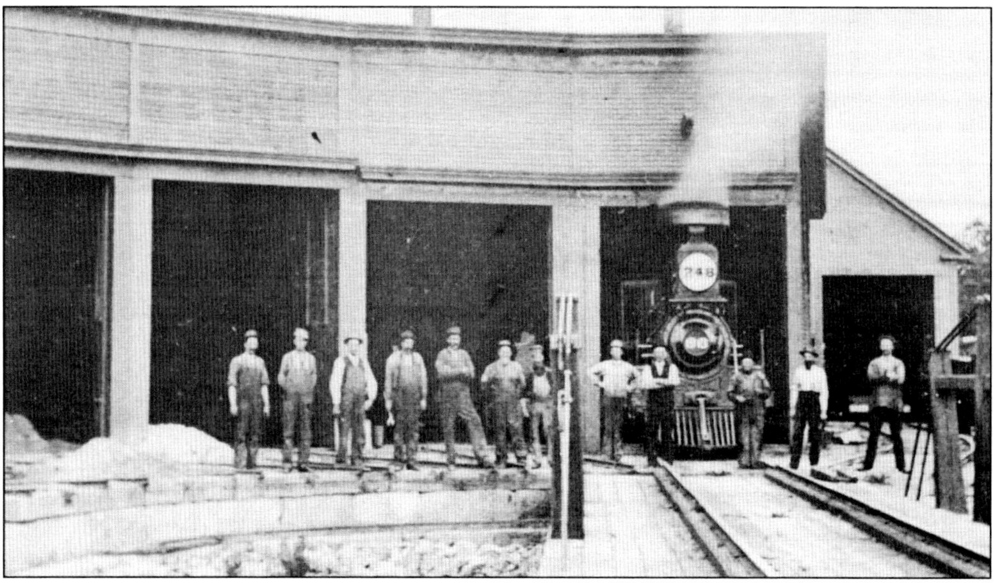

The Sanbornville Roundhouse, *c*. 1880. This seven-stall roundhouse and machine shop burned in 1911, and was replaced by a three-stall building.

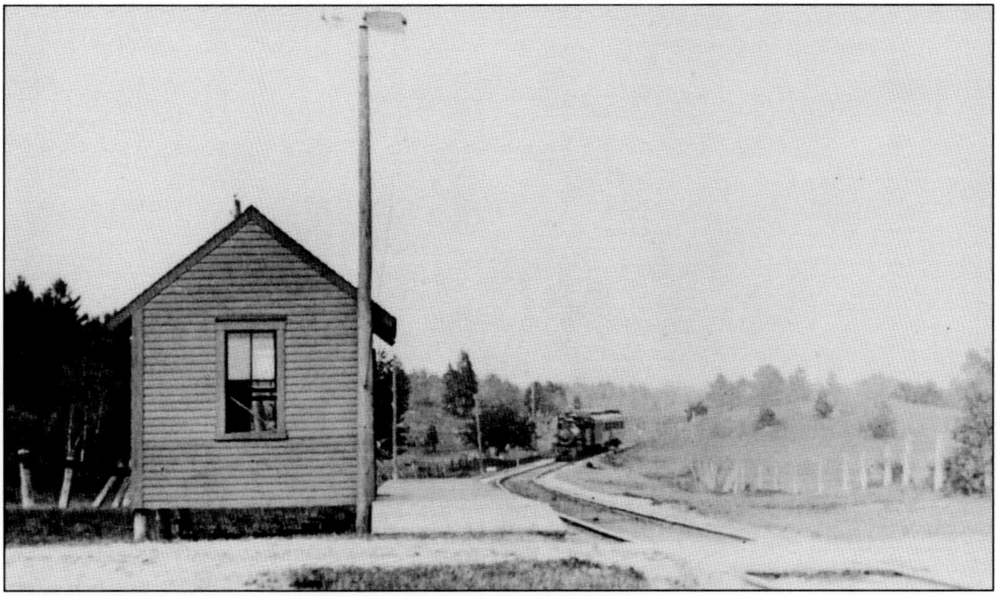

The Fernald Station, *c.* 1910. As many as ten trains a day stopped at this station. Note the hand-operated "flag" to signal the train to stop for passengers.

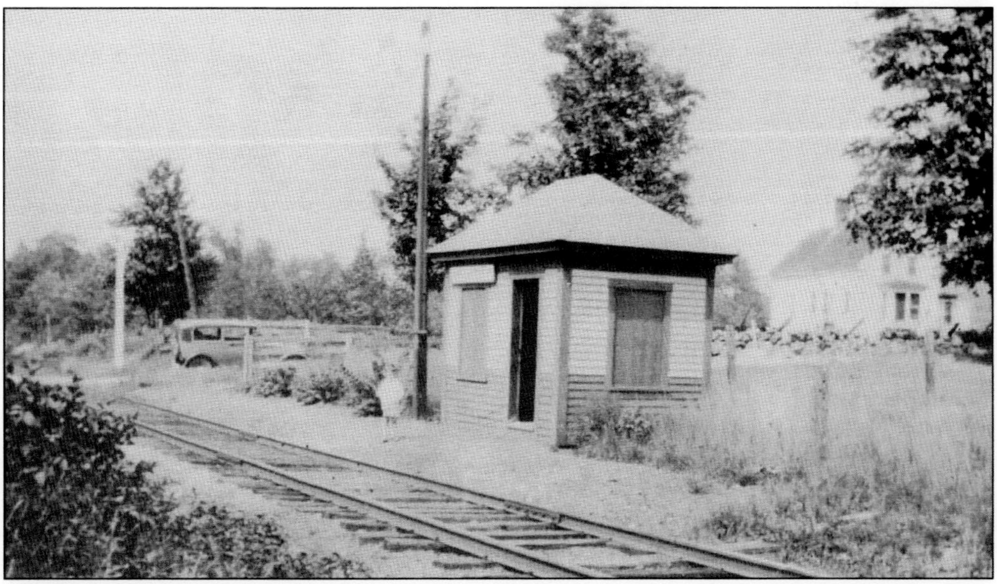

The Brookfield Station, a flagstop located 2 miles from Sanbornville, during the 1930s. This stop was originally known as "Pikes."

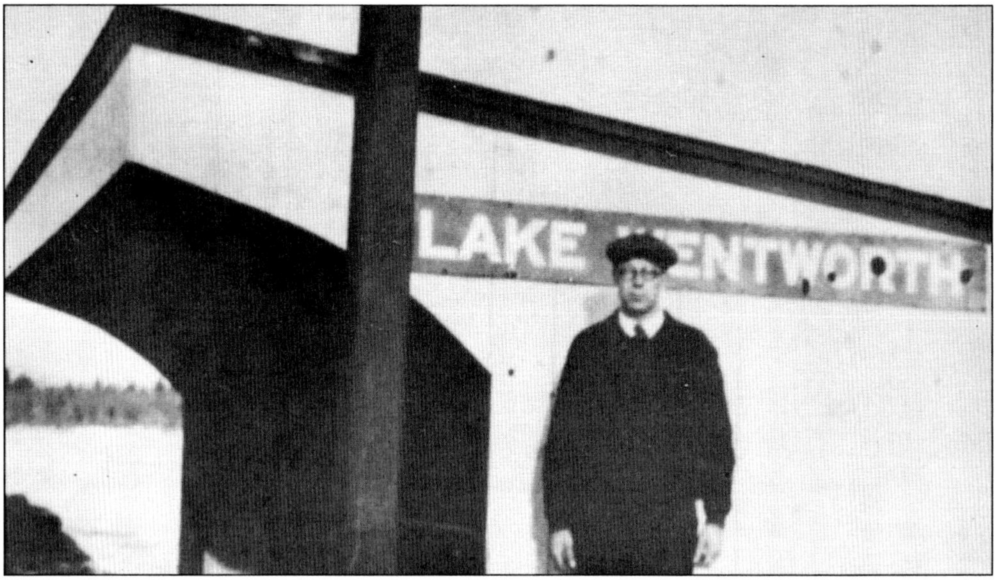

The Lake Wentworth Station, *c.* 1920. This was a most unusual station, in that the only access was by boat. There was no road to this station, which served the summer cottages on Lake Wentworth.

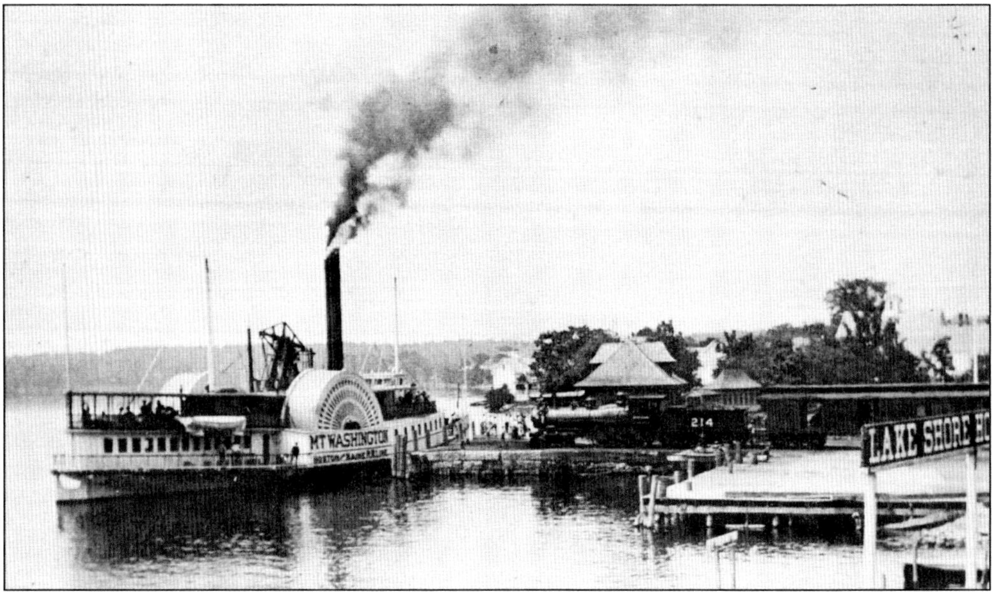

The Wolfeboro Dock Station, *c.* 1910. The Boston & Maine Railroad train meets the steamer *Mount Washington* at the new station, which replaced the original building that burned in 1899.

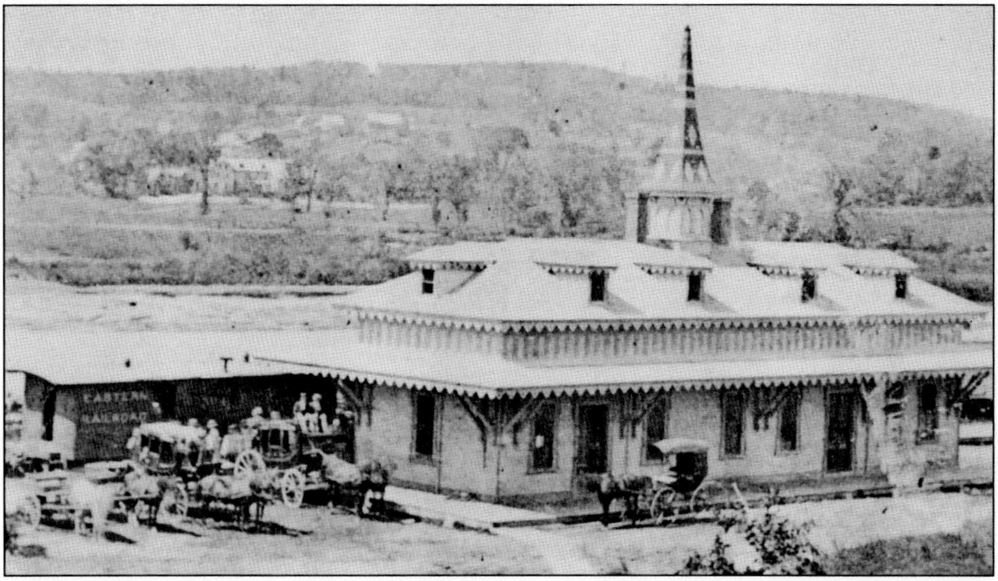

The Wolfeboro Station, *c.* 1875. Note the Eastern Railroad train, and the two stage coaches loading for the hotels and Melvin Village.

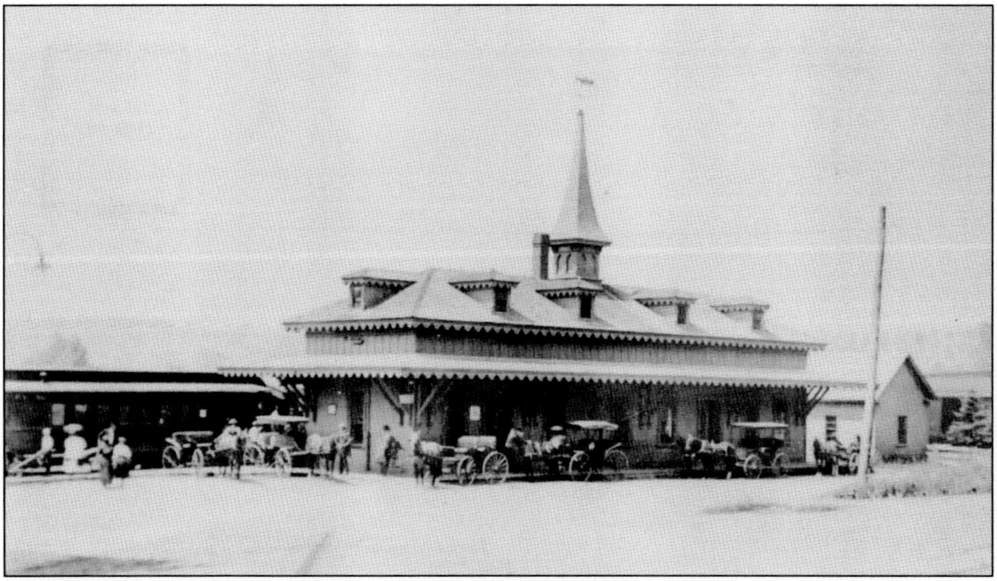

The Wolfeboro Station, *c.* 1900s, with the Boston & Maine train at station. The building to the right was the express office. The Town of Wolfeboro voted a gratuity of about $35,000 for the construction of this road, but it is not known whether it was ever paid. This stock continued to receive 6 percent in rentals until the purchase of the road and consolidation with the Boston & Maine Railroad in 1892. The Boston & Maine gave 15–17 percent of a share of its stock for each share of the Wolfeboro Railroad stock, amounting to $340,000 for the new capitalization.

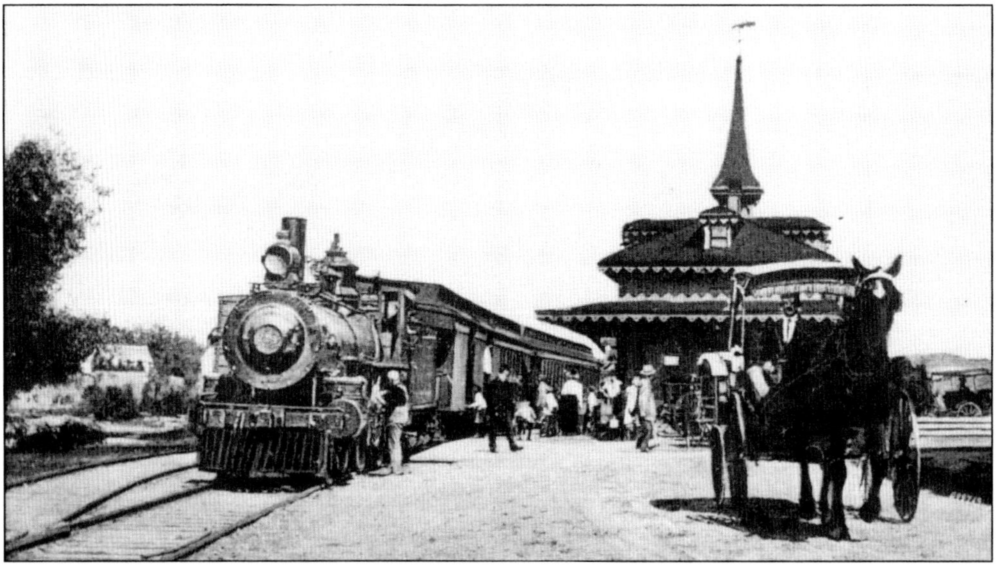

The Wolfeboro Station as seen in 1912, Wolfeboro, NH.

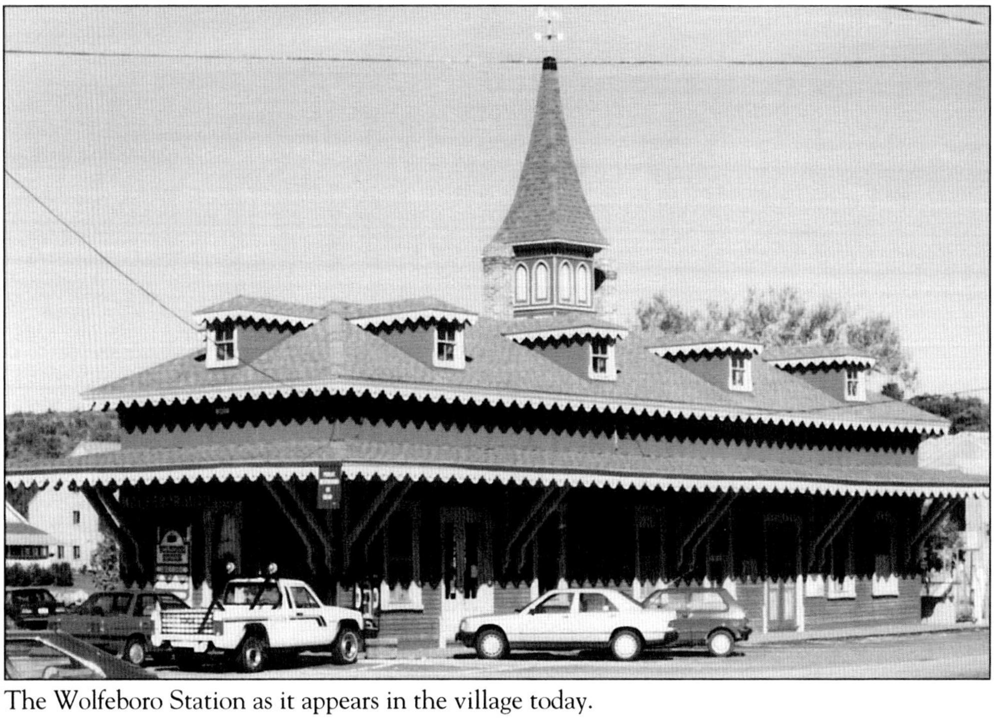

The Wolfeboro Station as it appears in the village today.

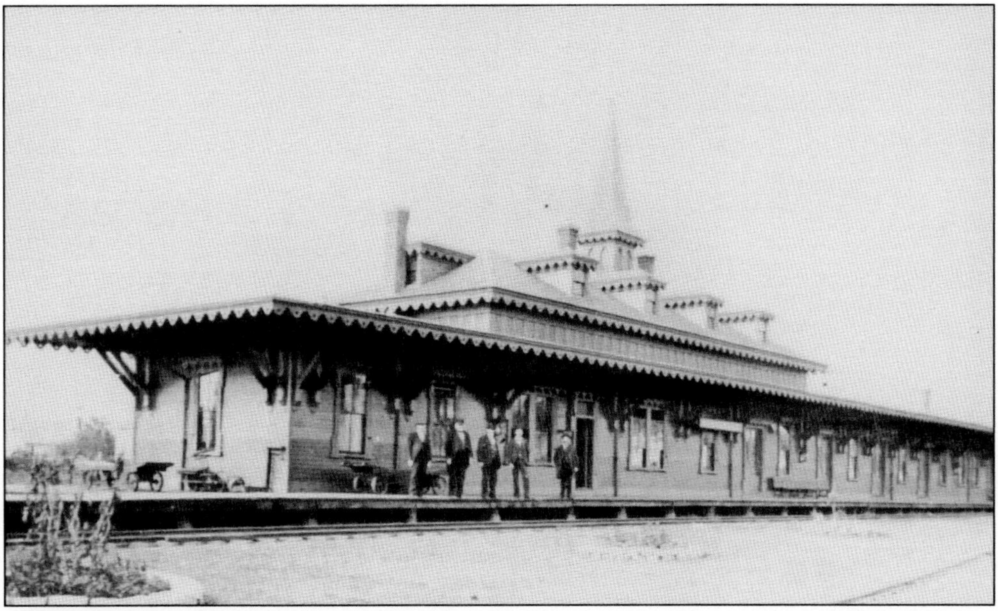

The Sanbornville Station after considerable enlargement. The offices of the Northern Division of the Boston & Maine, plus a large lunchroom, took up considerable space. Sanbornville was called "Wolfeboro Junction" for many years, 1895.

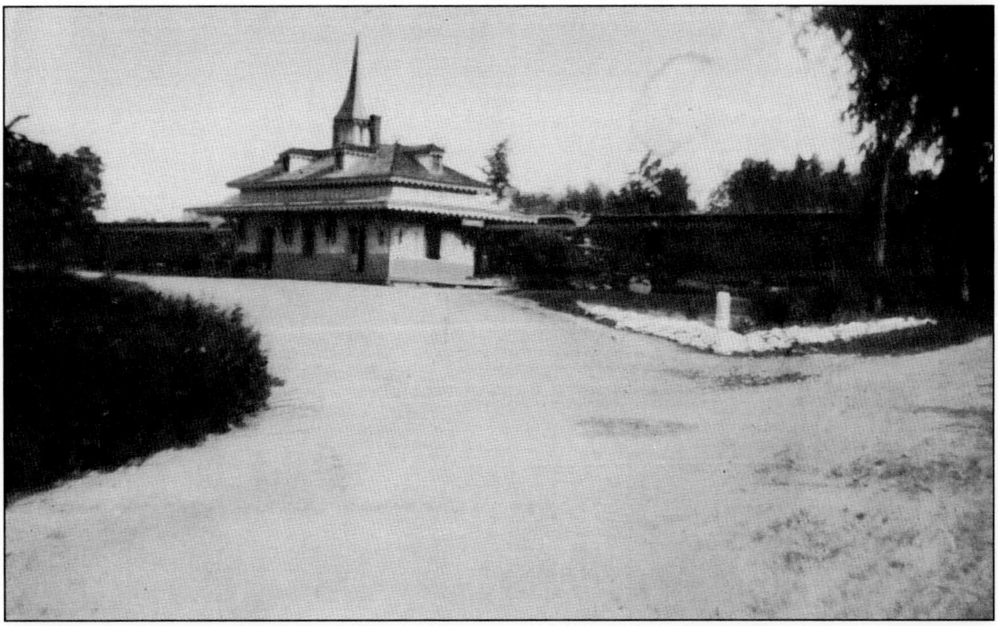

The Ossipee Station in Ossipee NH, 1898. The Portsmouth, Great Falls & Conway Railroad was organized in 1866 for the purpose of taking over the Great Falls & Conway Railroad and the South Berwick Branch Railroad. Immediately following reorganization, the line was extended from Union Village to West Ossipee at a cost of $767,200, a considerable portion of the money being advanced by the Eastern Railroad, and this extension was followed by a further one from West Ossipee to North Conway at a cost of $483,400.09, all advanced by the Eastern Railroad. In 1884, the Eastern Railroad was leased by the Boston & Maine Railroad.

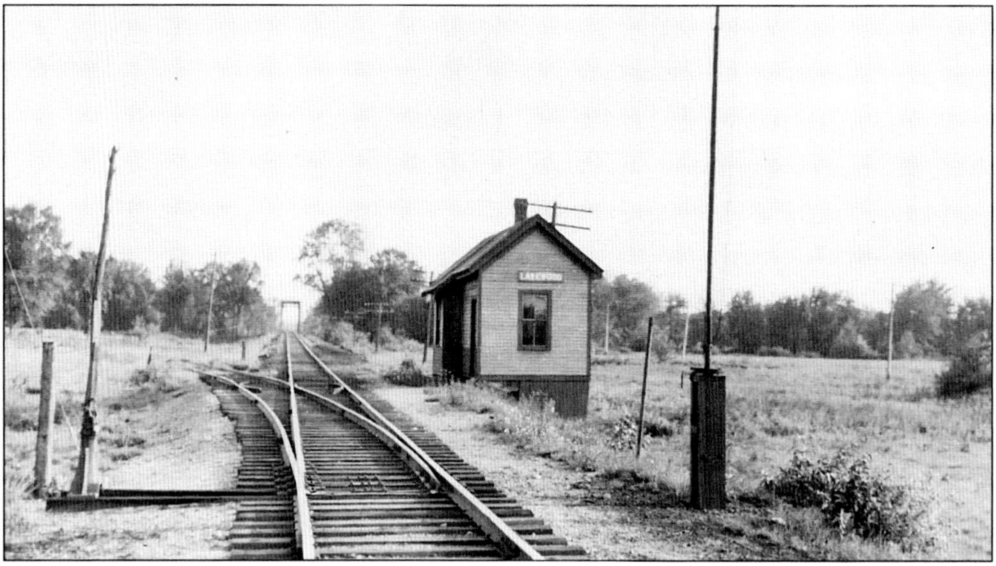

The Lakewood Station, West Ossipee, NH, 1910.

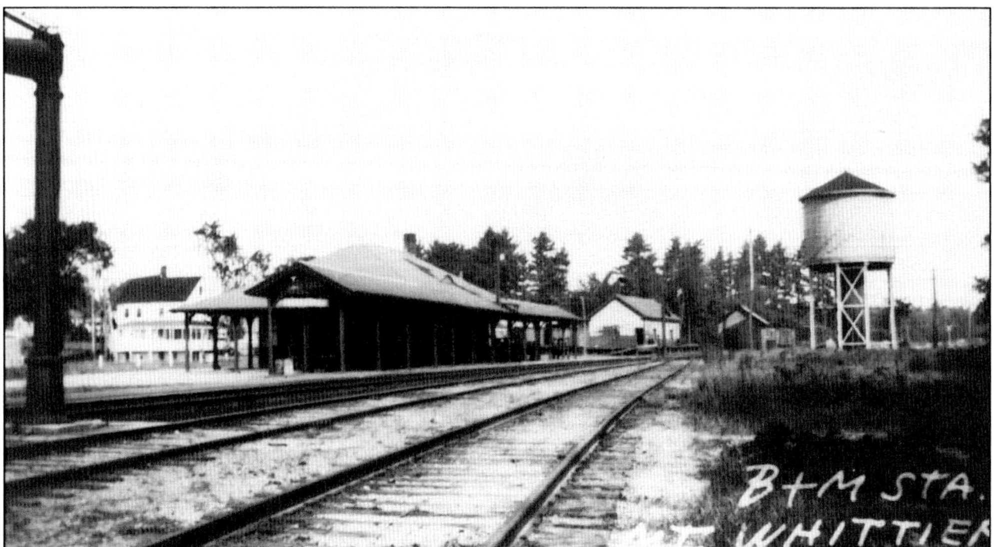

The Mount Whittier Station in West Ossipee, NH, 1930.

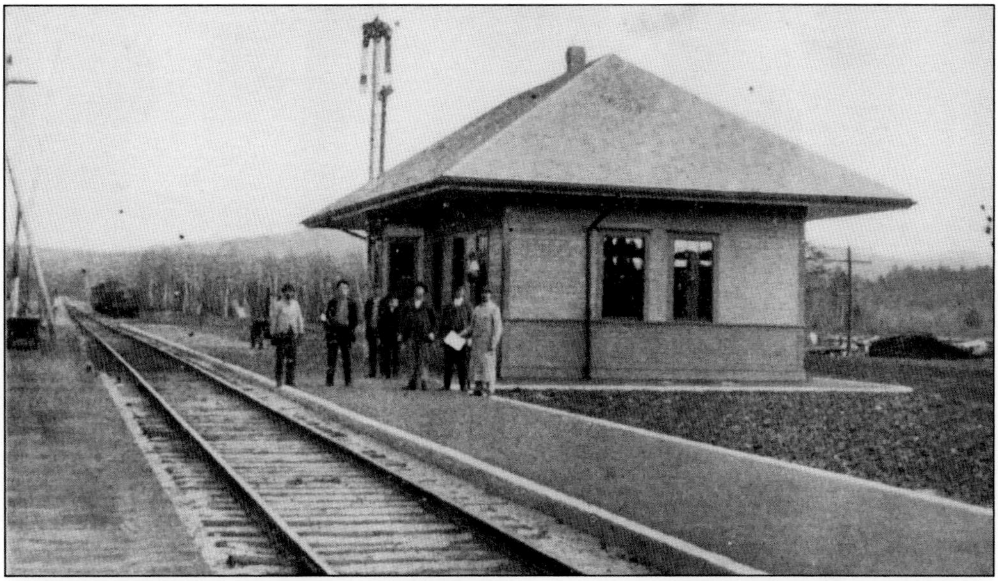

The Silver Lake Station, Madison, NH, 1919.

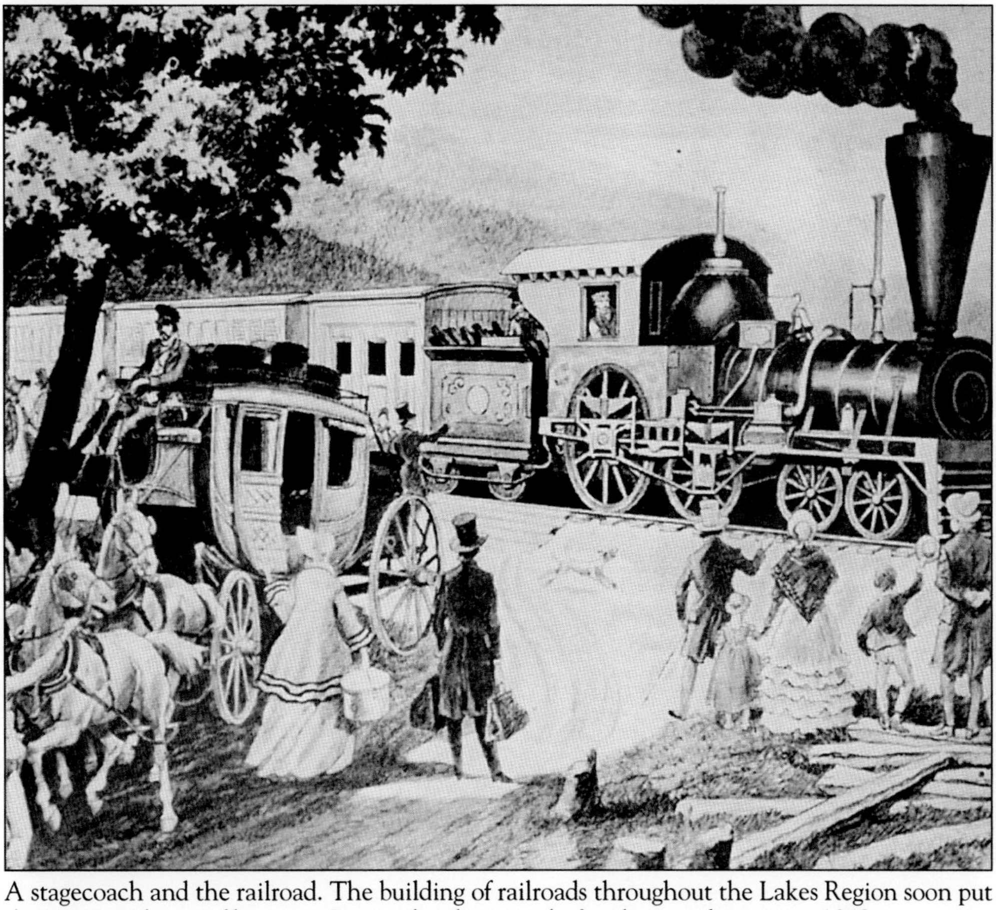

A stagecoach and the railroad. The building of railroads throughout the Lakes Region soon put the stagecoach out of business. Pictured is the arrival of such an early train, *c.* 1849.

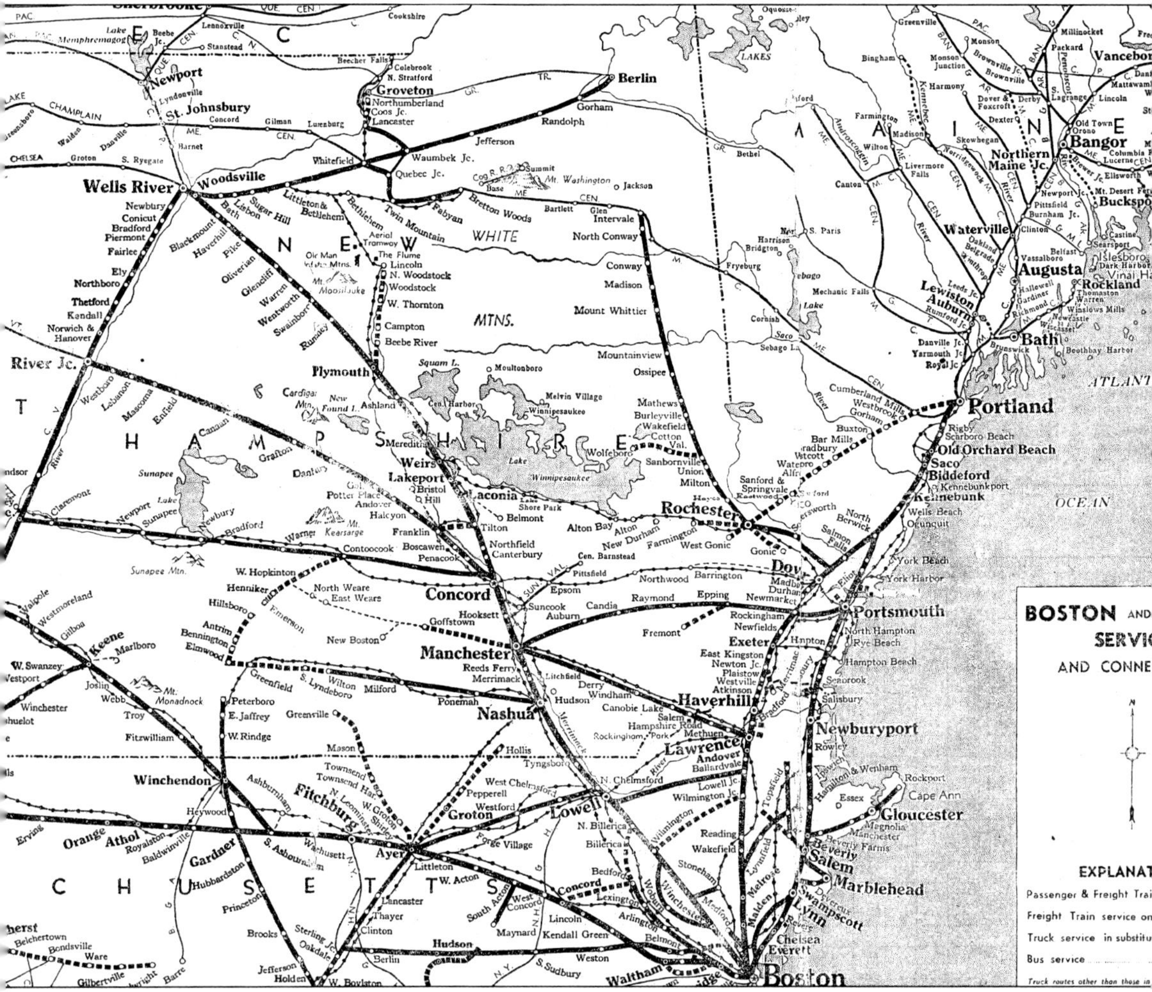

Railroad lines, stations, and routes from Boston to the Lakes Region and the White Mountains of New Hampshire. The Boston & Maine service and connections are shown here in the early 1900s.

Four

Recreation and Tourism

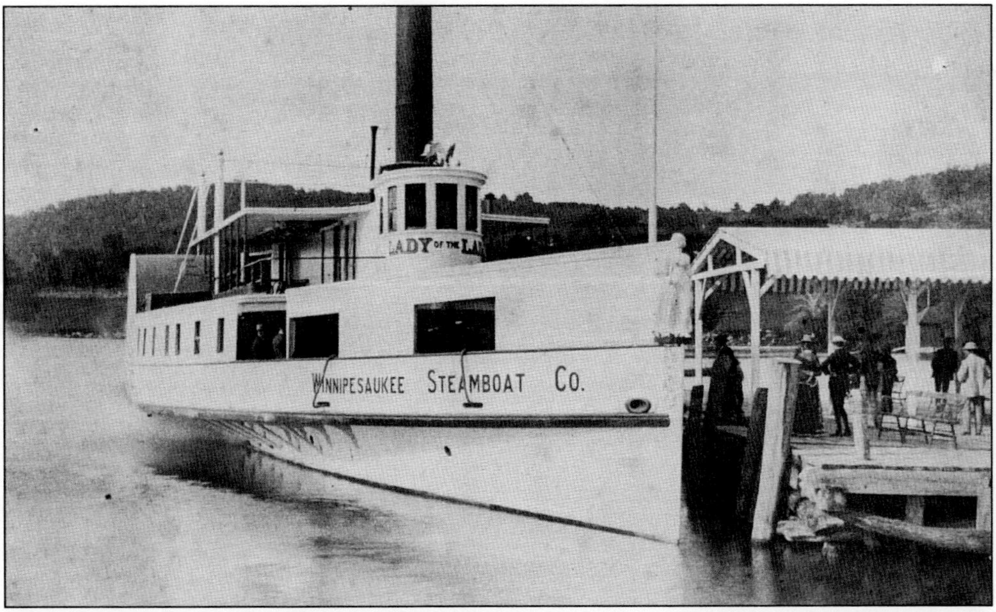

The steamer *Lady of the Lake* at the Center Harbor dock, 1880s. This vessel was originally built by the Winnipesaukee Steamboat Company and launched at Lakeport, NH, in June 1849. She was the first lake passenger steamer and was operated under the ownership of the Boston, Concord and Montreal Railroad Company. She was retired from lake service in 1893. Her final resting place is located in 40 feet of water in Glendale Bay. Today, divers tell us that her hull is still in perfect condition.

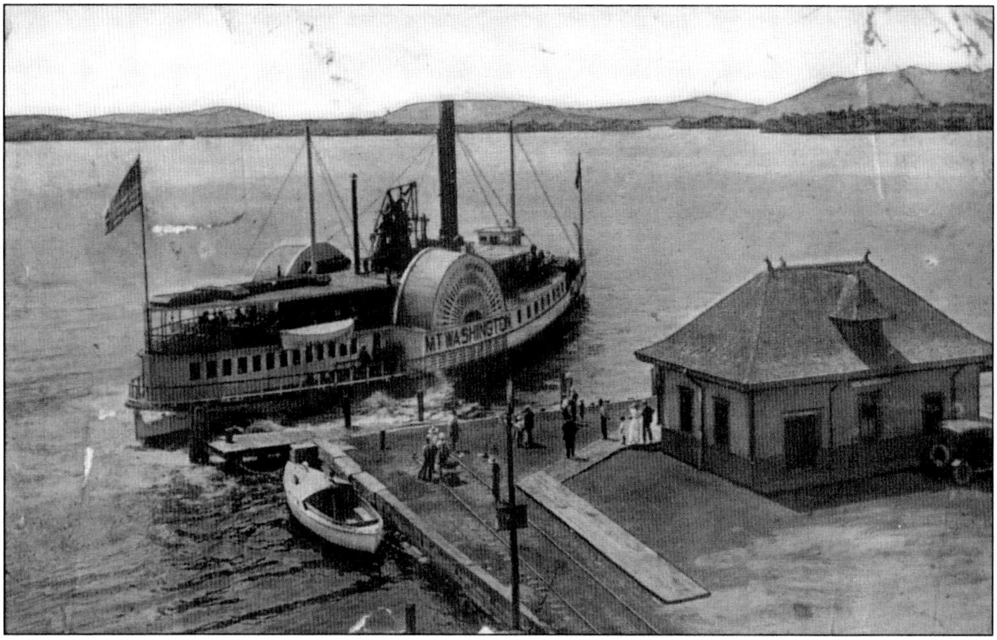

The steamer *Mount Washington* leaving the Wolfeboro town dock on its return trip to The Weirs, 1880s.

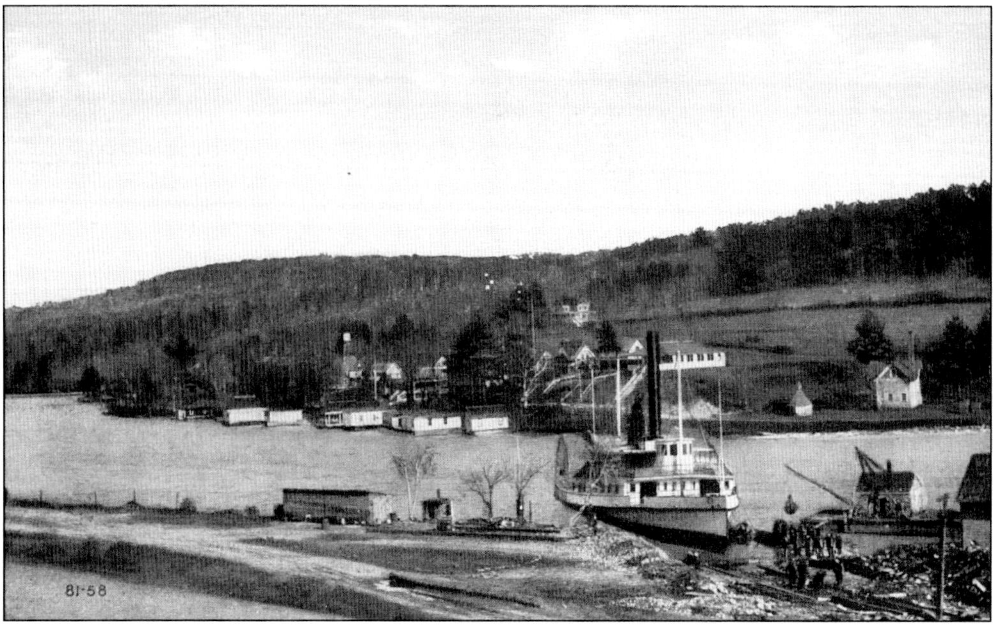

The steamer *Mount Washington* being hauled out for repairs, Alton Bay, NH, 1880s.

The steamer *Mount Washington* docked at The Weirs on a late Sunday afternoon with an engineer checking the walking beam on the top deck, 1929.

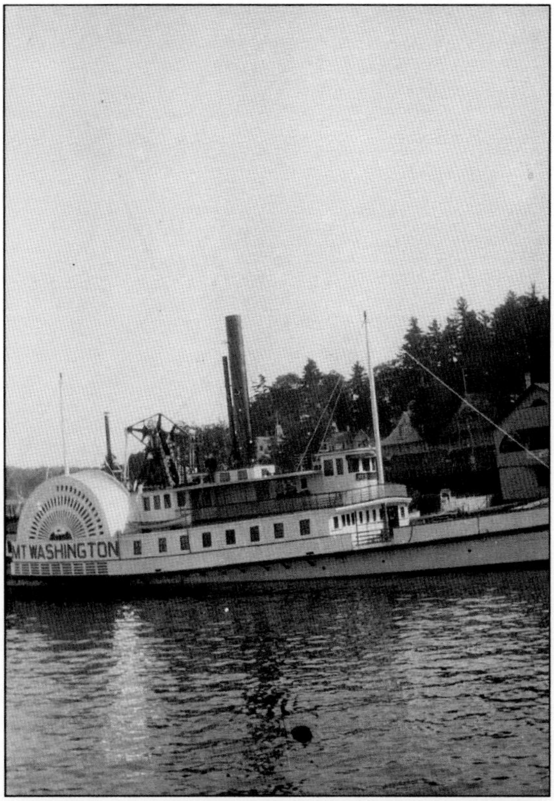

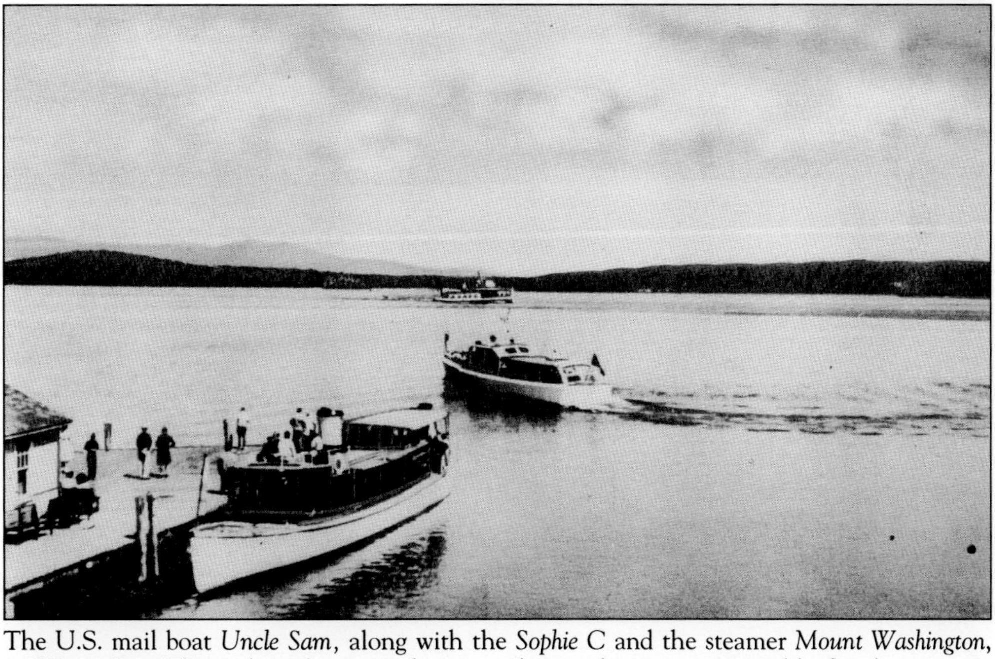

The U.S. mail boat *Uncle Sam*, along with the *Sophie* C and the steamer *Mount Washington*, in Weirs Bay. These three boats, and many other crafts, were responsible for the growing transportation of thousands of regular tourists among the islands and scenic grandeur of the Lakes Region.

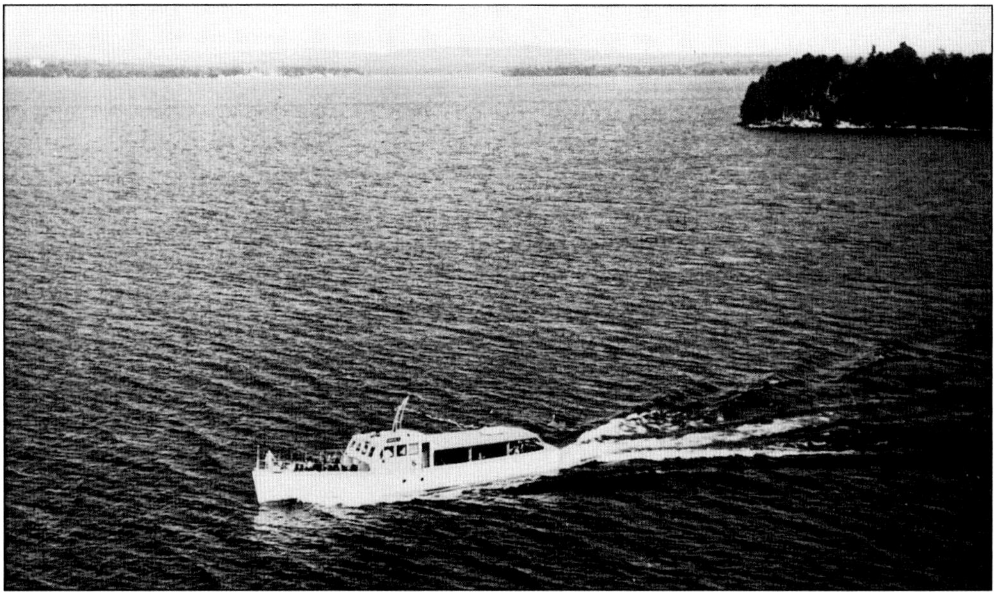

The *Sophie C* off Diamond Island, Lake Winnipesaukee, 1946.

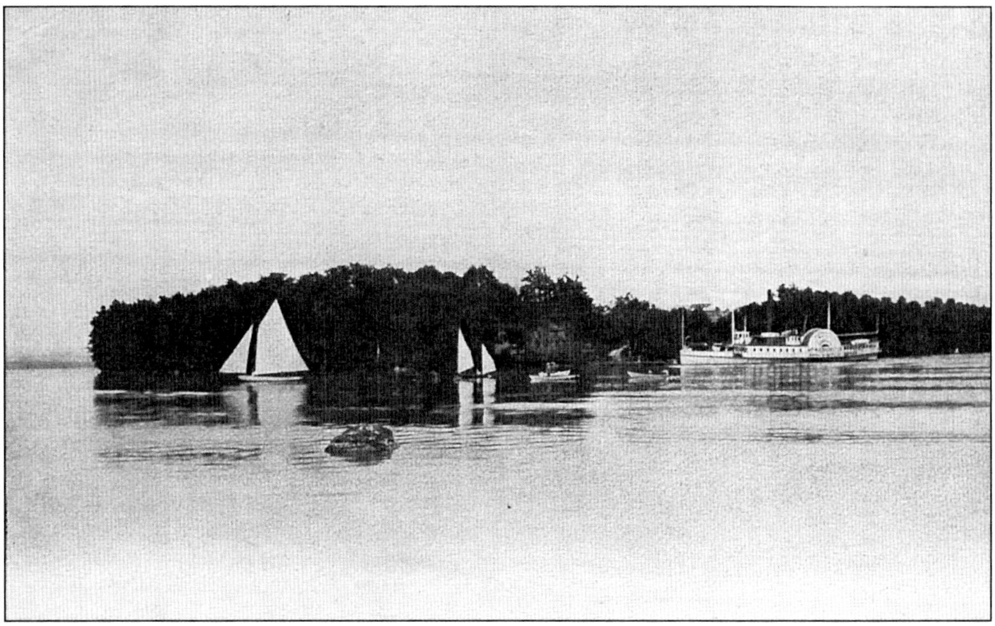

The steamer *Mount Washington* at Bear Island, early 1900s. Bear Island is the second largest island in the lake, and the only island which has its own church. The shape is similar to that of an hourglass with approximately 8.5 miles of shoreline.

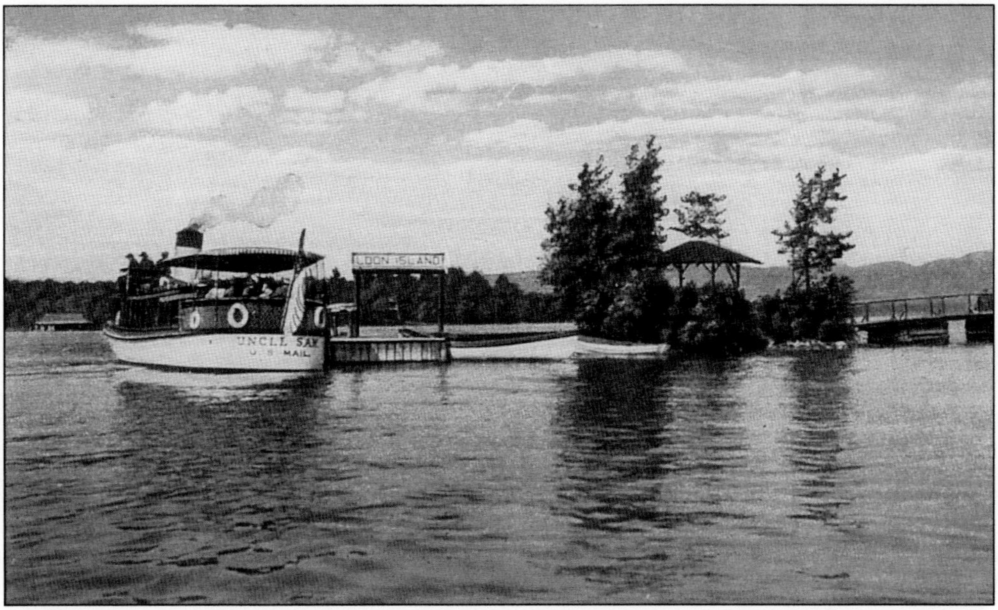

The mail boat *Uncle Sam* docked at Loon Island while on its regular mail delivery route, 1920s.

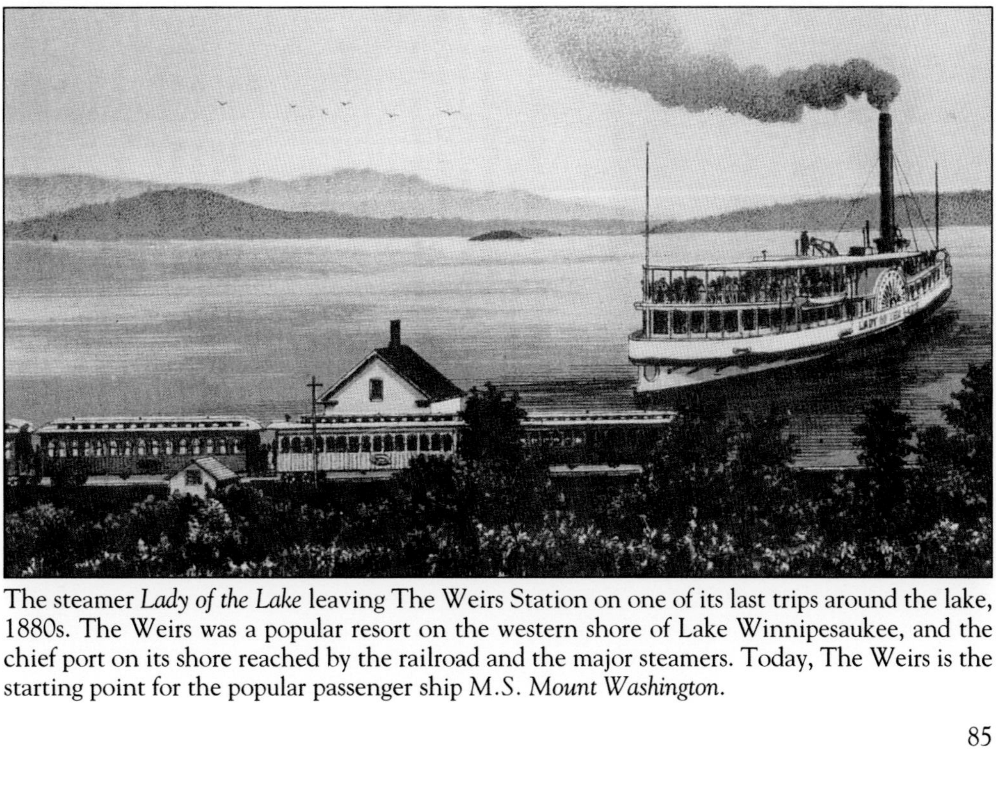

The steamer *Lady of the Lake* leaving The Weirs Station on one of its last trips around the lake, 1880s. The Weirs was a popular resort on the western shore of Lake Winnipesaukee, and the chief port on its shore reached by the railroad and the major steamers. Today, The Weirs is the starting point for the popular passenger ship M.S. *Mount Washington*.

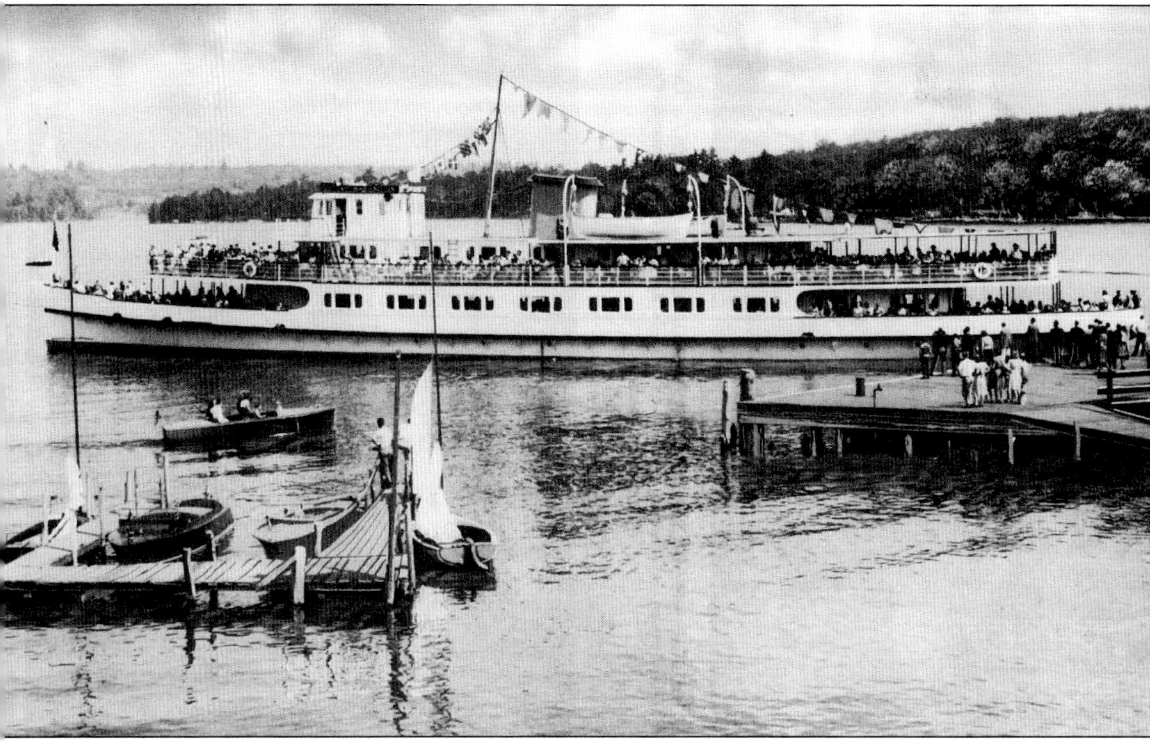

The M.V. *Mount Washington II* leaving The Weirs, 1948. At this time this vessel was capable of carrying 1,200 passengers, being 205 feet long and weighing 600 tons. The diesel-propelled, steel vessel carried on the traditional voyages of the past wooden sidewheelers which had sailed these waters for generations.

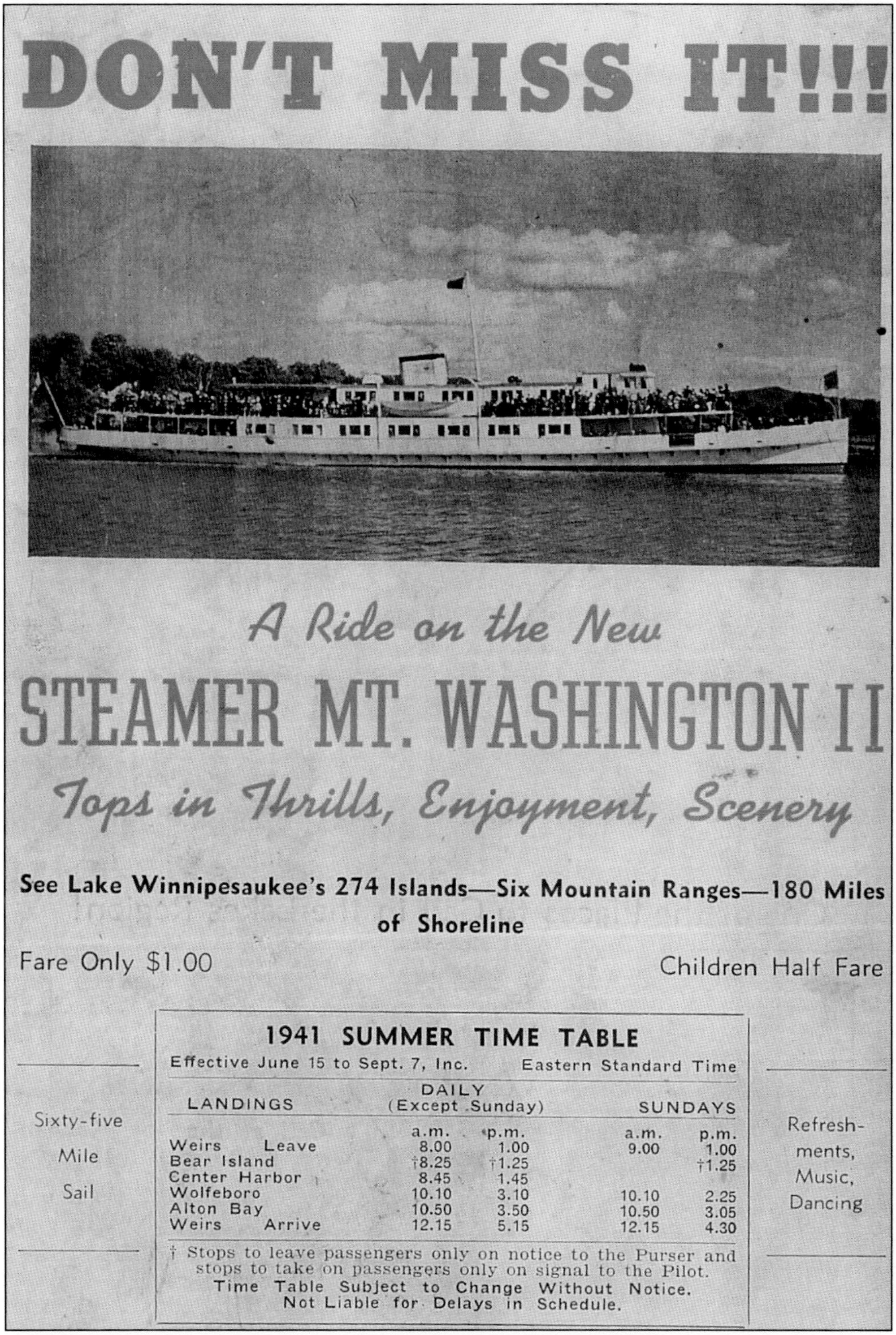

"DON'T MISS IT"—A poster issued by the Winnipesaukee Steamboat Co., during the summer of 1941. Note the schedule of stops—the *Mount* made periodic stops at Bear Island that season.

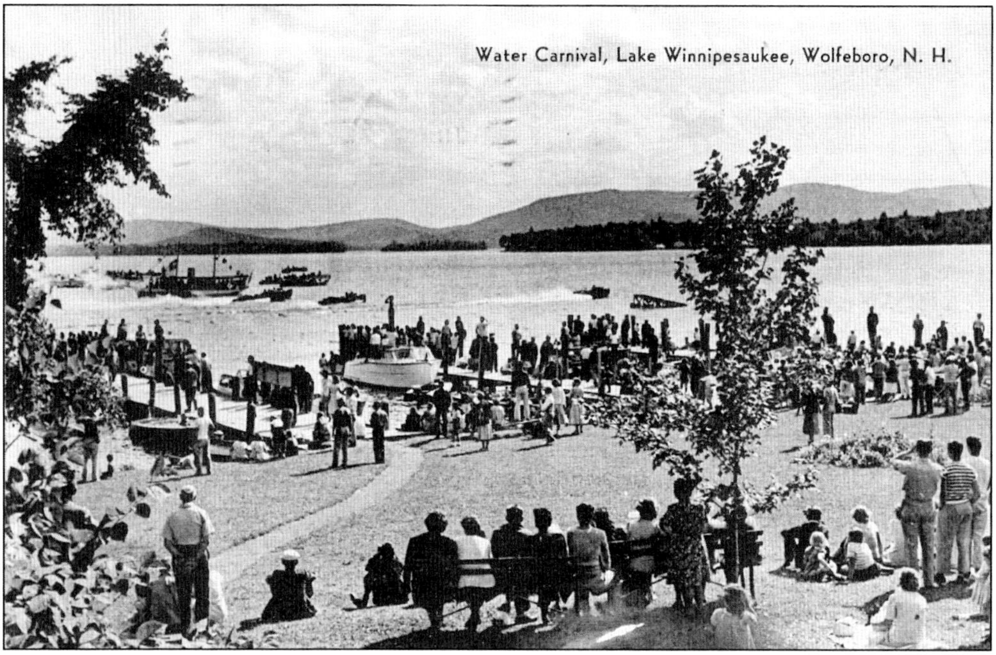

The water carnival in Wolfeboro Bay, 1951.

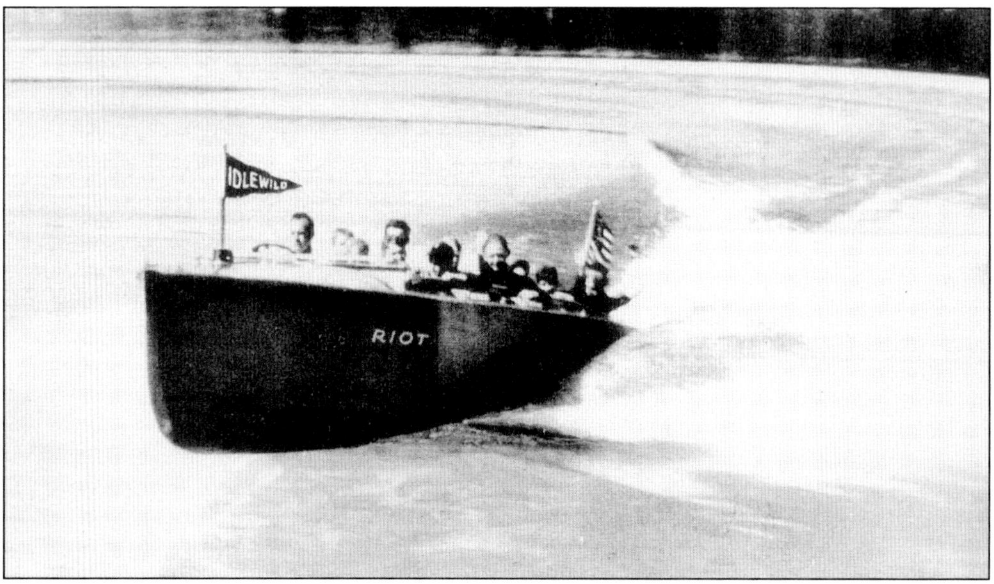

The *Riot* speed boat owned and operated by Camp Idlewild on Cow Island in Tuftonboro, NH. This 28-foot speed boat takes a summer afternoon to enjoy racing through the open waters of Lake Winnipesaukee with campers aboard.

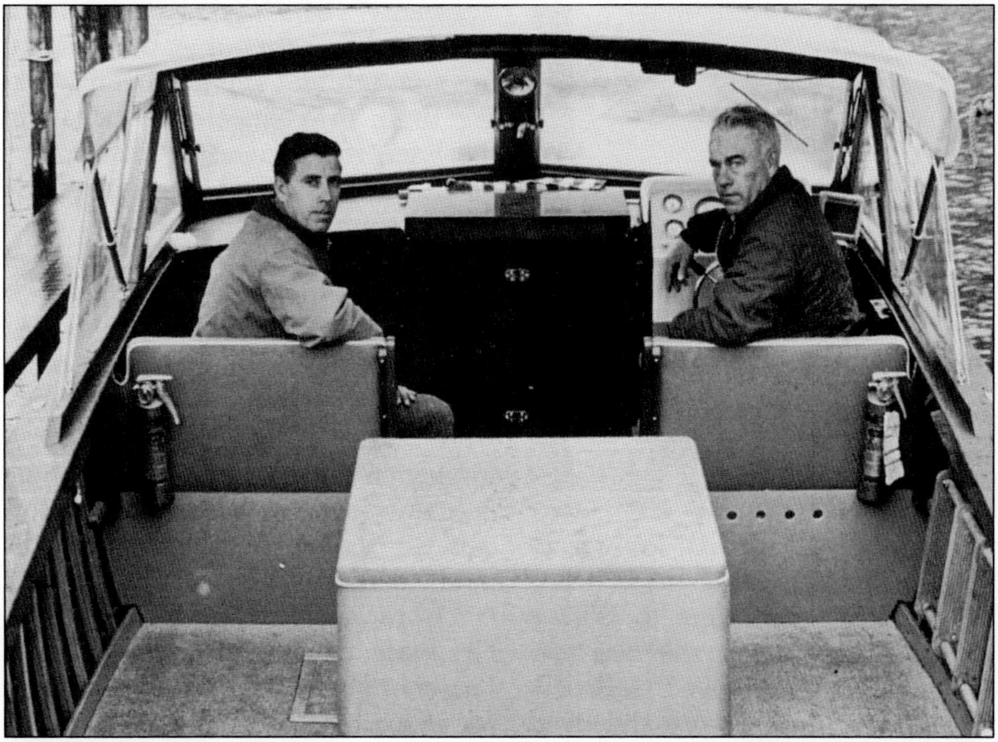

The New Hampshire Department of Safety's Marine Patrol, 1966. Lake Supervisor for the Department of Safety Brad Bryant of Meredith (right) and Foreman of Navigation Dick Dame of Laconia (left) are seen in their patrol boat, ready to set out for the big lake to ensure the safety of motorists and vacationists alike. Dick Dame was charged with maintaining navigational aids on all New Hampshire's waters. Both men operated out of a Gilford Marina, which the state had purchased in the fall of 1965.

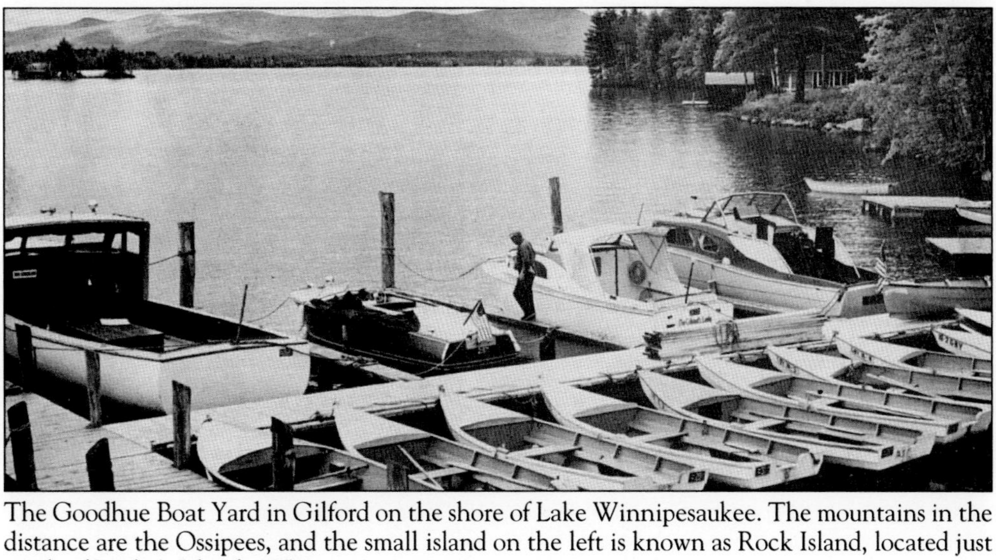

The Goodhue Boat Yard in Gilford on the shore of Lake Winnipesaukee. The mountains in the distance are the Ossipees, and the small island on the left is known as Rock Island, located just south of Locke's Island, 1951.

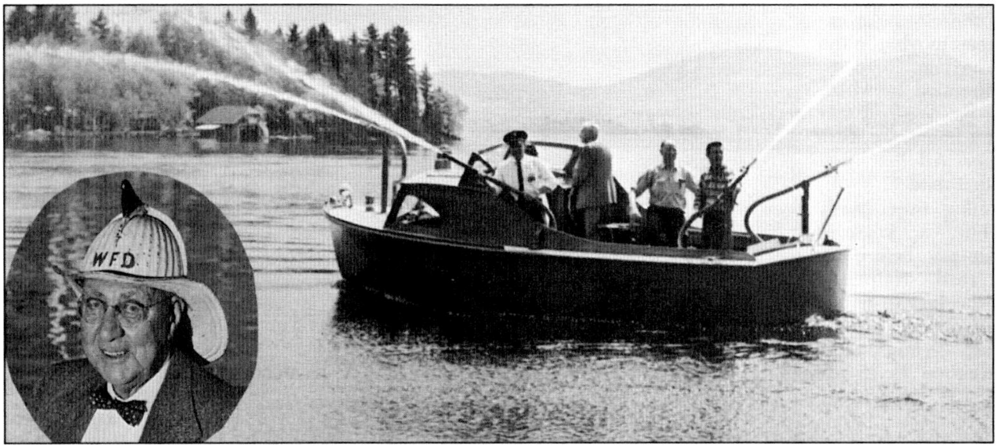

Dr. Herbert W. Drury's fire boat. In 1965, Captain Drury of Tuftonboro Neck is seen in this trim craft equipped with four custom-built nozzles which are powered by two, 9 h.p. Gurham-Rupp pumps with an output of 310 gallons per minute. This craft can send a stream 150 feet in any direction. The apparatus is mounted on a 22-foot fiberglass hull, drawing 27 inches of water. Propelled by a 90 h.p. marine engine, the vessel can reach speeds of 25.6 knots.

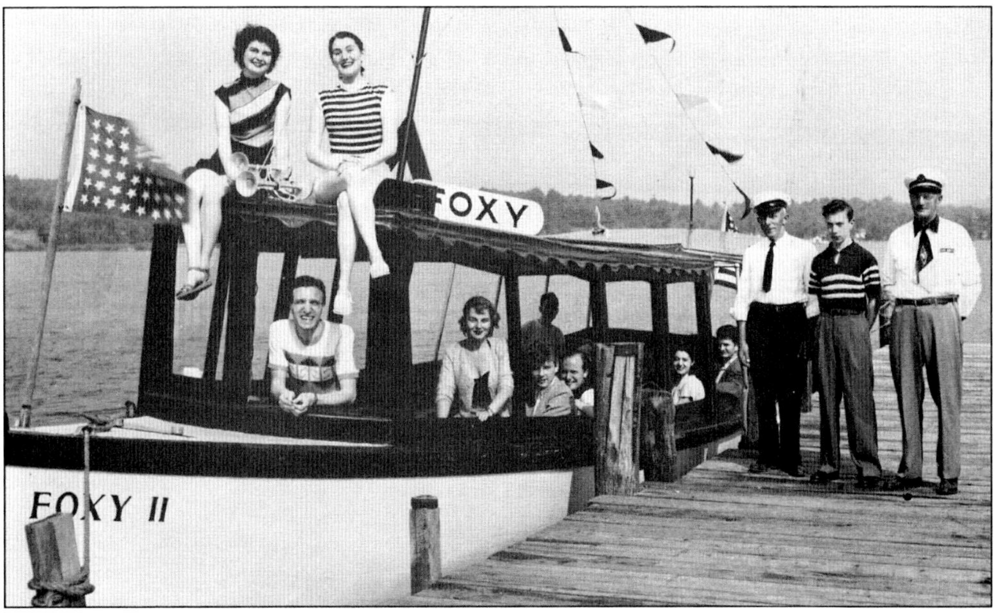

The *Foxy* with the Tilton Players, 1950. This 42-foot wooden craft, owned by Carl and Amie Wallace, operated out of Paugus Bay, where Burger King is now located. The craft made daily excursions from Lakeport to The Weirs. From The Weirs it sailed among the Forty Islands, to Glendale, then under Governor's Island Bridge, and back to The Weirs, and finally to Lakeport, its home port.

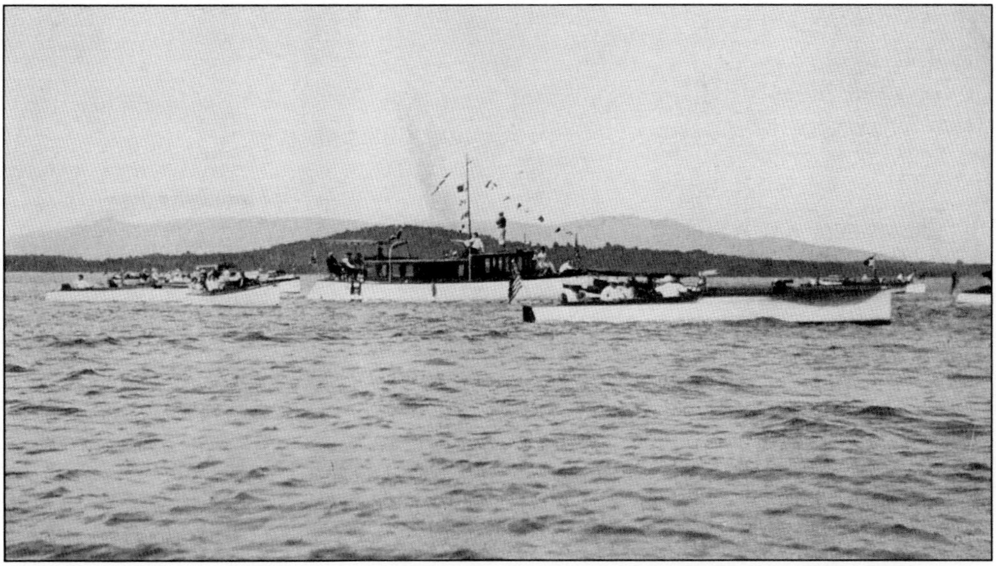

Spectators and the judge's boat at a race in the "Broads" of Lake Winnipesaukee, 1927.

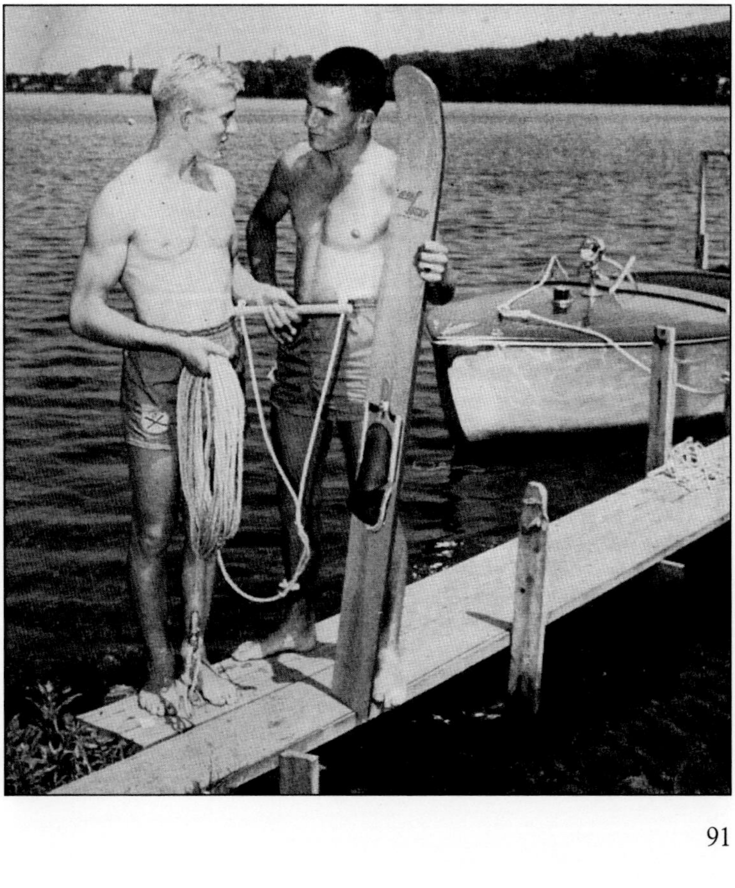

Water skiing stars Jack Beattie and Dick Binette, both of the Weirs Water Ski Club. Jack held the unofficial world's record of 94 feet, while Dick won both New England and Eastern jumping titles in 1951.

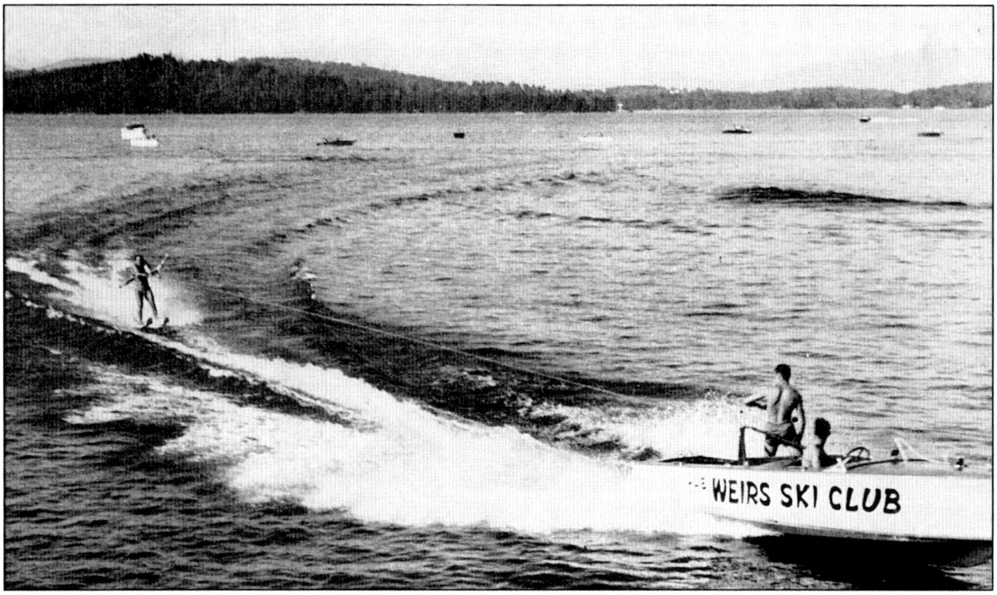

Jim and Pauline Stathis of The Weirs Ski Club. The two are shown here performing a "double turn" in the 1951 New England Championship water-skiing contest in Weirs Bay.

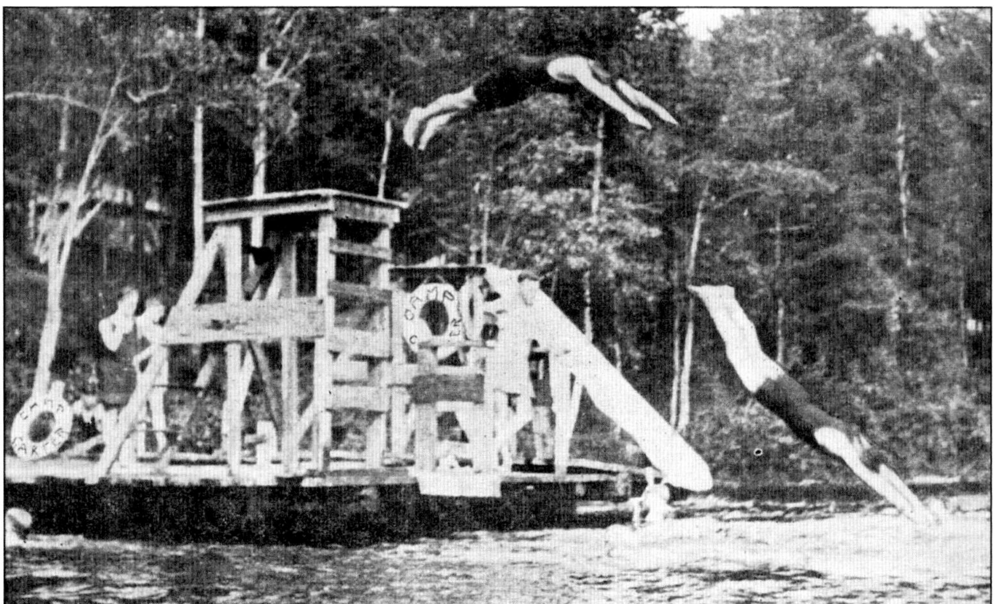
Camp Cater in Andover, NH, 1922. On a hot summer day nothing can be more refreshing than a plunge into the cool waters of Elbow Pond. It lies at the very foot of Ragged Mountain, and is well fed by clear mountain brooks and springs.

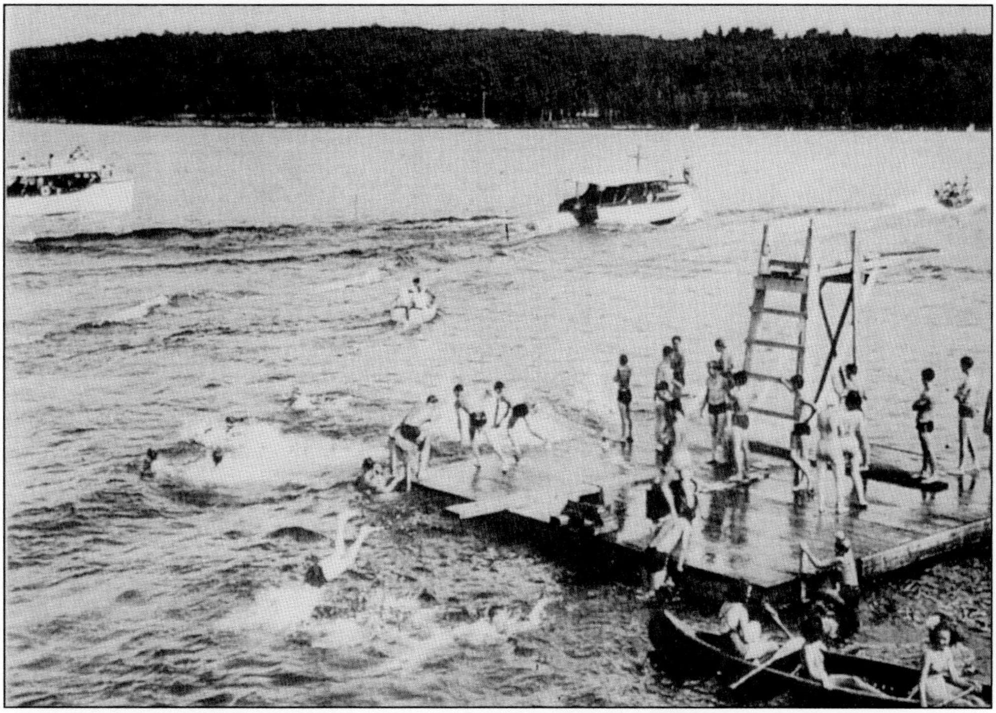

One of the many fine bathing beaches in the Lakes Region, 1950s.

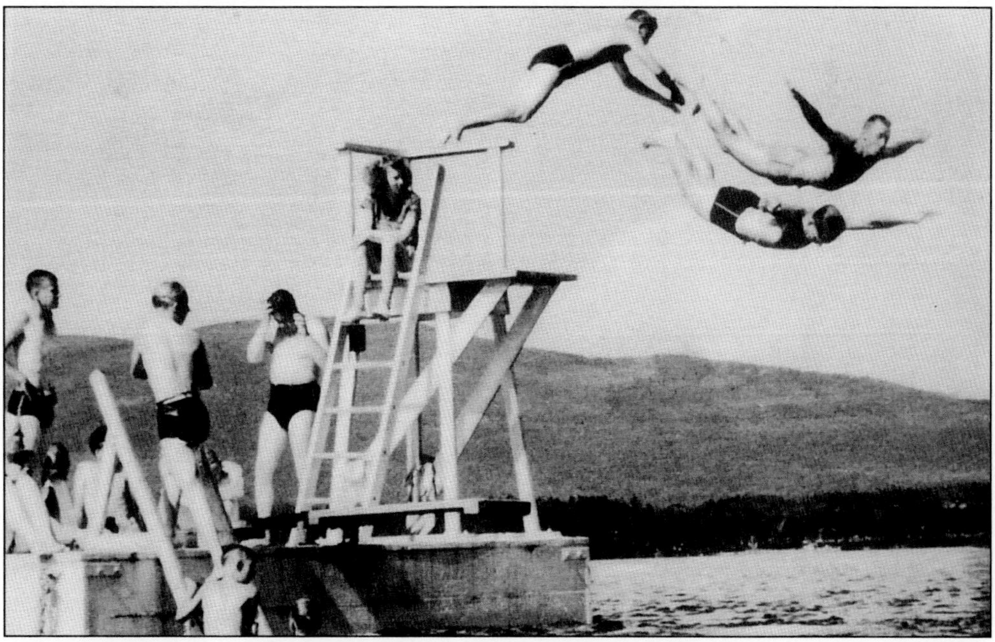

Three divers known as the "Swedish Luther League Fellows" doing their swan dive at Geneva Point Camp in Moultonboro, NH, 1940.

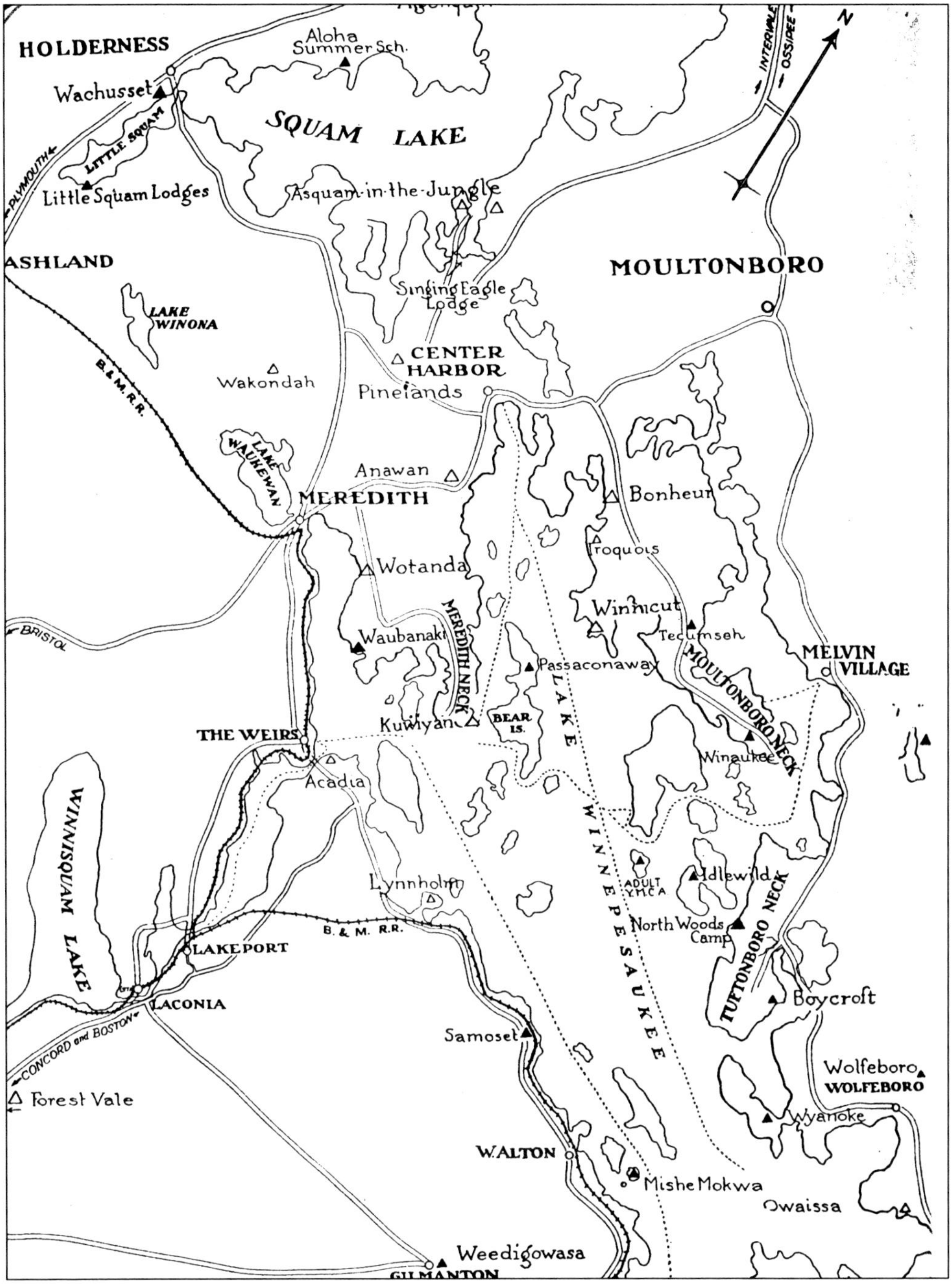

A map of the Lakes Region showing the locations of the organized camps on Lakes Squam and Winnipesaukee. During the 1930s there were more than 72 camps in the Lakes Region, and by 1950 there were 218 camps in the entire state, housing 23,000 young people and 3,000 counselors. It is interesting to note that Camp Chocorua, the first boys' camp, was organized on Squam Lake in 1881; the first girls' camp was organized on Newfound Lake in 1900. The first boys' camp on Lake Winnipesaukee was Camp Idlewild on Cow Island. New Hampshire was the birthplace of the organized camp movement.

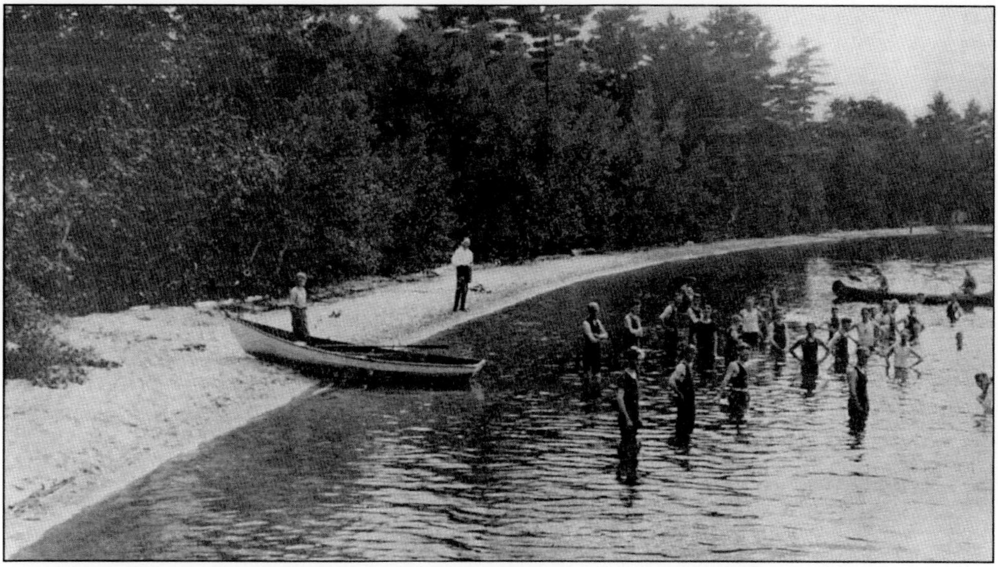

A swimming beach at the Geneva Point Camp, Moultonboro, NH, 1930s.

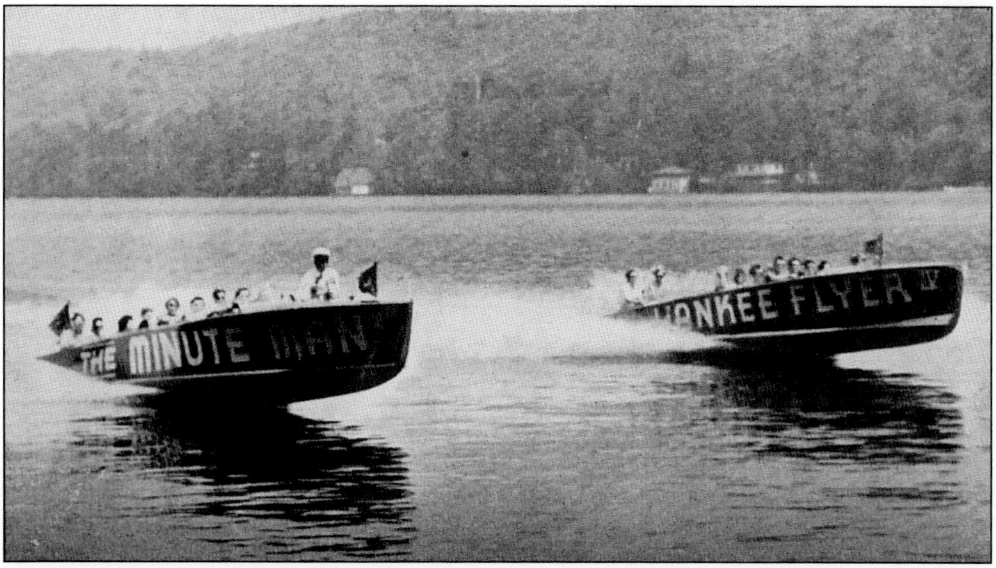

Cram's Speed boats racing down Alton Bay, 1940s. These boats operated daily out of Alton Bay. Pictured are the *Minute Man* and *The Yankee Flyer IV*, heading up Alton Bay en route to the "Broads."

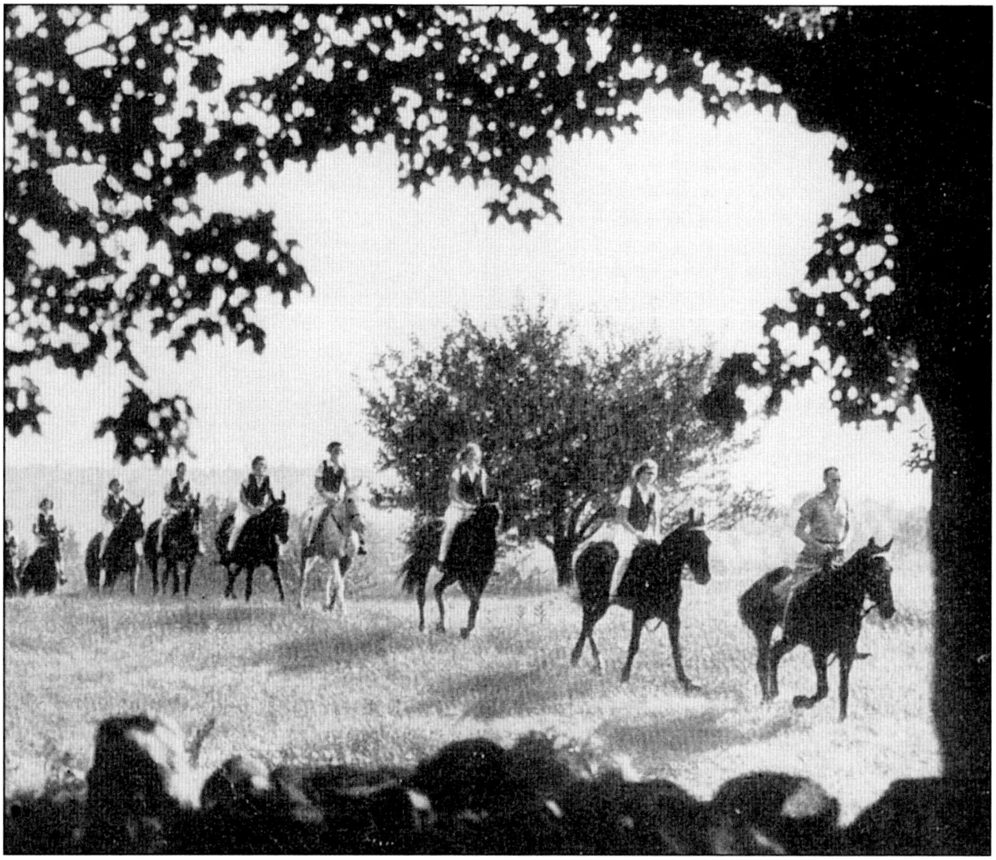

Horseback riding, an activity included at practically all the summer camps in the Lakes Region.

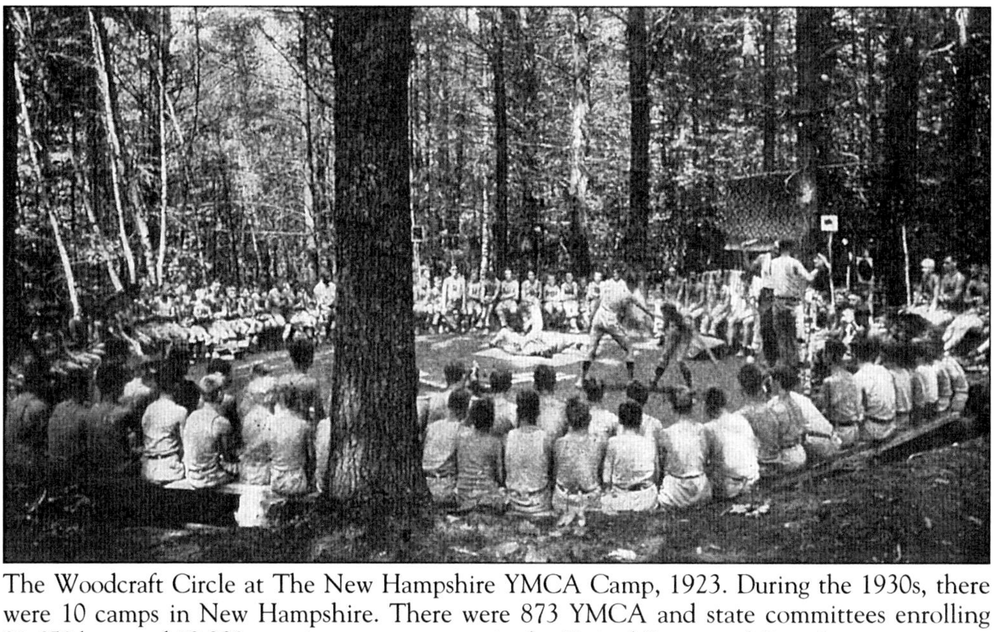

The Woodcraft Circle at The New Hampshire YMCA Camp, 1923. During the 1930s, there were 10 camps in New Hampshire. There were 873 YMCA and state committees enrolling 91,658 boys and 13,339 men in summer camps in the United States and Canada.

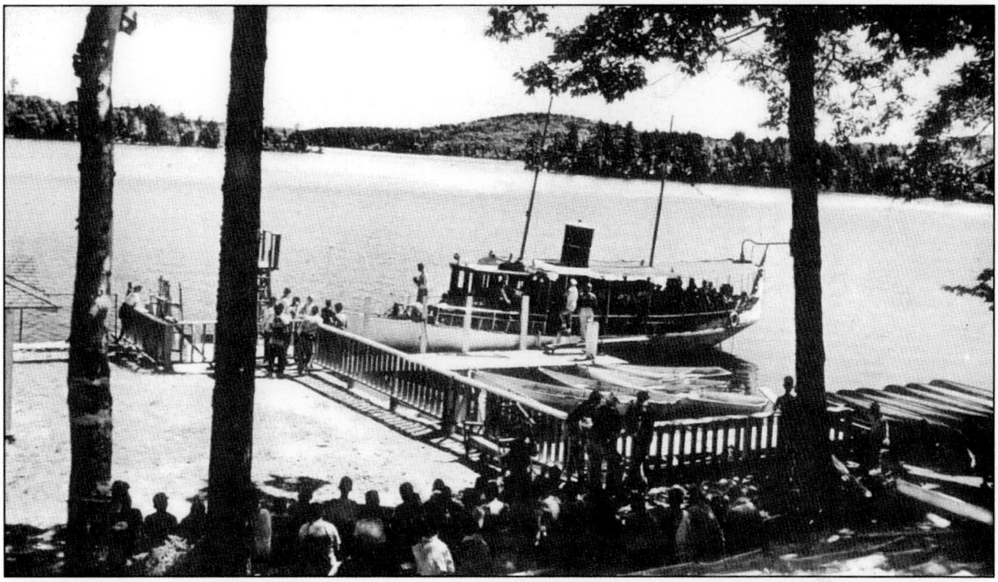

The steamer *Swallow* docked at Camp Alton, Wolfeboro, NH, loading the Alton boys for their annual boat ride on Lake Winnipesaukee.

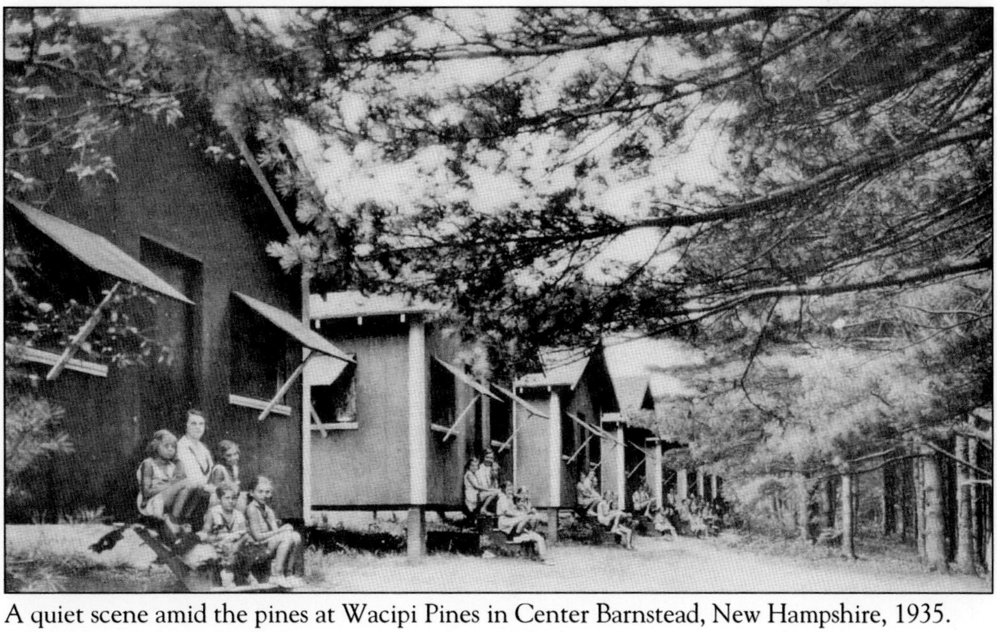

A quiet scene amid the pines at Wacipi Pines in Center Barnstead, New Hampshire, 1935.

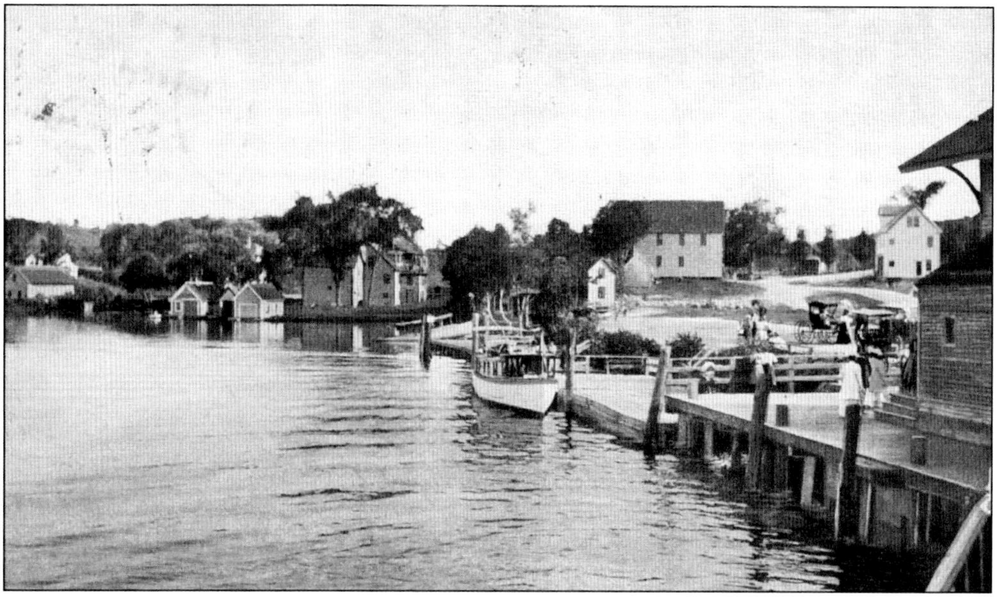

A view of Alton Bay from the steamer *Mount Washington*, 1911.

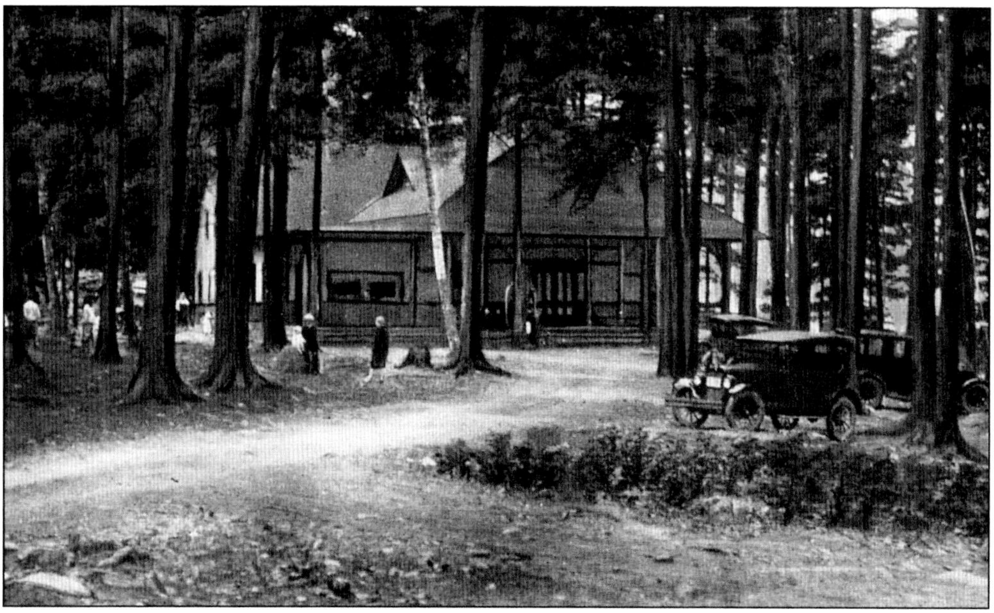

The Pavilion at Lake Shore Park on Lake Winnipesaukee, early 1920s. This was a popular recreation hall for campers and visitors alike.

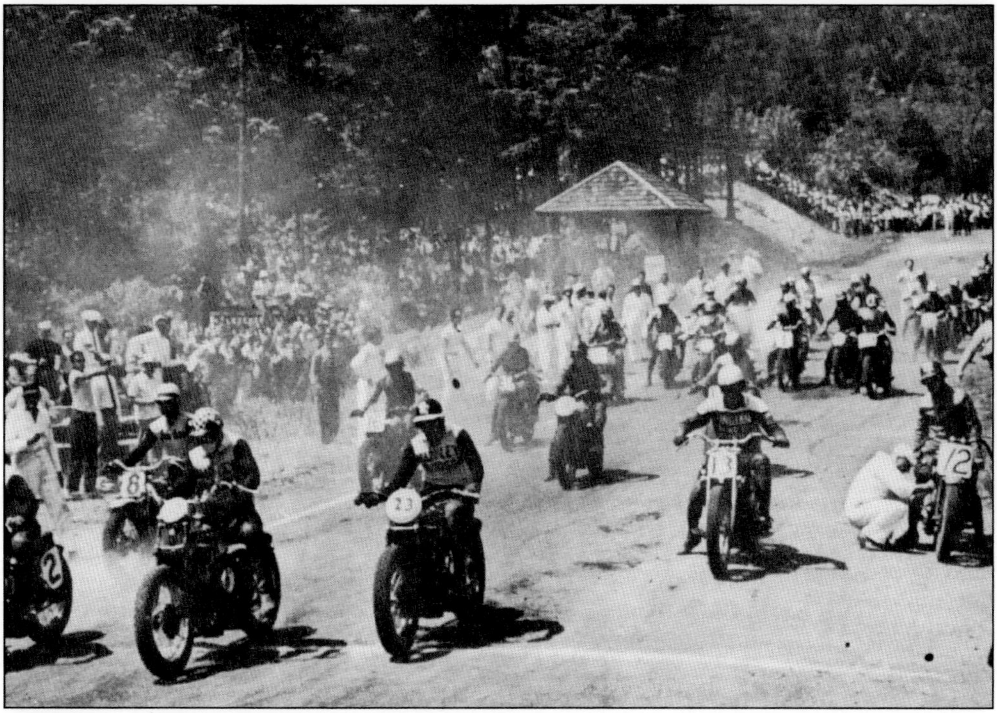

Motorcycle racing at the Belknap Recreation Area in Gilford, NH, during the 1950s. During the late spring of 1998, the Laconia Motor Cycle Association celebrated their 75th annual tour in the Lakes Region.

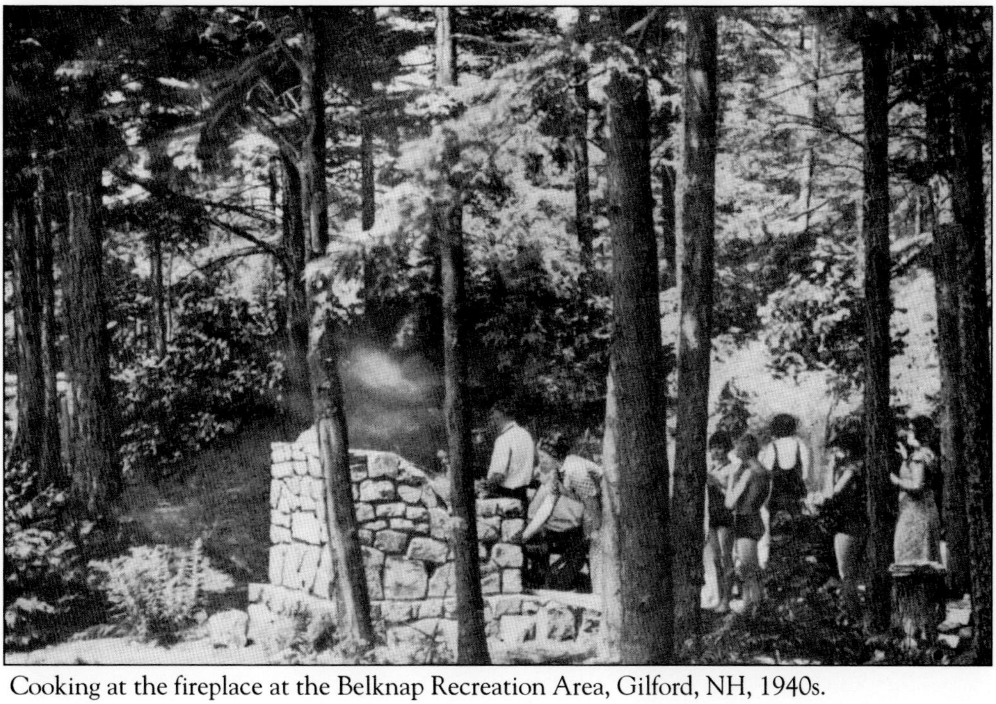

Cooking at the fireplace at the Belknap Recreation Area, Gilford, NH, 1940s.

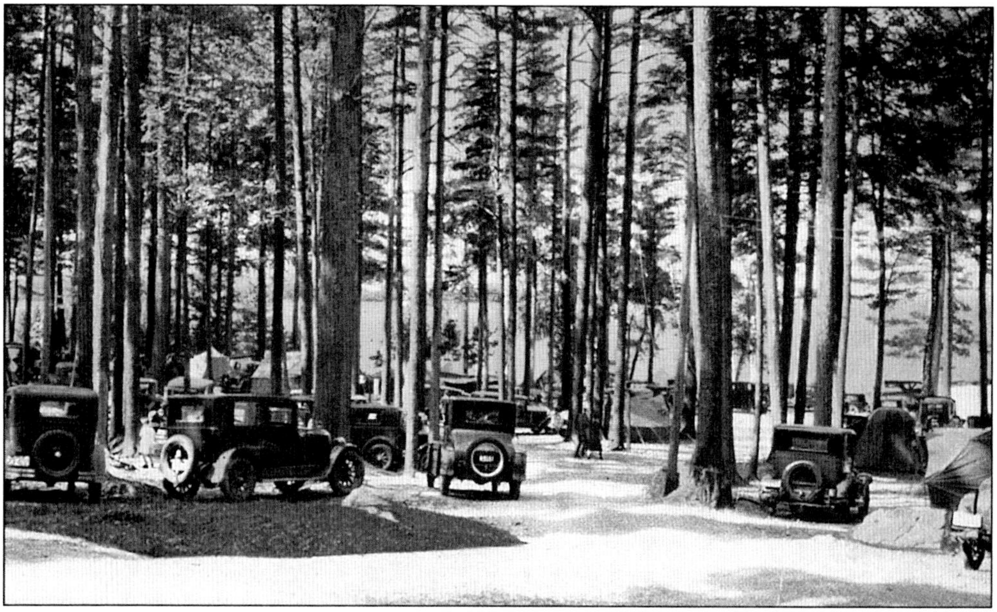

The beach at Lake Shore Park, early 1920s. This beach is considered one of the largest and most beautiful in the Lakes Region.

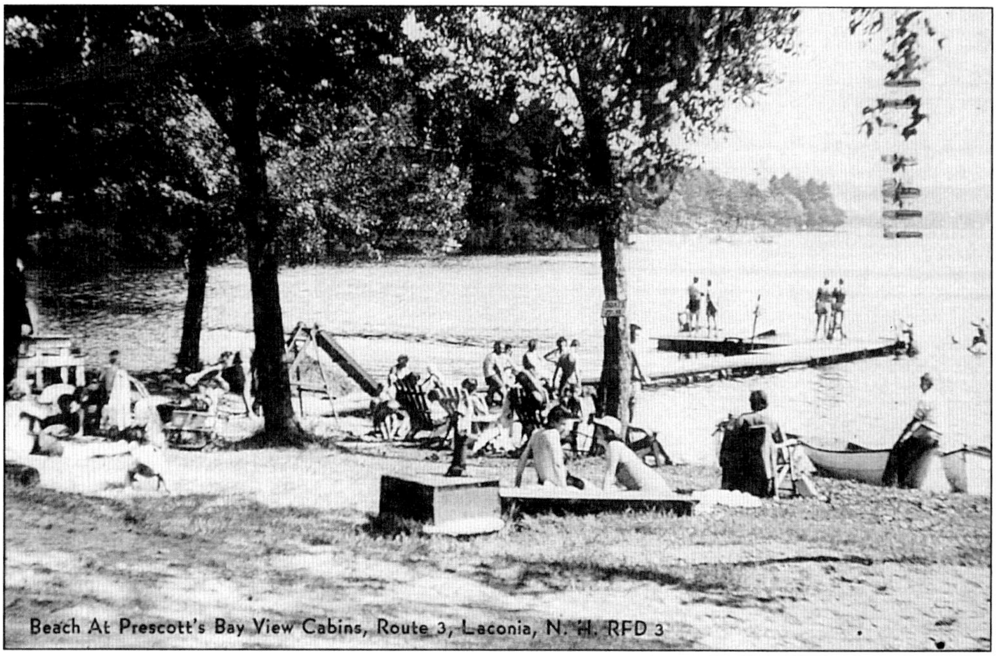

Beach At Prescott's Bay View Cabins, Route 3, Laconia, N. H. RFD 3

The beach at Prescott's Bay View Cabins on Route 3, between Lakeport and The Weirs on Paugus Bay, Laconia, NH, 1950.

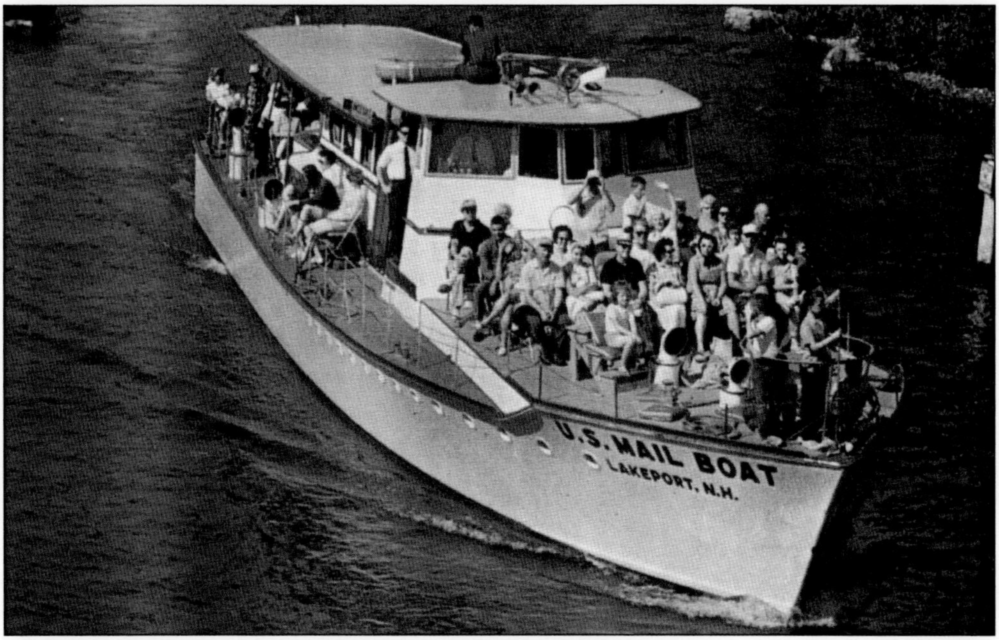

The U.S. mail boat *Uncle Sam II* in the channel at The Weirs. This vessel was originally built as a PT boat (PT-719) for World War II, but never saw action. For six years (1963–69) she delivered the mail on Lake Winnipesaukee. After her brief service on the lake, she was slated to return to the Atlantic Ocean. The craft was sold at auction to Frank Damrell of Andover, Massachusetts, and Southport, Maine, for $5,500. Pictured standing by the wheelhouse is owner Allan Perley.

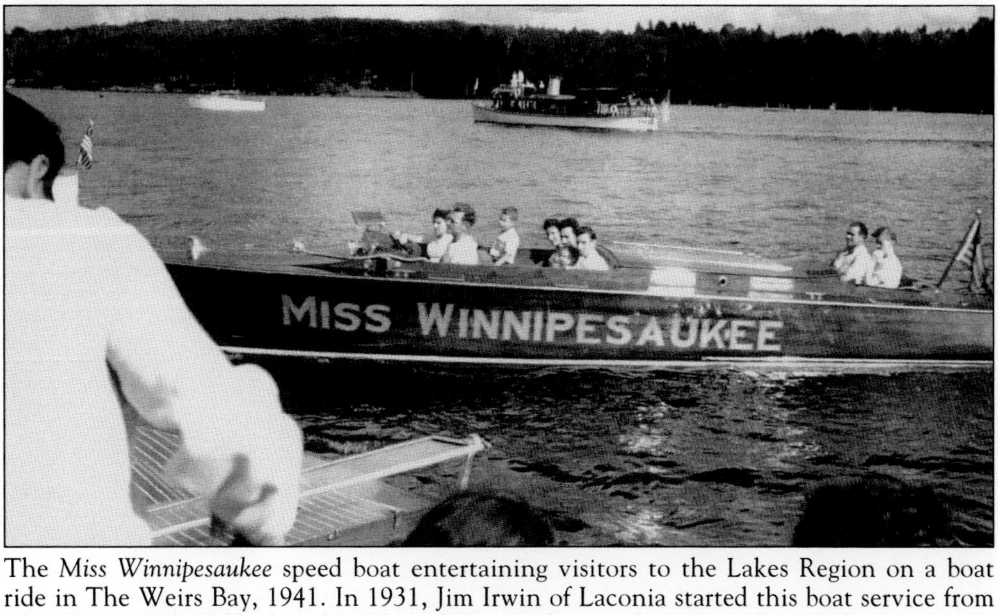

The *Miss Winnipesaukee* speed boat entertaining visitors to the Lakes Region on a boat ride in The Weirs Bay, 1941. In 1931, Jim Irwin of Laconia started this boat service from The Weirs. Bob Belford is the pilot of this 28-foot craft. Notice the *Uncle Sam* in the background as she enters the bay on her trek to deliver mail to the many islands. The small white boat in the far distance was a public utilities boat (a patrol boat) before the Safety Service came into operation.

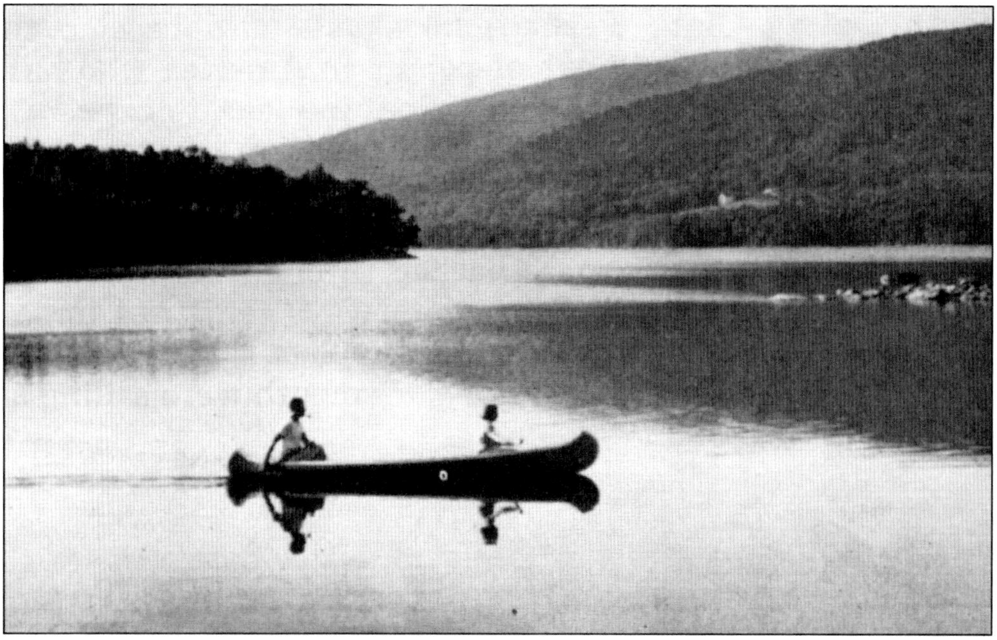

A quiet moment of canoeing the waters of Lake Kanasatka, in Moultonboro, NH. In the distance is Red Hill, majestically watching over Center Harbor and the northern bays of Lake Winnipesaukee and Squam Lake.

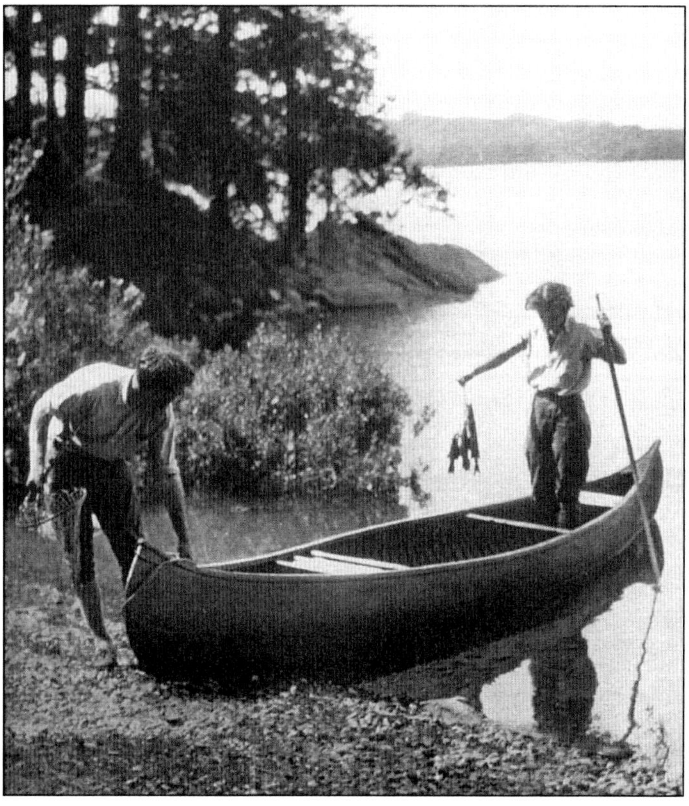

Fishing in the Lakes Region. Salmon is stocked and taken from early spring through the summer months. Lake trout are native to the region, and are taken from January through September. Bass, pickerel, white fish, shad, and perch are all taken in their proper season.

Fishing mountain streams—great sport for both serious fishermen and vacationers alike.

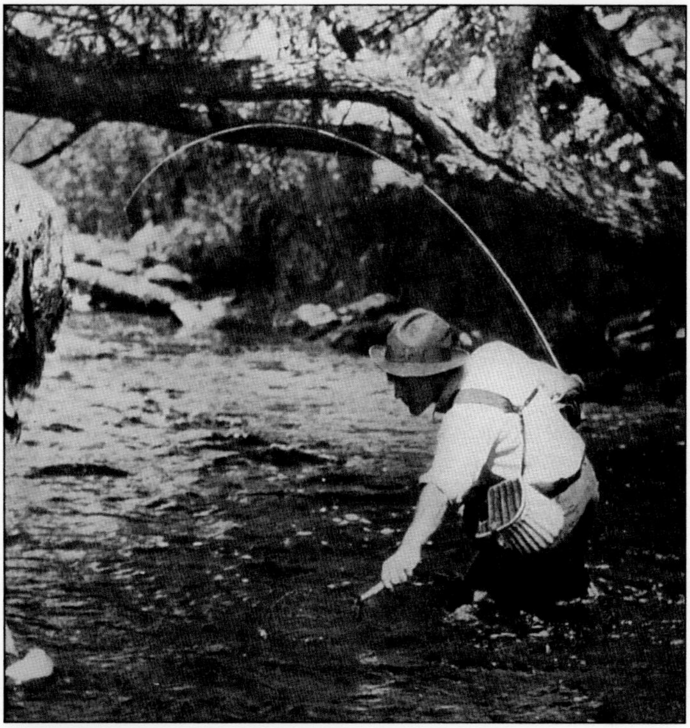

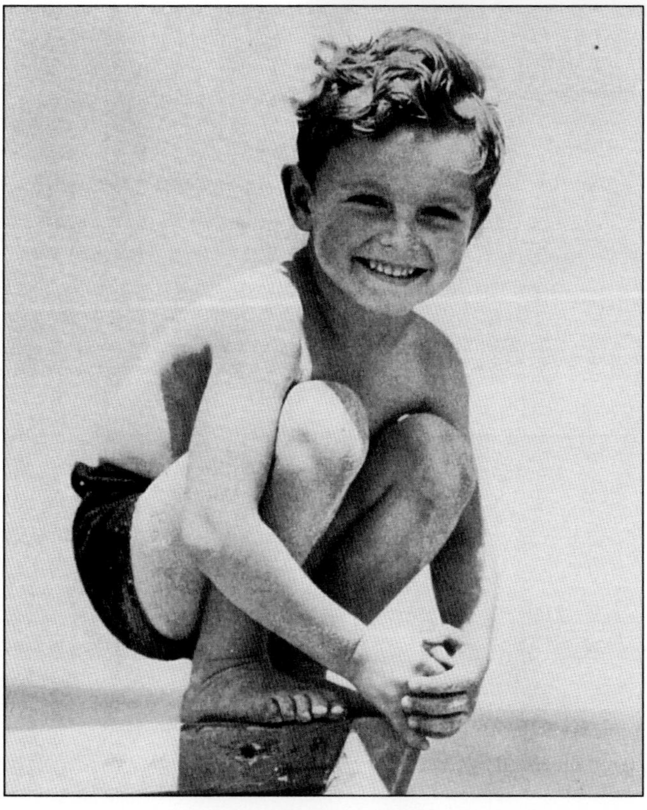

"You want to swim with me?"

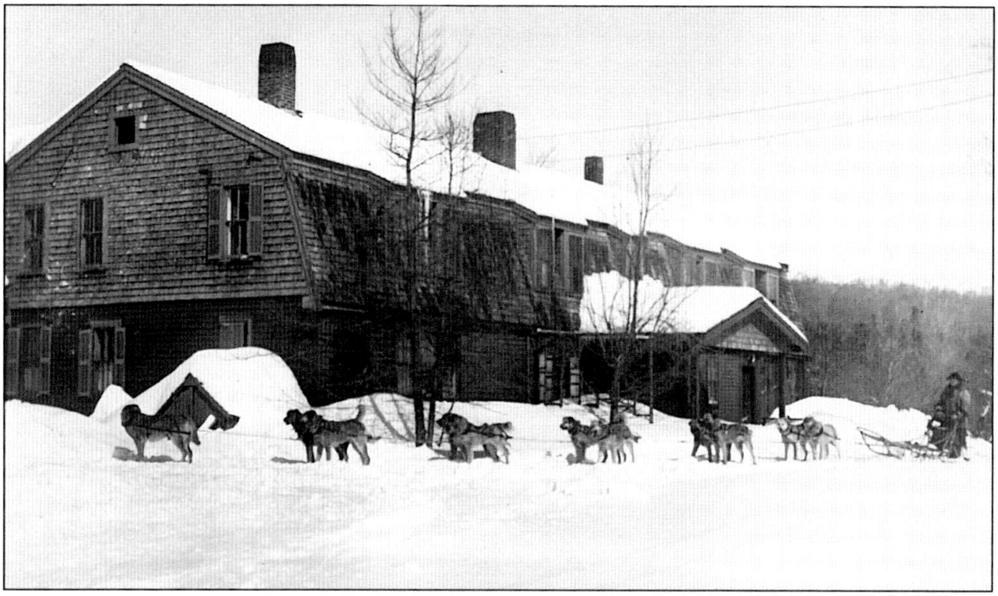

The Wonalancet Farm, Wonalancet, NH, 1920s.

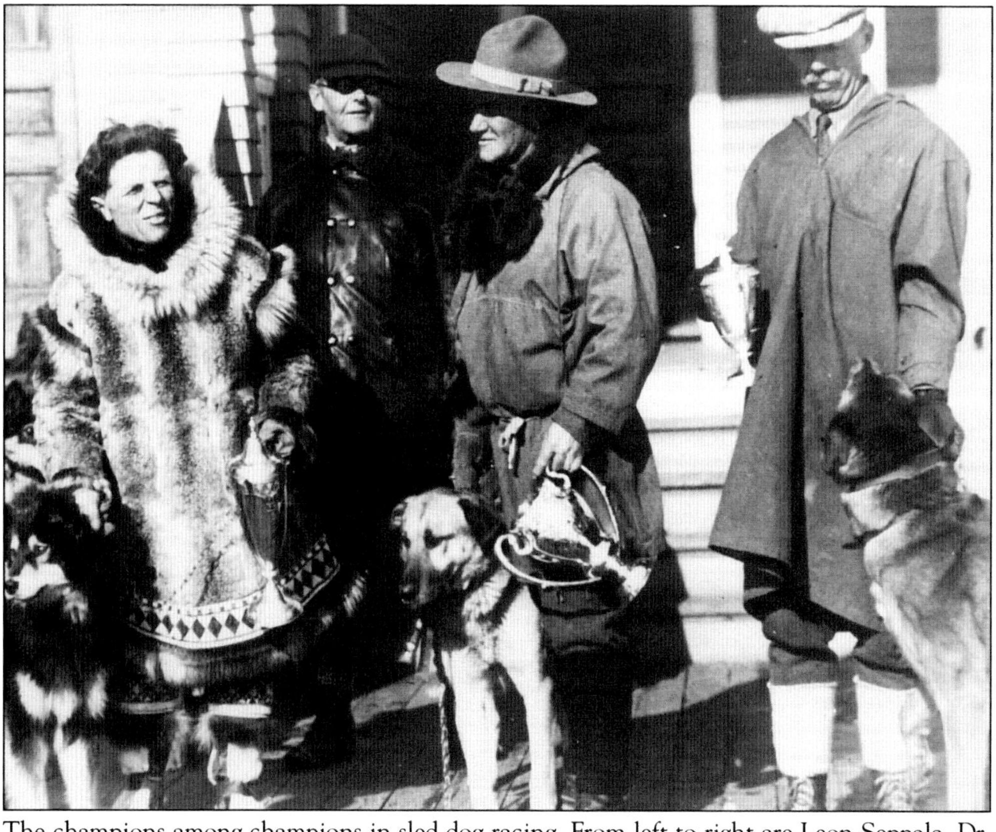

The champions among champions in sled dog racing. From left to right are Leon Seppala, Dr. Sproull, Arthur Walden, and Walter Channing at the World Championship Sled Dog Race in Laconia, NH, 1930s.

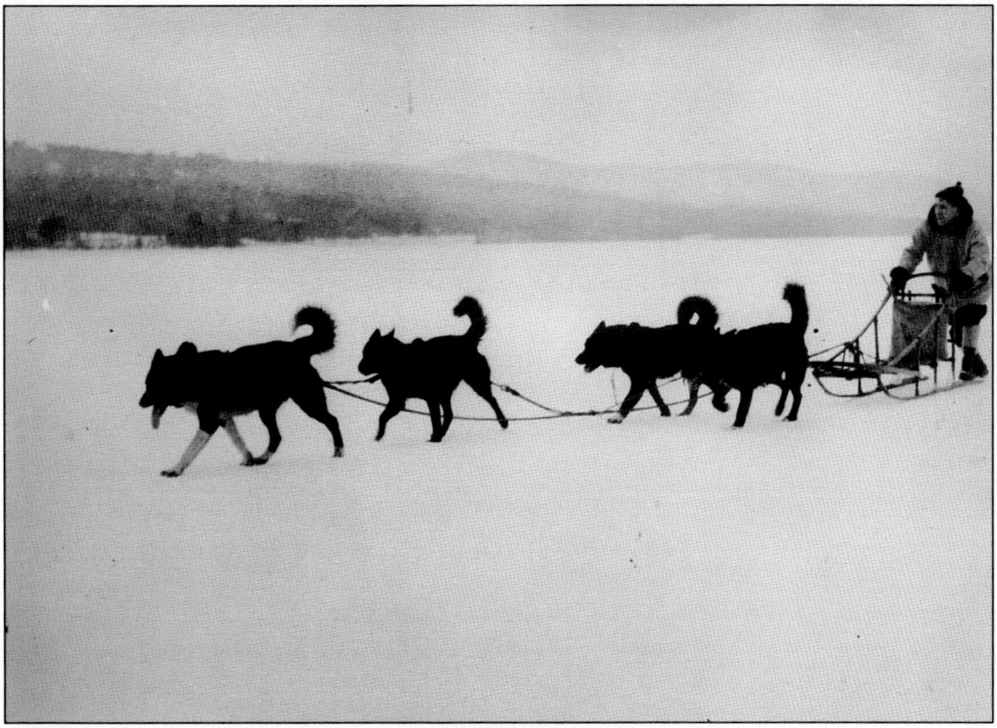

Ed Gordon and the Meredith town team, 1930s.

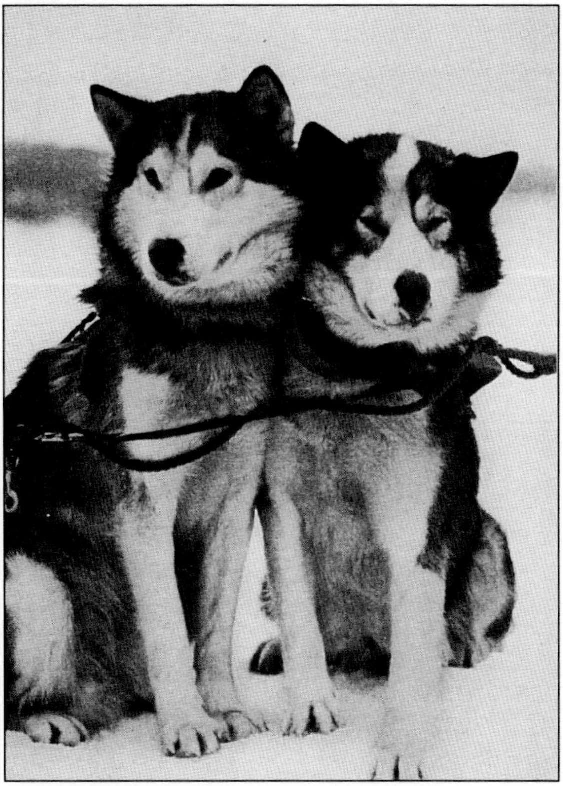

Sled dog racing was an exciting feature of the winter program, scheduled throughout the season at Wonalancet, Meredith, Tamworth, Plymouth, and Laconia. The pair shown have just finished a 20-mile race. The two lead dogs were bred at the famous Chinook Kennels, 1935.

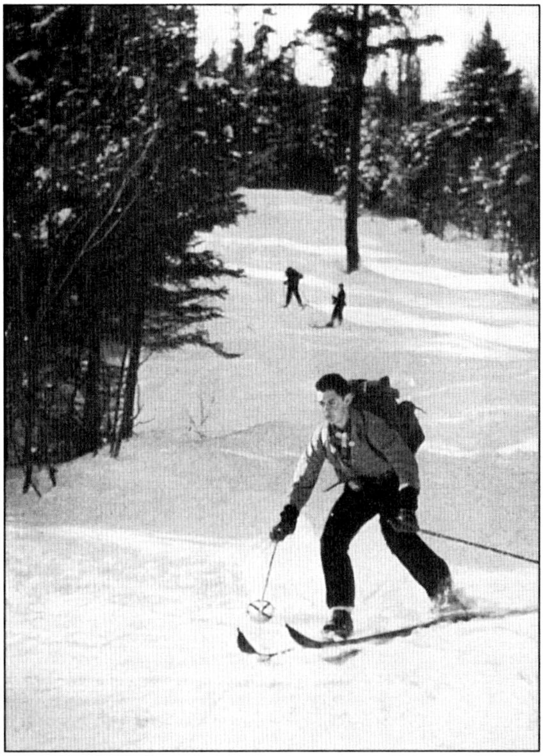

The Lakes Region, a network of carefully planned trails, well mapped, groomed, and marked. There are slalom courses and jumps. No matter what your skill, anywhere in the region, there are hills and trails for you.

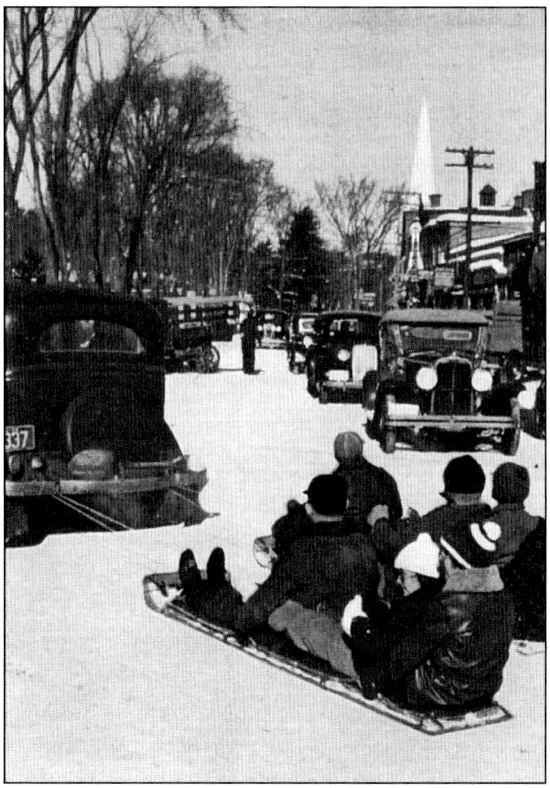

Tobogganing on main street, 1935.

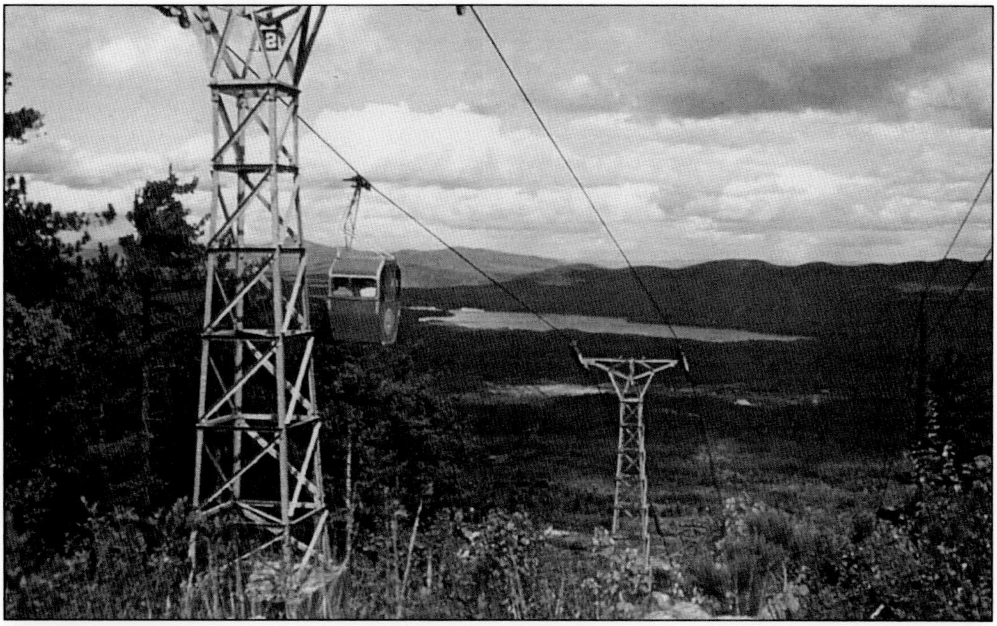

The Gondolas as seen on Mount Whittier in West Ossipee, NH, with Silver Lake in the distance, *c*. 1960s.

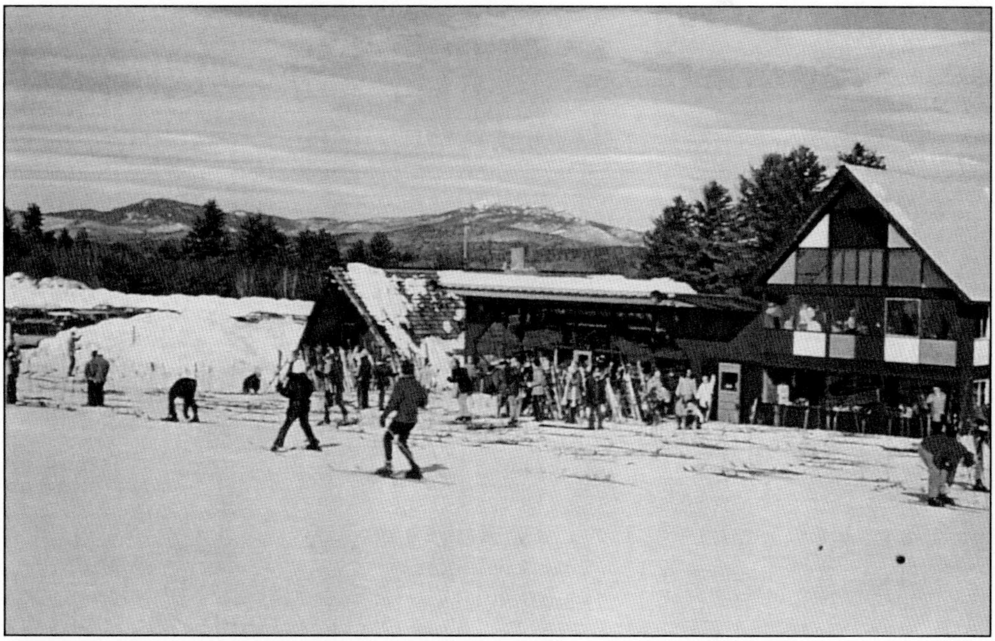

The base lodge at the Mount Whittier Ski Area in West Ossipee, NH, 1960s.

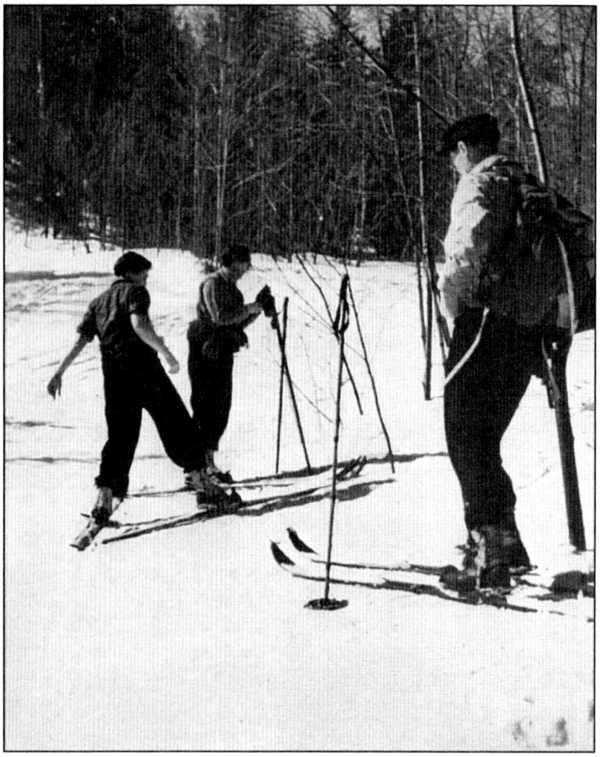

Cross country skiing, a family experience in the Lakes Region, 1935.

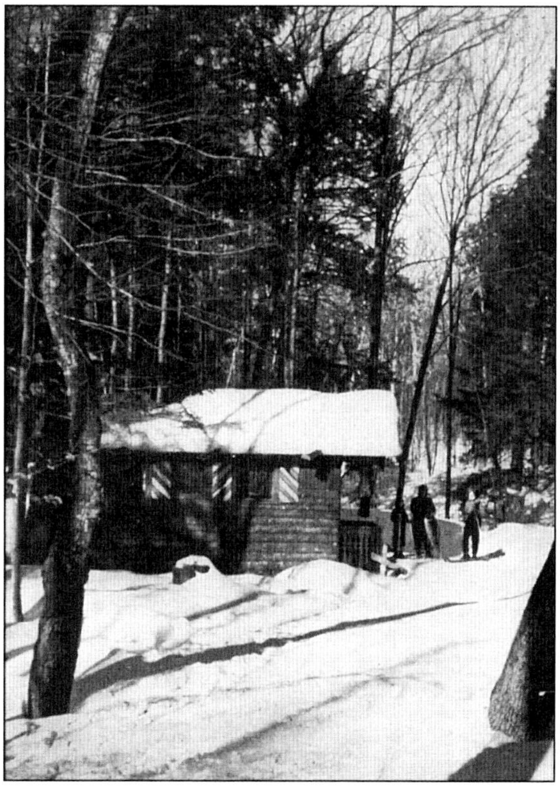

Snow shoeing in the Sandwich Mountain Range. Here, before the mountains, are beautiful open fields and trackless paths in the quiet woods.

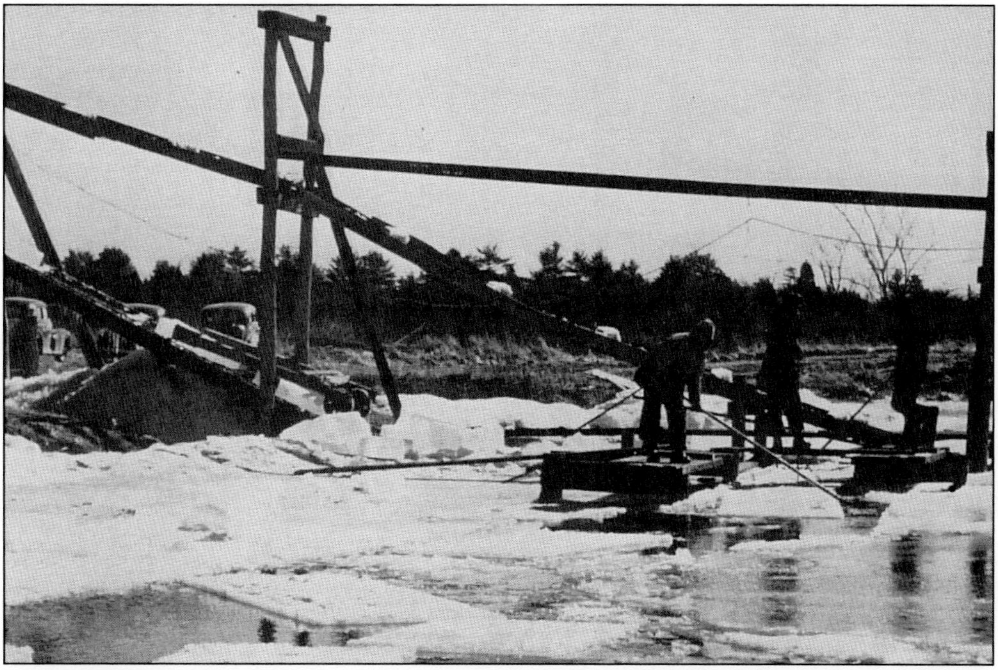

Ice harvesting on Squam Lake, a big business after the January thaw during the early 1900s. Many ice houses were clustered around most lakes in the region, and during the spring and summer months ice trucks were loaded with ice bound for the cities to fill ice boxes.

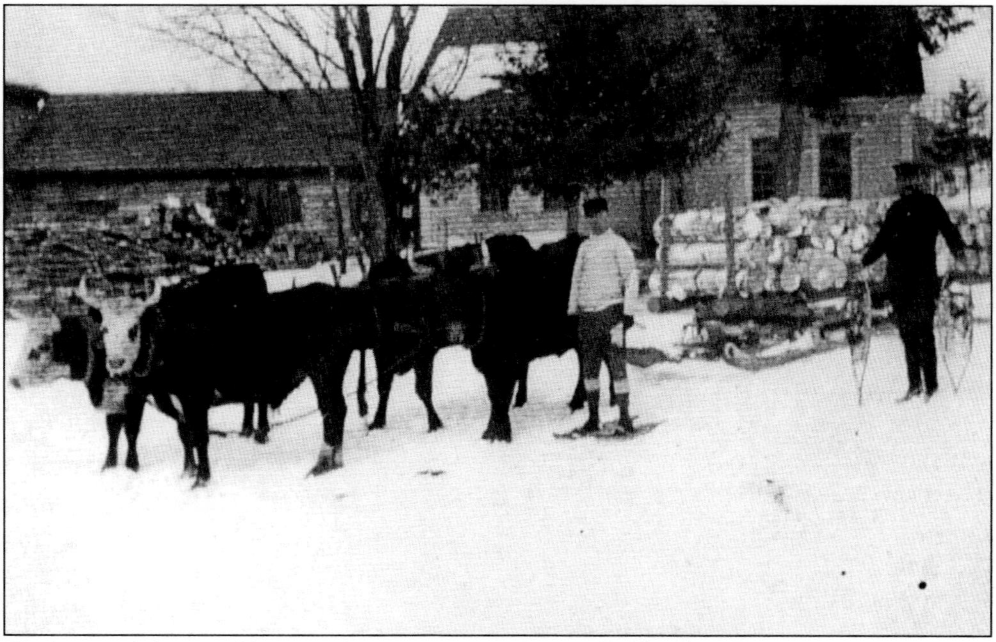

Wesley Tewksbury and his award-winning oxen team in Sandwich, NH.

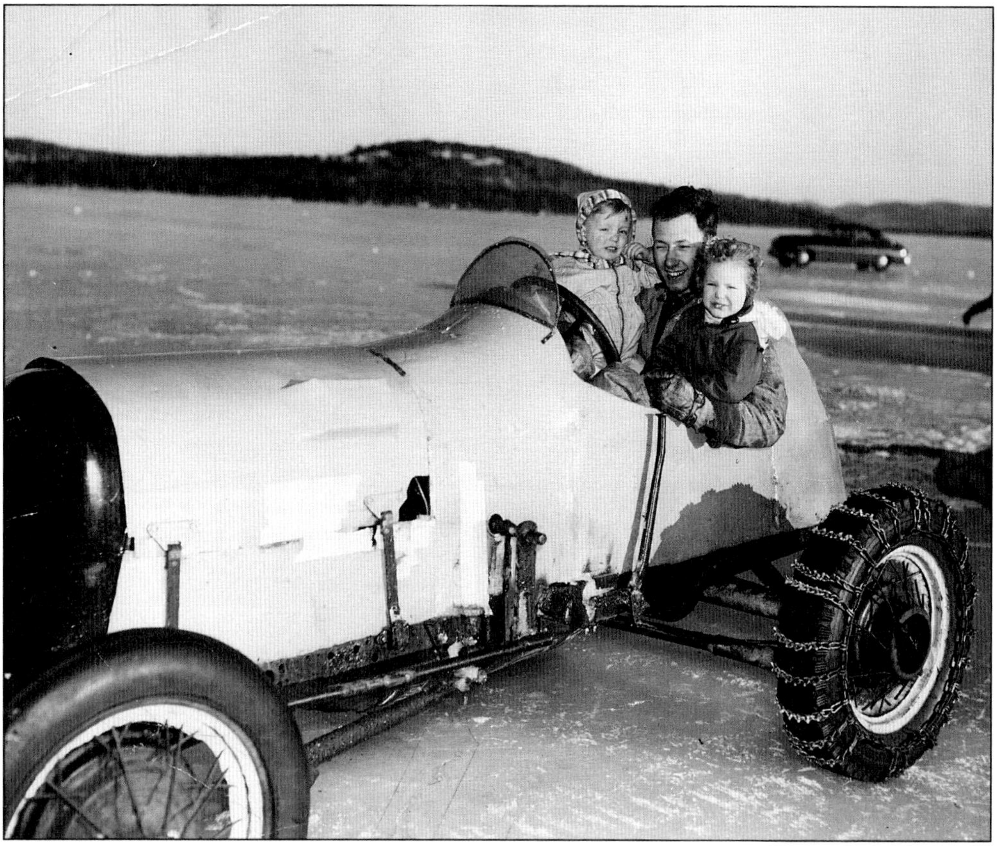

Race car No. 40, called the *Meredith Ford*, on Meredith Bay, Thanksgiving Day, 1951. Pictured are Tony Amabile (the driver) and his two children, Thomas (left) and Anthonette. According to the AP News, this vehicle was electrically timed at 90 mph, its top speed.

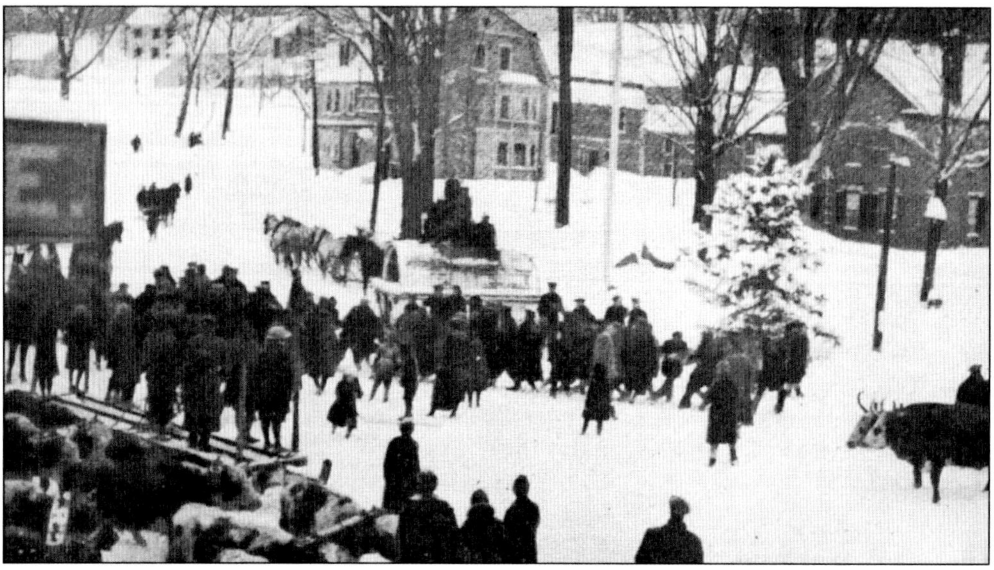

Winter sports and snow rolling on Main Street in Bristol, NH, early 1900s.

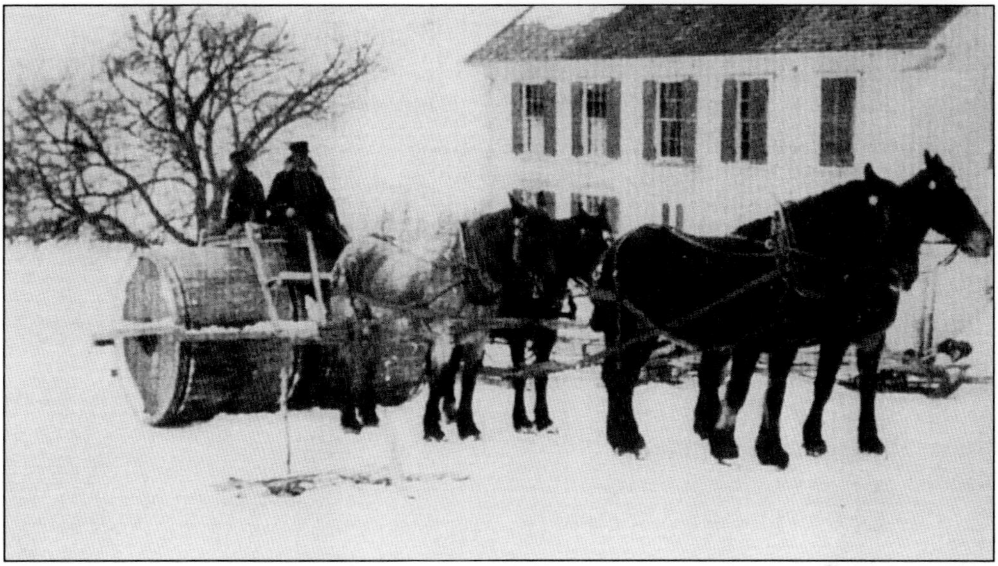

Felix Rattee and Leon Pailleur. The two are shown leaving after a heavy snowstorm to roll the roads at the Smiling Hill Farm in Gilford, NH, 1918.

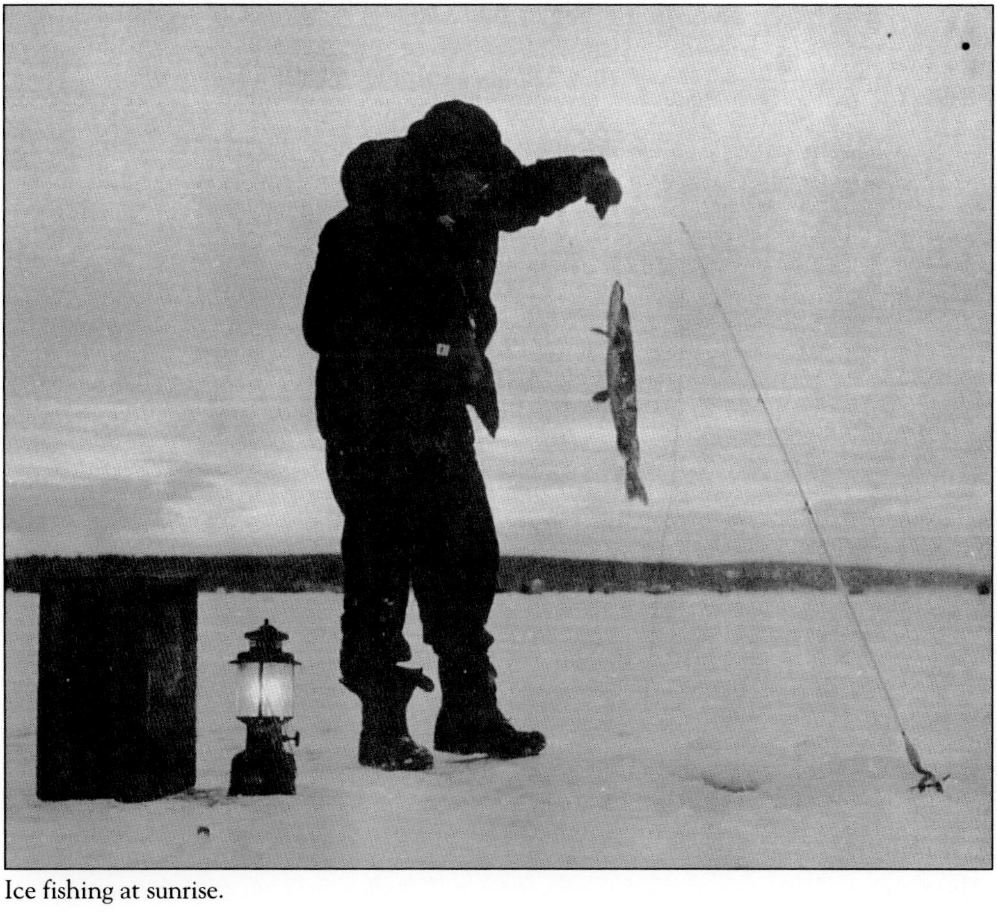

Ice fishing at sunrise.

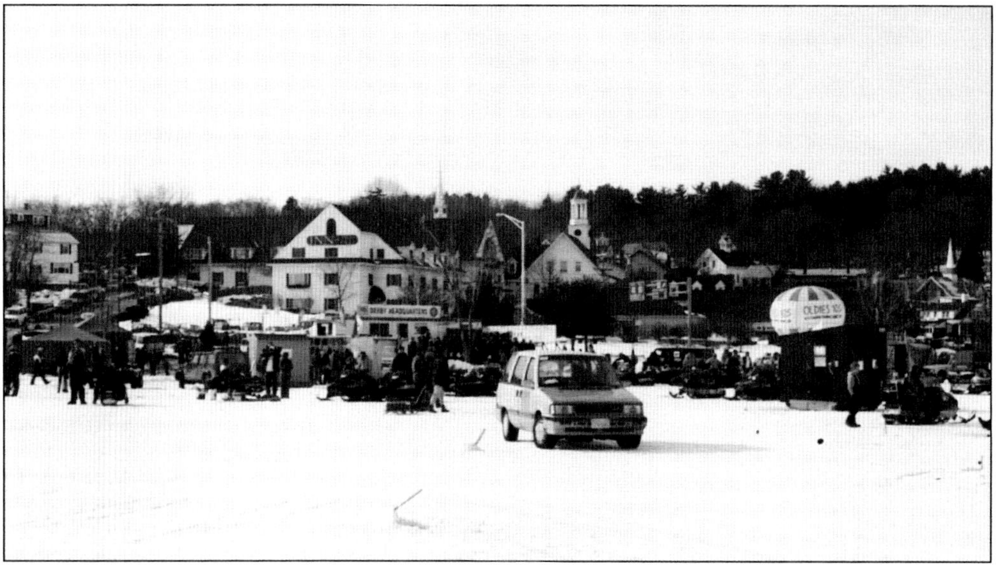

The Meredith Rotary Fishing Derby. For the past 20 years, the Meredith Rotary Club has sponsored "The Great Rotary Club Fishing Derby" as an annual fund-raiser for the many projects of the club. Pictured are the busy activities of fisherman, snowmobilers, and spectators on Meredith Bay with the village in the background, 1980s.

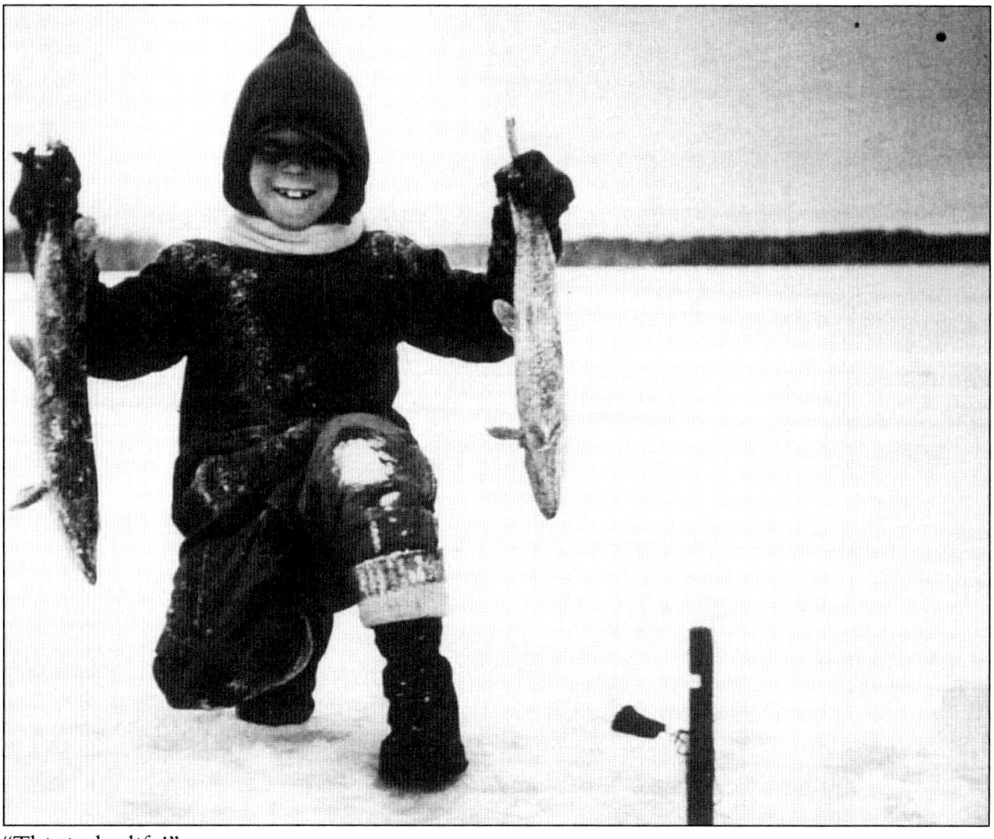

"This is the life!"

Five

Reminiscent Moments

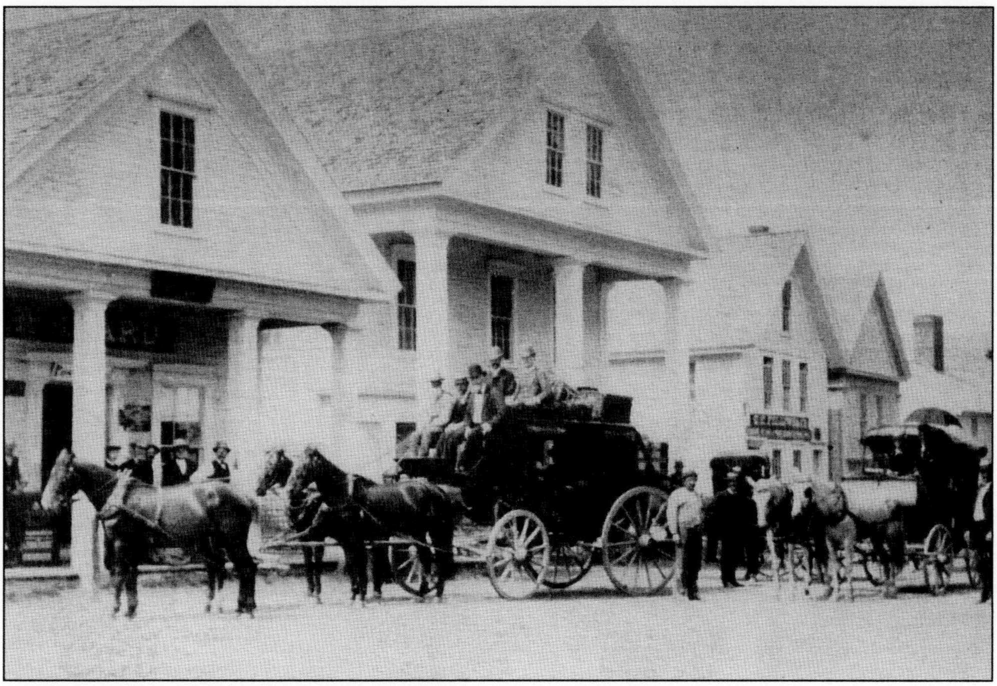

A stagecoach in Sandwich, NH, early 1900s.

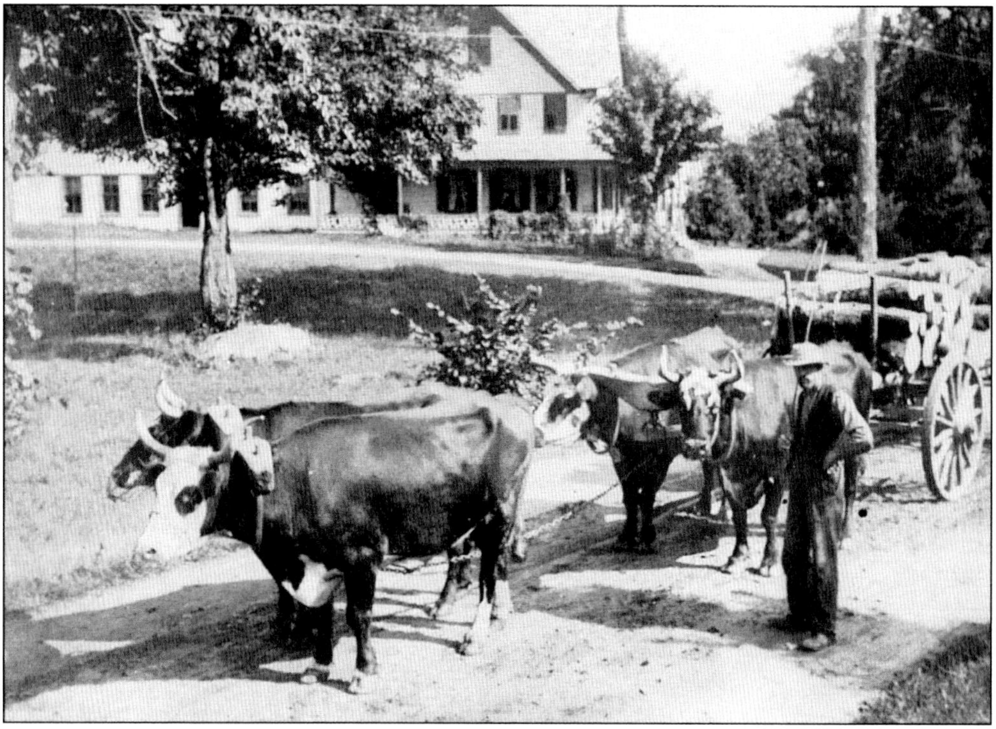

A double-ox team, 1880s.

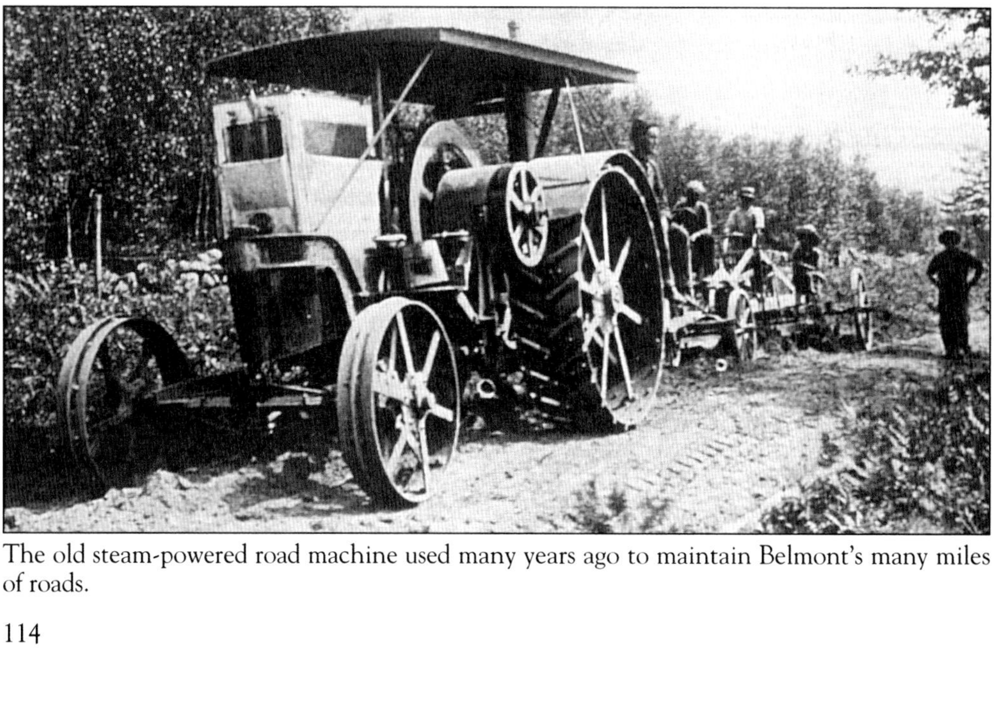

The old steam-powered road machine used many years ago to maintain Belmont's many miles of roads.

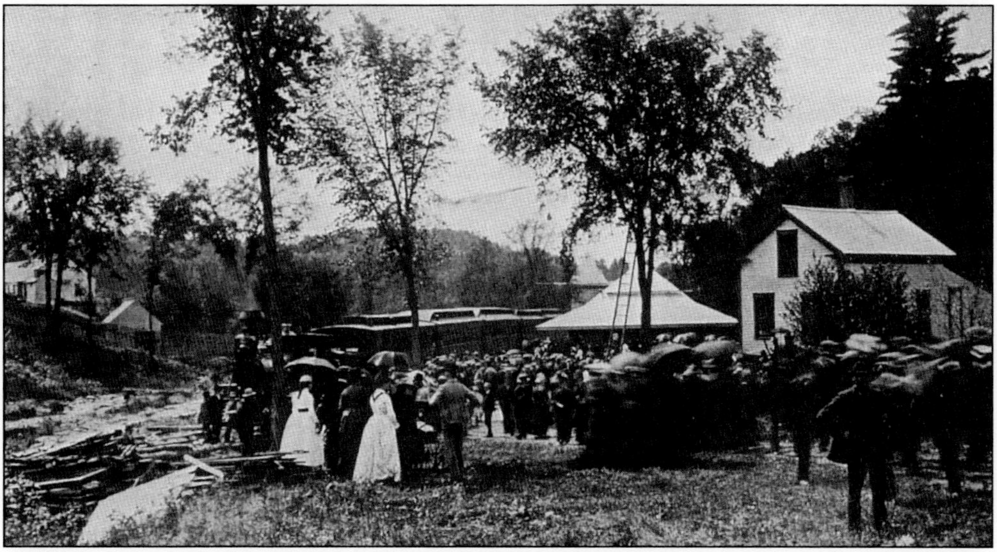

Crowds of townspeople at the arrival of the first train on the Belmont and Tilton Railroad in Belmont, NH, August 17, 1889.

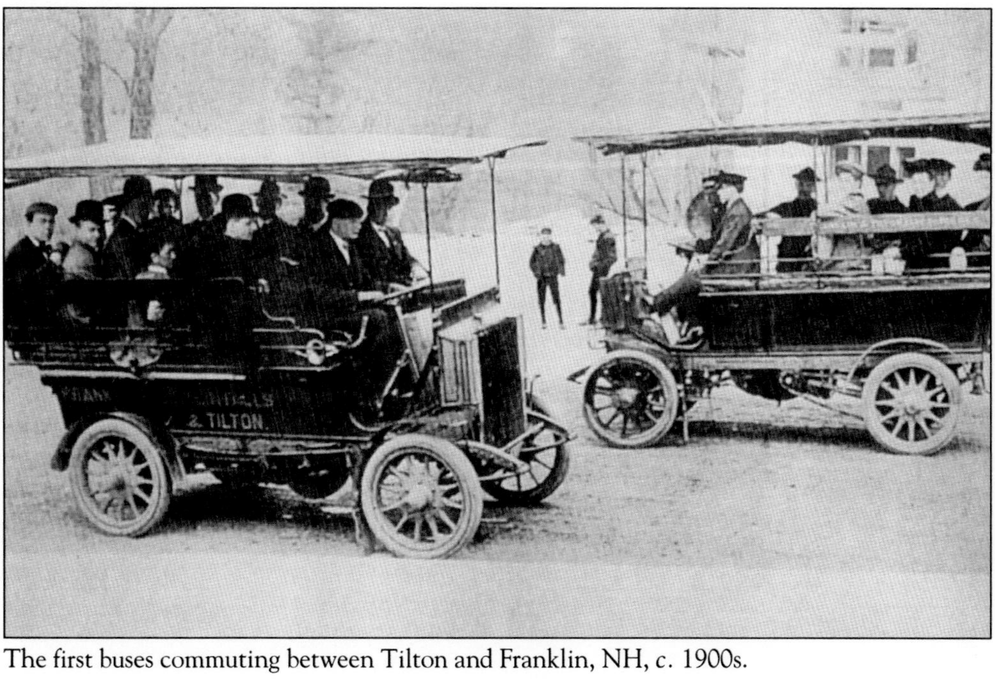

The first buses commuting between Tilton and Franklin, NH, *c.* 1900s.

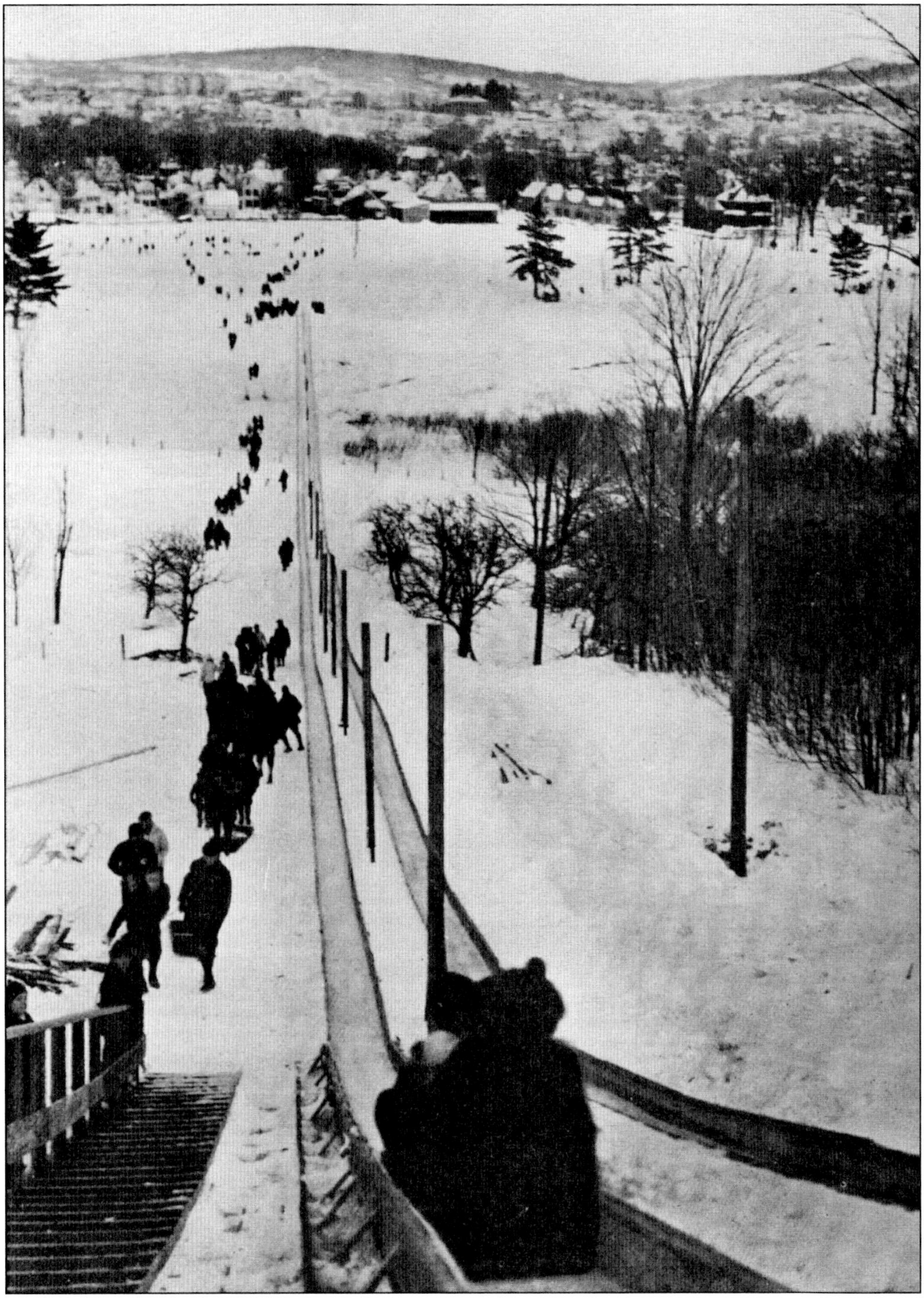

Laconia's 1/2-mile toboggan chute located on Durkee Street Hill, formerly called Peace Street Park, now known as Memorial Park off Court Street, *c.* 1920. Winter carnivals were held in this park with a man-made skating rink. The chute was maintained by Harold Tefft. On cold nights, he'd sprinkle the chute with water so it would freeze; unfortunately, too many people got hurt on the chute and it was eventually closed.

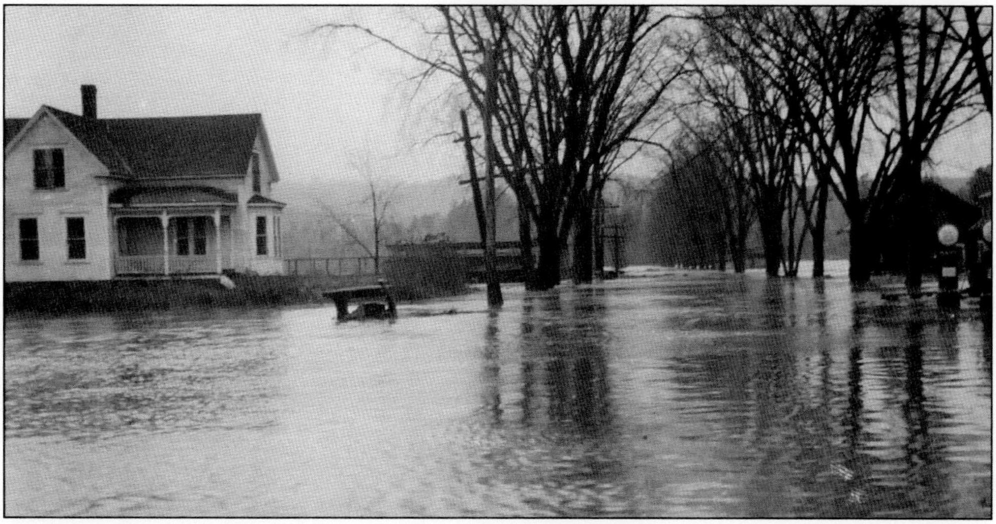

Flood scenes in and about Plymouth, NH, in November 1927.

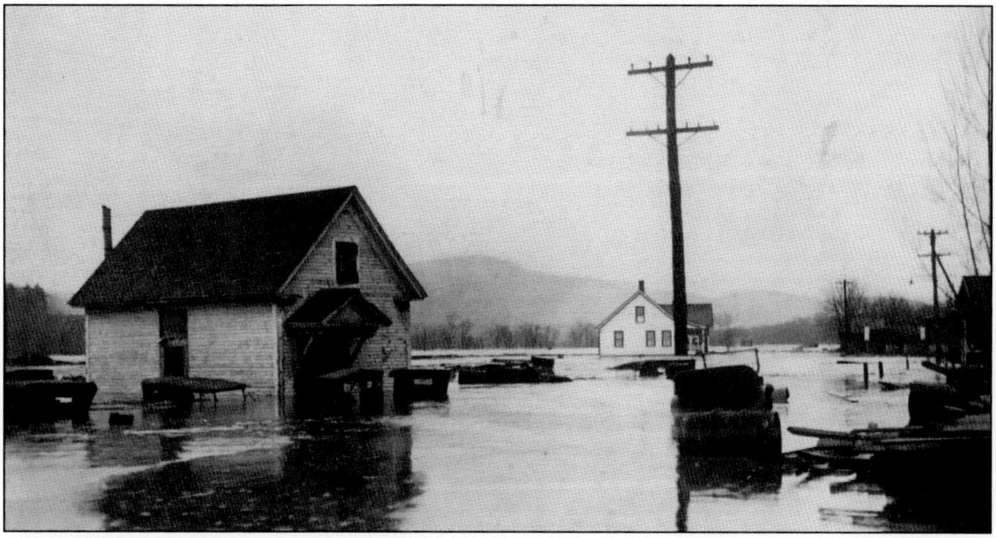

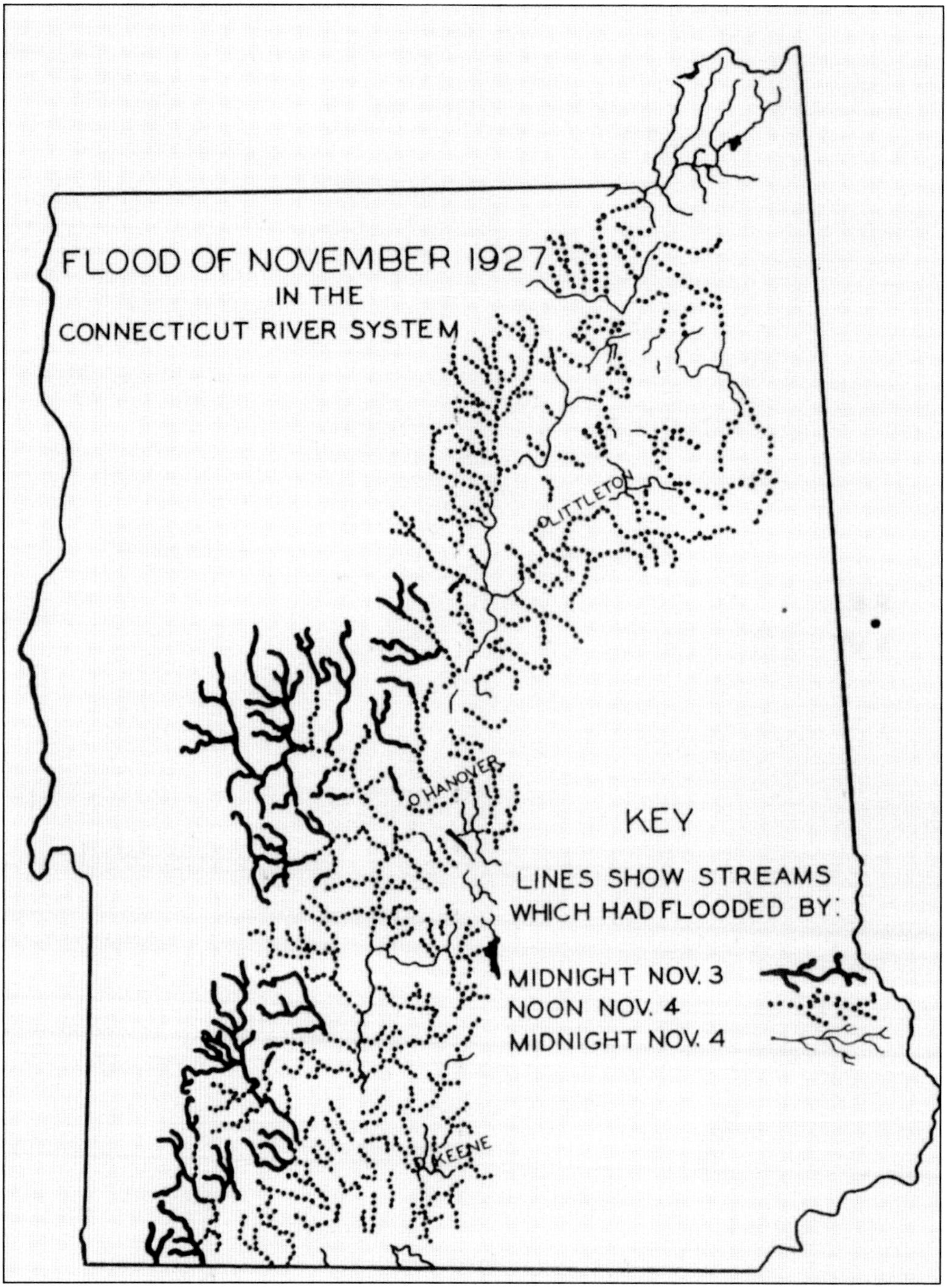

A map of the flood of November 1927, showing the progress of the crests down the Connecticut Valley for each 12-hour period. Since the storm traveled from southwest to northeast, the streams in southern Vermont flooded first, then those in northern New Hampshire flooded.

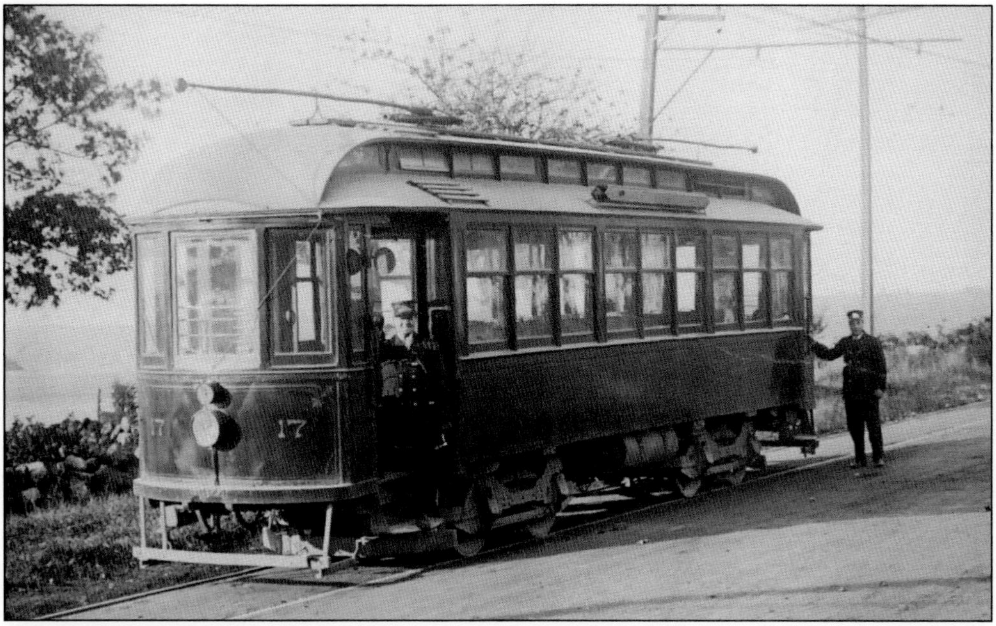

An electric car at The Weirs, NH. Pictured are Nelson Ducette, operator, and George Conant, conductor.

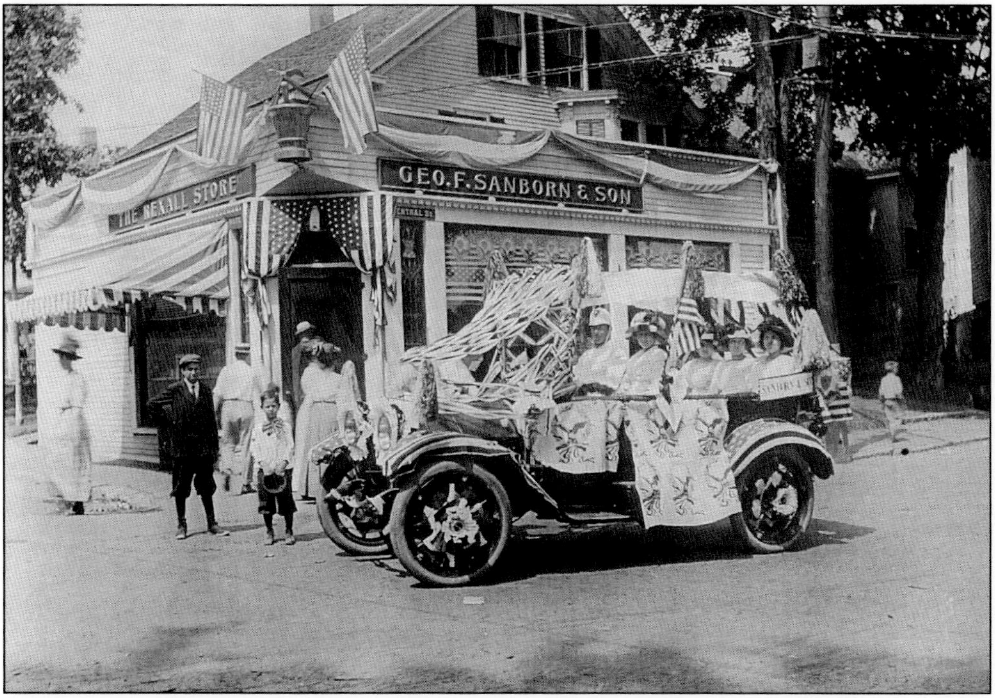

The first-prize float, Fourth of July parade, on Main Street in Meredith, NH, 1915.

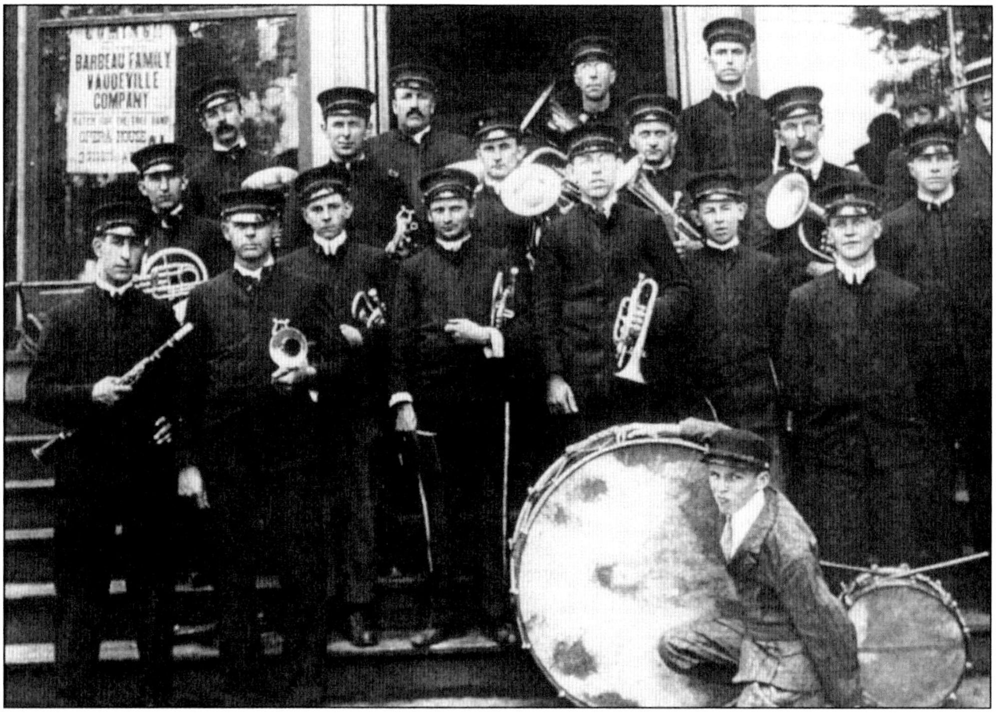

The Belmont Community Band in front of the community hall (town hall), 1920s. Notice the stairway to the hall at the center of the picture. The entrance was later moved to the rear of the building.

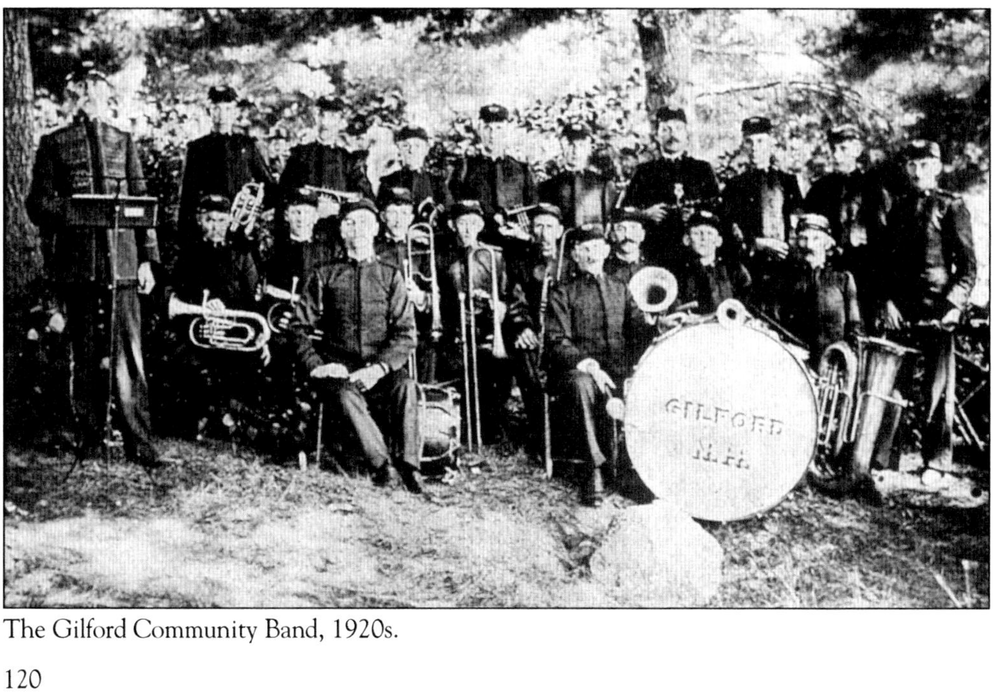

The Gilford Community Band, 1920s.

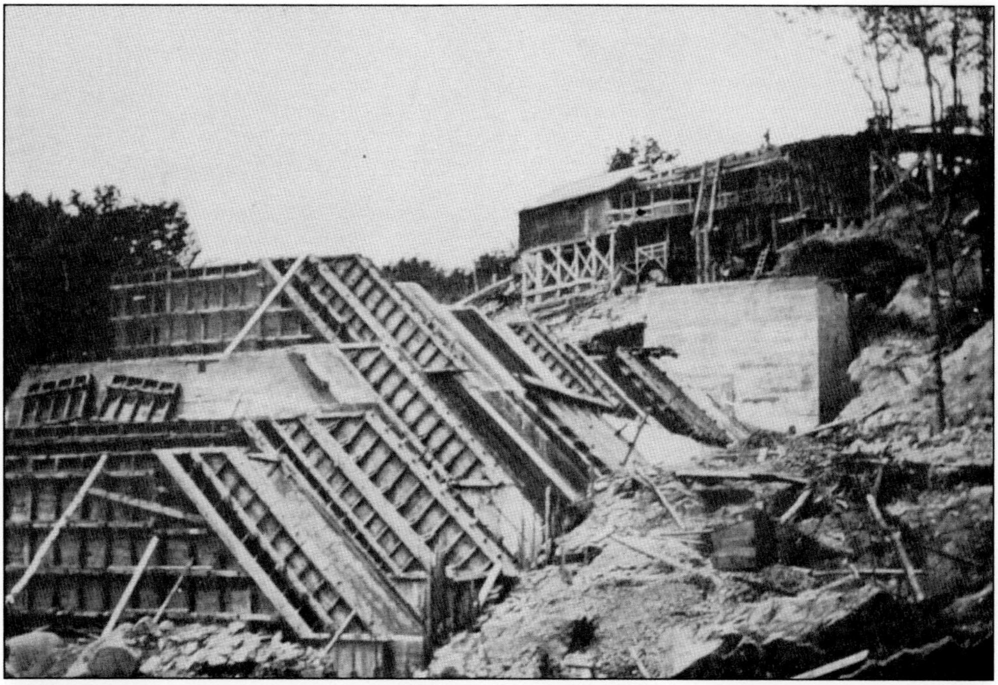

The Bristol Dam, Bristol, NH, 1923. This hydrodam was rebuilt in 1930–32, and is presently owned and operated by the Public Service of New Hampshire.

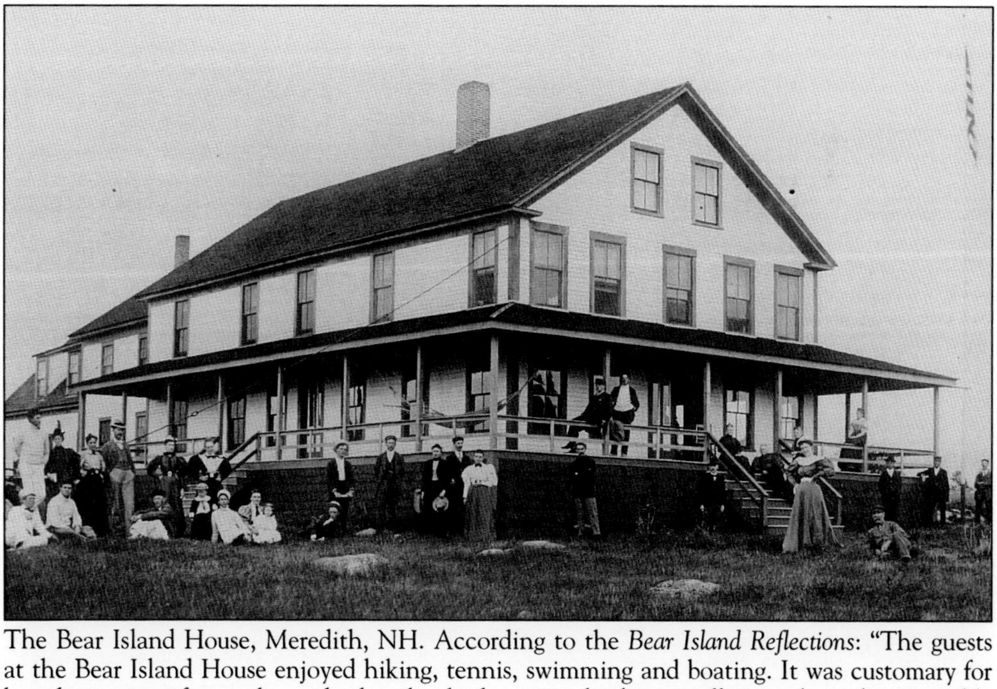

The Bear Island House, Meredith, NH. According to the *Bear Island Reflections*: "The guests at the Bear Island House enjoyed hiking, tennis, swimming and boating. It was customary for boarders to stay for weeks at the hotel, which required a large staff to work in the vegetable garden, milk the cows, gather the eggs, roll the tennis courts, run the boats, and, of course, clean the room and wait on tables."

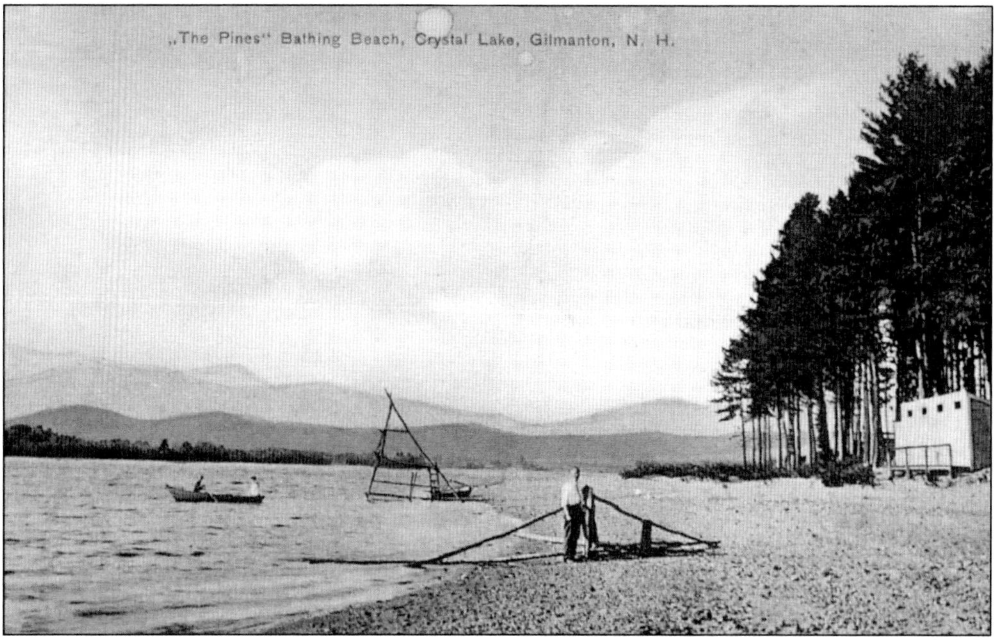

"The Pines" bathing beach on Crystal Lake in Gilmanton, NH, 1911.

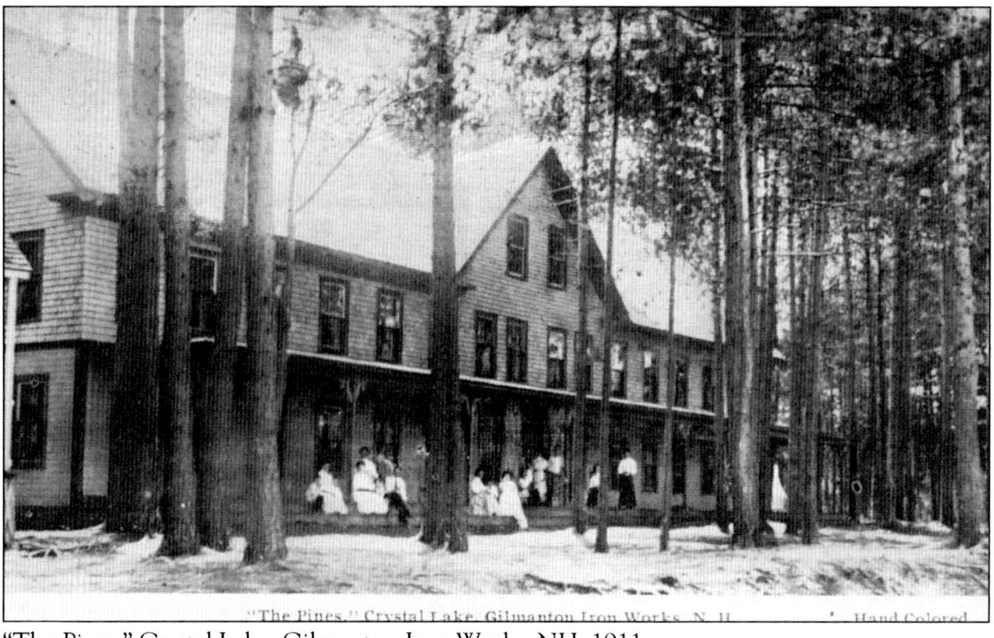

"The Pines," Crystal Lake, Gilmanton Iron Works, NH, 1911.

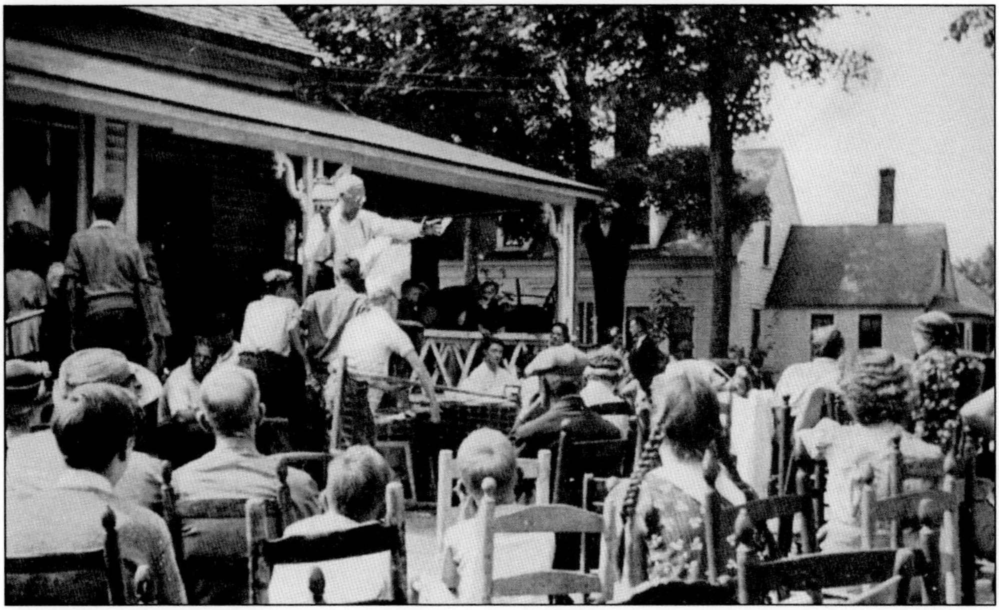

Auction time in the Lakes Region, 1960s.

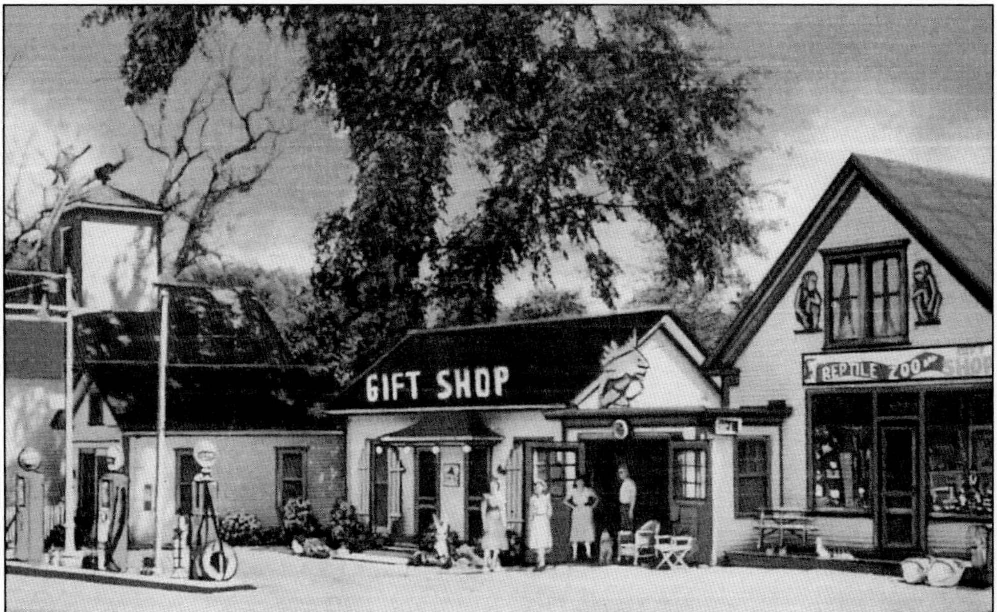

The Reptile Zoo and Gift Shop in Alton Bay, NH, 1940s.

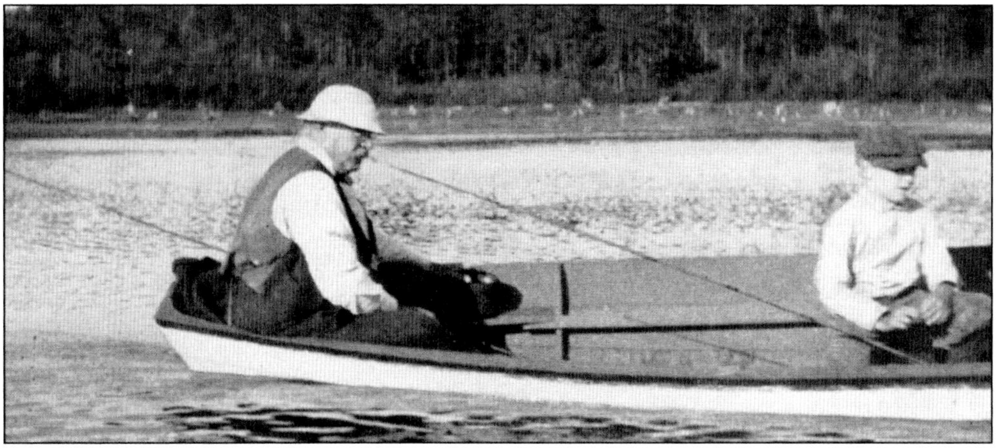

Grover Cleveland and his son Richard fishing in Duncan Lake, Ossipee, NH, early 1900s.

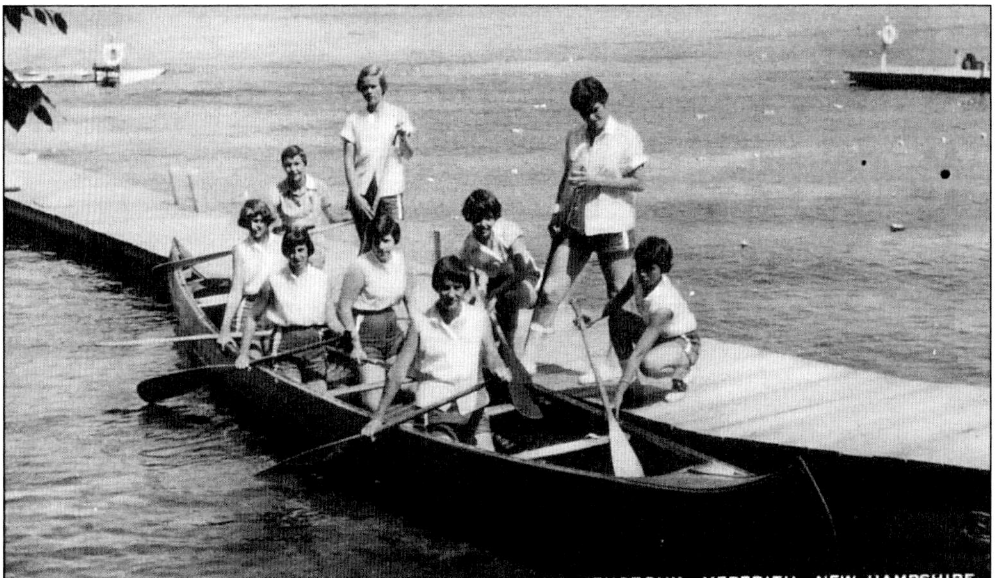

Campers from Camp Menotomy in Meredith, NH, prepare to make a canoe trip across the lake, 1950s.

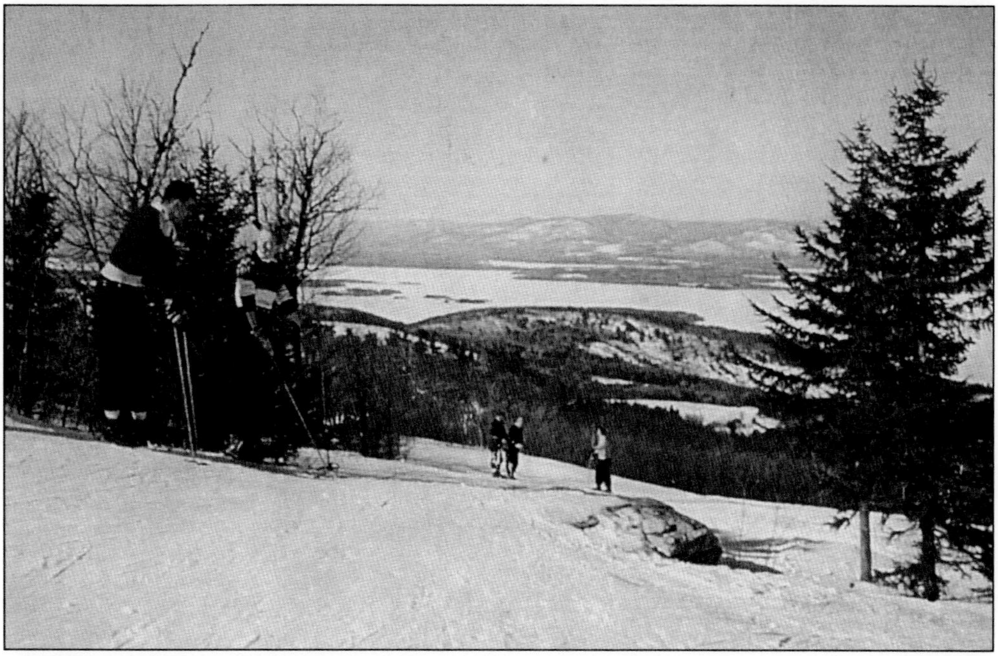

The Belknap Ski Area, Gilford, NH, 1968. In the background is a panoramic view of the broads in Lake Winnipesaukee framed by the Ossipee Mountain Range in the far distance.

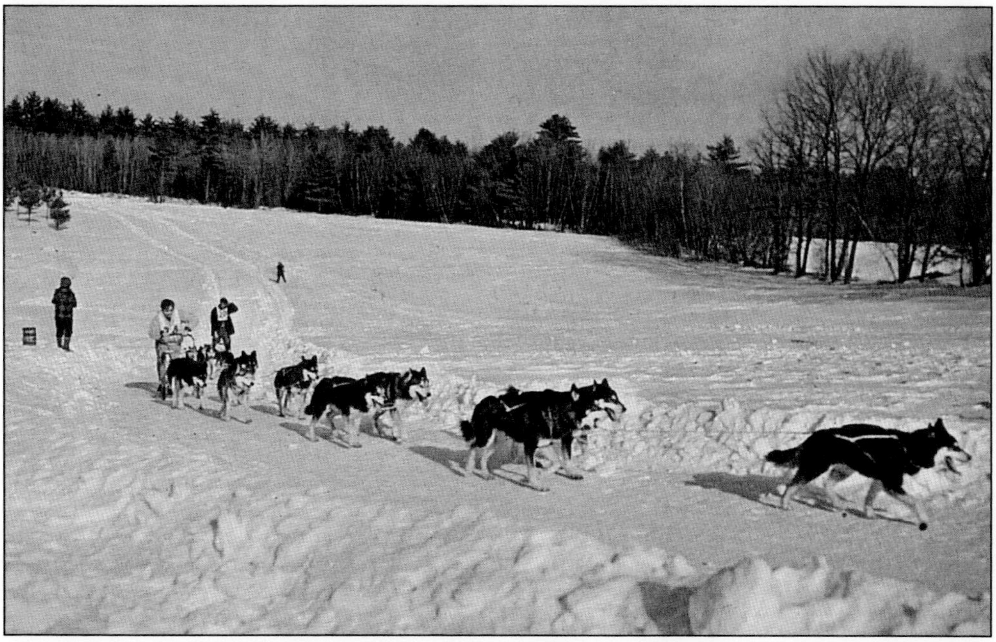

The 1968 World Championship Sled Dog Rance in Laconia, NH. Sled dog races continue to be an exciting feature of the Lakes Region winter activities.

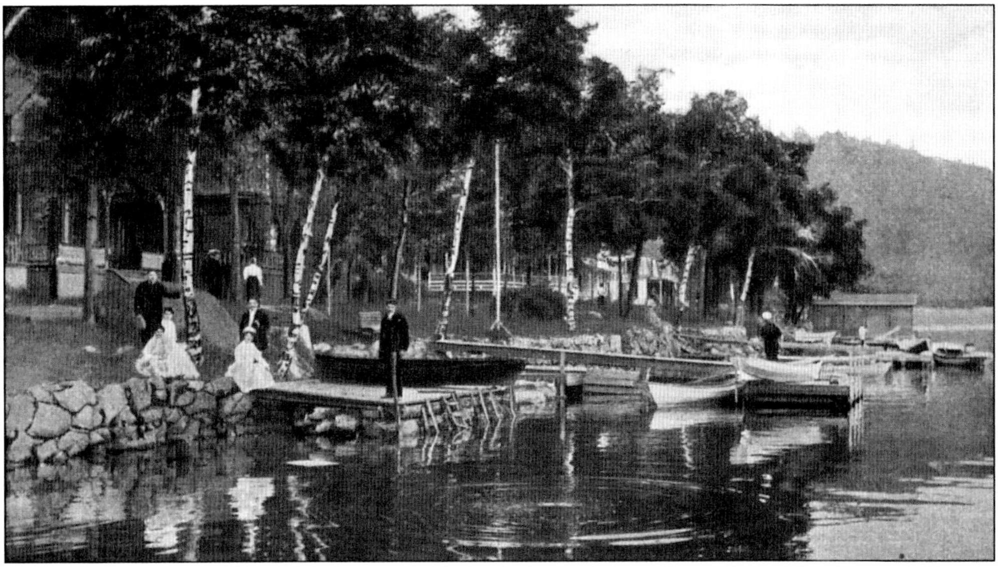

The Shore Path at The Weirs, early 1900s.

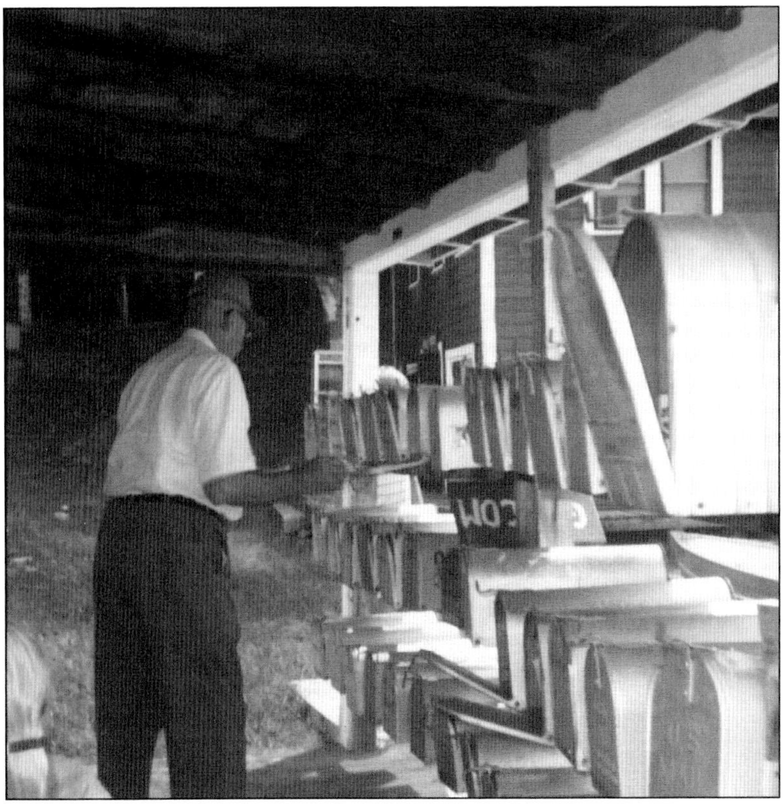

Postmaster Edward Lavallee delivering the mail at Bear Island Post Office, 1971.

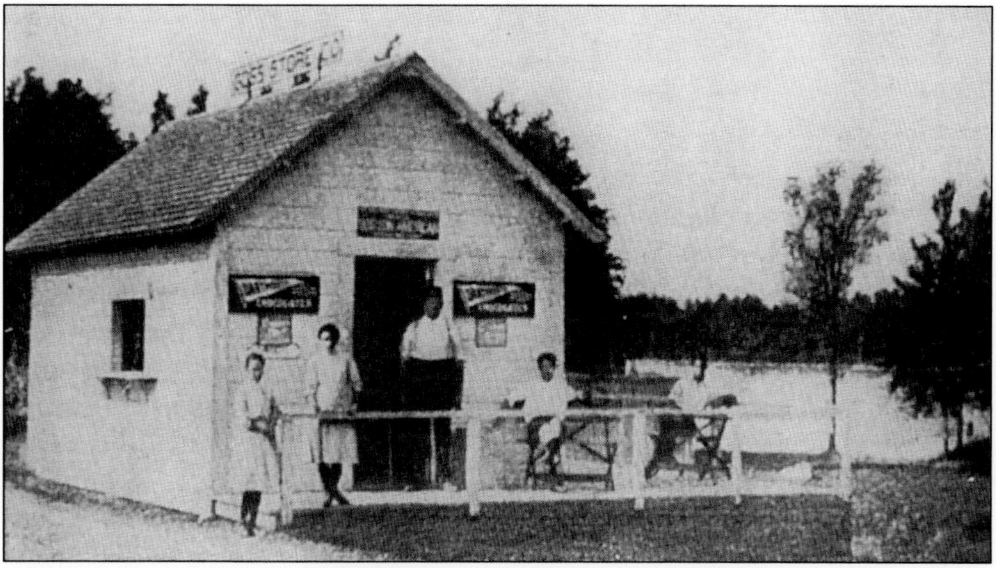

The Noah Goss Store Co., in Glendale, better known as Dorothy's Restaurant, 1950s.

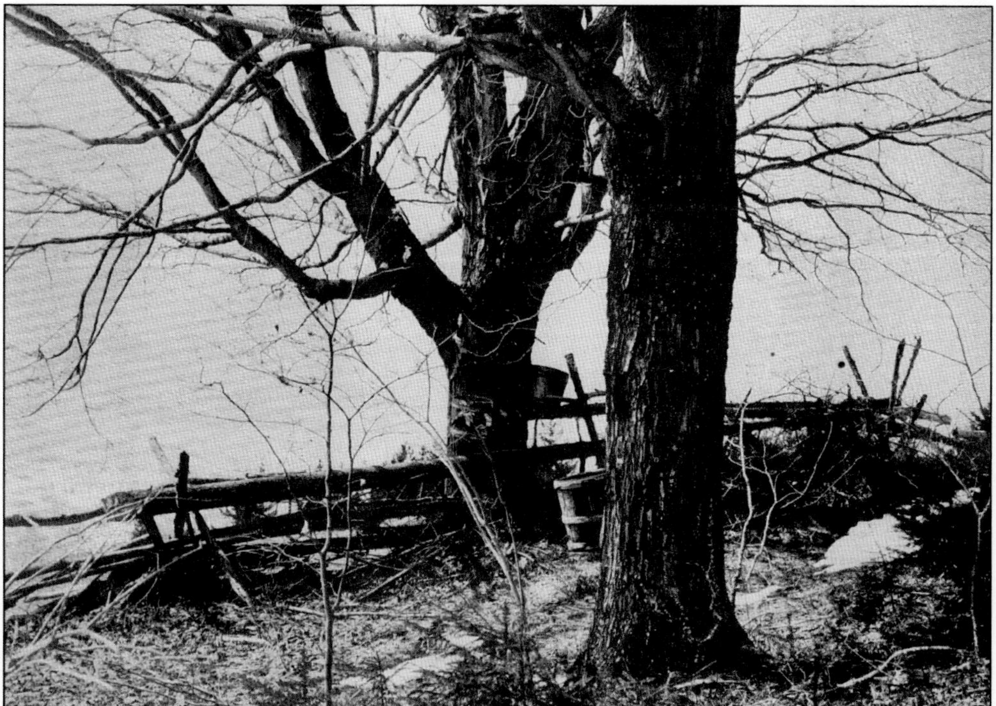

Spring in the Sugar Orchard.

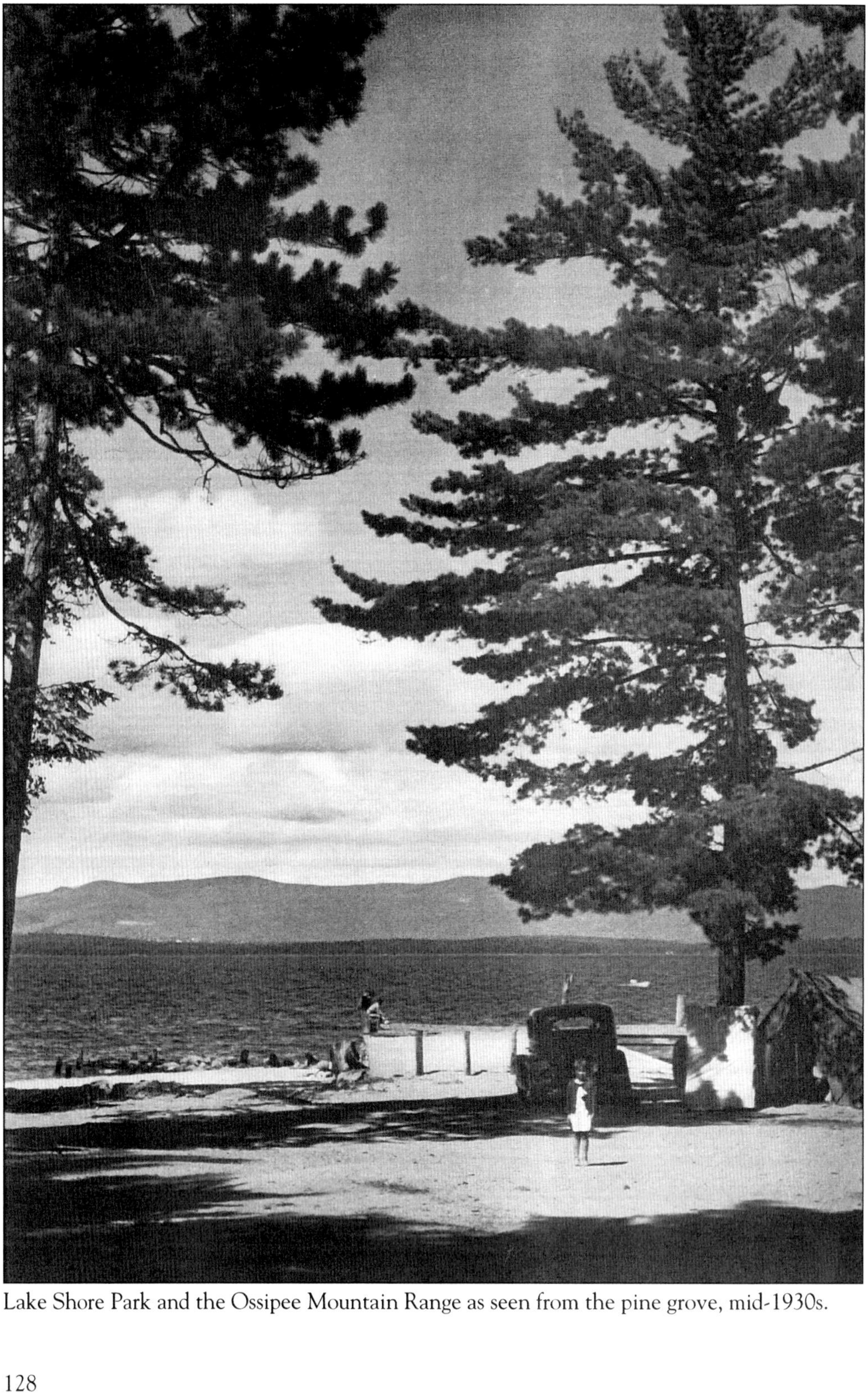

Lake Shore Park and the Ossipee Mountain Range as seen from the pine grove, mid-1930s.